Joined-up Youth Research, Policy and Practice

a new agenda for change?

by

Bob Coles

Supporting and improving work with young people

Barnardo's

GIVING CHILDREN BACK THEIR FUTURE

YOUTH • WORK • PRESS

Published by

YOUTH . WORK . PRESS

the publishing imprint of the
National Youth Agency,
17–23 Albion Street,
Leicester
LE1 6GD.
Tel: 0116.285.3700.
Fax: 0116.285.3777.
E-mail: nya@nya.org.uk
Website: http://www.nya.org.uk

in partnership with Barnardo's

ISBN 0 86155 244 X
Price £16.95

The views expressed and the terms used are the author's own and do not necessarily
represent the views of the National Youth Agency or Barnardo's.

Typeset by Avon DataSet Ltd, Bidford on Avon, Warwickshire B50 4JH.
(www.avondataset.com)

Contents

Preface and acknowledgments

Like many authors, in researching and writing this book, I have experienced wild mood swings: from exhilaration to exasperation to exhaustion; from terror at the outset of each chapter, to relief when I had it in draft form, to anxiety when it was about to be read by a real expert in the field. This book compounded the feelings of terror several times over as it attempts to deal with an array of youth policy issues rarely covered within a single volume. This was exacerbated by wanting to cover three main strands on all the topics covered in the book: what current research can tell us; what policies are being developed; and what practical projects are doing in this area and with what degree of success. Many colleagues and friends have helped inspire and sustain me through these times and deserve my thanks.

Di McNeish and Steve Harwood at Barnardo's helped form the idea for the book and Angela Bolton helped me see it through to completion. I also thank the fifty or so heads of agencies, units, departments or sections within government departments and the voluntary sector who nominated interesting youth projects for me to visit, and the staff who gave up their time to talk to me. This 'youth tourism' phase was a delight as I moved from Fort William to Feltham, Cardiff to Kings Lynn, Whitley Bay to Wrexham. I was hugely impressed by the commitment of those working with young people. I hope the cameos of these projects can do justice to their work. They may not be able to convey the tenacity with which they cope with difficult problems in challenging times. Such are the vagaries of funding that some of these projects no longer exist or have substantially changed since I visited them during the Spring and Summer of 1999. To all who helped I give my thanks for the frankness and honesty with which they described their trials and tribulations, as well as their aims and ambitions. These cameos are the heart of the book. It is through these projects (and the thousands of others like them) that youth policy is turned into practice.

If that was not enough, the writing of the book has taken place during a time of considerable change. Even when I thought I had a complete draft, the world would change – sometimes dramatically. Never in my memory has youth policy been so high on the political agenda. Never before has so much research been undertaken on young people's lives. Policy initiatives and new ways of working have been falling thick and fast around my ears as I attempted to sift through what I thought I already knew. Many of these developments are gratifying in that they are broadly in line with the policies many of us have been recommending should be developed for the past twenty years. But on occasions I wished that it would all just stop – or at least until I had finished the book. But, of course, policy development will continue even after it is published. I should also acknowledge that this is not the only thing I have written over the past two years and much of the critique of the role of the Social Exclusion Unit in developing youth policy was also included in a chapter (Slouching towards Bethlehem) in *Social Policy Review 12*. H. Dean, R. Sykes and R. Woods (eds), Newcastle, Social Policy Association.

Although writing is both terrifying and lonely (and never more so than in the writing of this book), a huge number of people have surrounded me with support. At the University of York, numerous social policy colleagues have fed me a rich diet of relevant research. I must thank Jonathan Bradshaw, Roger Burrows, Eirian Edwards, Janet Ford, Helen Kenwright, Wendy Mitchell, Sarah Nettleton, Debs Quilgars, Julie Rugg, Martyn Seago, Mike Stein, Ian Sinclair and Jim Wade. The University of York has provided a wide 'comfort blanket' of support, a hugely helpful subject librarian in Jeannette Colclough, and a research term to carry out the fieldwork – or the 'youth tourism' as I preferred to call it. Other colleagues in other universities and elsewhere also proved invaluable, both in keeping me up-to-date with developments and in filling in the gaps in my knowledge. Special thanks go to Karl Atkin, Debbie Baldwin, Balbir Chatrik, John Coleman, Paul Convery, Gary Craig, Andy Furlong, Ravi Gurumerthy, Charlie Lloyd, Donna McAlpine, Patrick West, Howard Williamson and Tom Wylie – and to John especially for reading, and commenting on, the whole manuscript. Barnardo's also helped in providing an impressive team of 'guardian angels' in an attempt to avoid my worst errors in some of the chapters. Thanks are given to Pam Hibbert, Helen Roberts, Darshan Sachdev and John Strongman of Barnardo's, Steve Harwood, now at Coram Family, Helen Norris at South Bank Careers, Mark Perfect at the Youth Justice Board and Martin Stevenson of the Connexions Service. I thank them all for helping me fill glaring omissions or avoid crass mistakes. I, of course, remain responsible for any errors that remain. I thank Barnardo's for their financial support of the fieldwork undertaken for this book, and Youth Work Press for arranging for its speedy publication. The views expressed in the book are not the views of those who have helped in its production. Responsibility is entirely that of the author.

This book has taken the best part of two years from initial planning to completion and my obsession with it has intruded into the whole of my life rather than simply 'office hours'. My thanks also go to Mary Maynard who tolerated my obsessiveness, to Ethel for being a calm, supportive and nourishing London base. Chris repeatedly sorted out my technological incompetence and Donna stopped me becoming too wild and unkempt (most of the time). Jo was exemplary in getting on with the *real politique* rather than merely writing about it. When completing *Youth and Social Policy* some years ago, Chris and Jo were still undergoing their 'youth transitions'. I doubt that they consider they have yet completed them even though they are both in their late 20s. It is they, the many young people I met on my travels, and those working with them who have been my biggest inspiration. The complexity of young people's lives deserve the more integrated, holistic and 'joined-up' patterns of support this book seeks to promote. The opportunities are now there for us to provide better connections through, for instance, the new youth support service. We have the opportunity of a lifetime to make certain this works. We cannot afford to fail again.

Bob Coles
December 2000

Chapter One

Youth and youth policy: Towards a more 'holistic' approach

This book aims to provide a review of youth policy. It is written at a time when there is growing concern in the UK for the welfare of young people, an acceptance that many systems of support offered in the past have failed lamentably and that new structures and patterns of working must be found to avoid the mistakes of the past. A leading role in the recent review and development of youth policy has been played by the Social Exclusion Unit (SEU) set up within the Cabinet Office following the 1997 General Election (Coles, 2000). The role of the Unit and its style of working will be reviewed in the final chapter. Three of its first five reports were directly concerned with youth policy issues and, within the other two, young people were a significant aspect of enquiry. The content of the reports will be reviewed in subsequent chapters. But it is worth noting at the beginning some of its refreshing honesty as manifest by Policy Action Team 12 on Neighbourhood Renewal (PAT 12, 2000). This report makes clear that Britain stands alone in Europe in having no minister or ministry for youth, no parliamentary committee and no body responsible for cross government youth policy. Instead responsibility spans a huge number of different agencies and departments which have often developed different policies in isolation, sometimes pulling policy in different directions. Indeed it would be easy to conclude that, if a defining characteristic of 'youth policy' involved having some explicit, coordinated strategy, then, until very recently, the UK did not have a 'youth policy' at all. Instead we merely had a haphazard collection of policies and initiatives which impacted upon young people's lives in an often unplanned, uncalculated and largely chaotic manner (Jones and Bell, 2000).

In the foreword to this report, the 'Champion Minister' of the team wrote the following: 'As we enter the 21st century, there can be no more important task facing us than to ensure that, no matter who they are, each young person has the best possible start in life and the opportunity to develop and achieve their full potential. For a minority of young people, achieving this ambition will not be easy. Through a combination of poverty, family conflict, poor educational opportunities and poor services, too many find themselves destined for a life of underachievement and social exclusion.' (PAT 12, 2000).

This book will review the Government's attempt to address such a bold and far-reaching agenda. But to set this challenge in context, this chapter will briefly describe some of the major changes that have taken place in the last quarter of the 20th century and which have fundamentally changed the social and economic conditions of youth. What will also become clear is that young people's lives are profoundly affected by public policy. But before embarking upon this review it is important that we are clear what we mean by youth, what counts as youth policy, and in what ways it influences and impacts upon young people's lives.

Youth and youth policy

Many authors define and conceptualise youth not as a specific age group but as a phase in the life course between childhood and adulthood (Coleman and Hendry, 1999; Coles, 1995; Furlong and Cartmel, 1997; Jones and Wallace, 1992). 'Youth' is thus a series of inter-linked processes or 'transitions'; 'young people' are those who are undertaking them. Youth is also the period of time during which young people are expected to do different things and take on different responsibilities as they prepare for, and gradually take on, adult roles. Yet, as we will see, no clear age parameters can be set for this. 'Youth policies' are prescriptions and plans designed to help young people and to manage the transitions from childhood to adulthood. These take different forms. Some policies are embedded in legal codes which define at what age young people are permitted to do certain things such as leave school, drive a car, get married, sign contracts including tenancy agreements, be held responsible for wrongdoing including crime, engage in sexual activities or buy or consume alcohol, and so on. (For an excellent review of the changing legal framework on young people see Bell and Jones, 2000). The law is, however, often inconsistent about the 'ages of responsibility' and accords different rights at different ages. There is also wide international variation. A young person may be held criminally responsible for their actions in England at the age of 10, yet in Scotland the age is 8, whereas criminal prosecutions may not take place until a young person is 13 in France, 15 in Germany and Sweden and 18 in Belgium (Lansdown and Newall, 1994). Young people in Britain can vote at the age of 18 but social security benefits are not paid at an adult rate until the age of 25. Other youth policies are not so much embedded in any laws but concern the running of the major social institutions that frame young people's lives, such as schools and other educational institutions, the health service, leisure provision or other services designed to promote and enhance their welfare. Many laws and social institutions are intended to apply to all young people. Yet, some laws are easier to apply and some are more vigilantly policed than others. For instance, young people can only legally engage in employment between 7 am and 7 pm after the age of 13, yet little attempt is made to apply and police the law (Lavelette, 1994; Lavelette, 1999). They may legally engage in consensual heterosexual sex after the age of 16 and homosexual activity after the age of 18 but many do so earlier (Coleman, 1999; Johnson et al., 1994). A young person may cease full-time education at the age of 16 but many truant or may be permanently excluded from school and receive little, or no, education (SEU, 1999b). Sometimes the law is at odds with other stated government objectives. The law may allow young people to quit full-time education at 16 but the vast majority do not and government unemployment. Domestic and household partnerships too break down. We must avoid linear assumptions, that once a positive status is achieved, youth is over and adulthood and full citizenship achieved.

4. Avoiding normative assumptions

The youth transition model is also implicitly normative. It assumes that getting a job, securing accommodation independent of the family of origin, and forming households, partnerships and families independent of them are 'good things' and important stepping stones to adulthood and full citizenship. This needs to be questioned and tested against criteria which sociologists, especially, seem reluctant to employ, such as measures of self esteem, control and self efficacy.

5. Focusing on both sides of the careers equation

There is a need to focus on *both* young people and the issues they face *and* the agencies that may, or may not, help them address them. This implies addressing what elsewhere is referred to as both sides of the 'careers equation': young people, and the opportunity structures afforded to them.

6. Examining both sides of the careers equation holistically

Both sides of this 'careers equation' need to be examined 'holistically'.

This means that we need holistic studies of the complexities of young people's lives and holistic studies of agencies with which they deal (or could, or should deal.) Not only are the various strands of young people's lives 'joined up' but so too should be the policies, agencies and practices seeking to promote their welfare.

7. Including young people as full participants in the process

There is a need to engage with young people as key participants in any partnership rather than rely upon solutions invented by others. This means attention should be given to how young people can be given a voice and encouraged and supported in participating in policy development and the evaluation of practice delivery.

8. Realism

Understanding must be grounded in a realistic appraisal of the social, familial and economic circumstances in which young people live and what can be realistically and sensitively accomplished in the short, medium and long term by policy intervention.

9. Understanding patterns of difference

The experiences of different groups of young people may be fundamentally different. Boys and young men may face different sets of issues than those faced by girls and young women. Being brought up in rural areas may be a very different experience from being brought up in the suburbs, in towns or in metropolitan areas. The experiences of different ethnic groups may differ fundamentally, as may those of young people with disabilities or special needs.

10. Being inclusive of all groups, not merely focusing on those defined as vulnerable or at risk

Much of the attention of research, policy development and practice in recent years has focused on those young people thought to be vulnerable, or at risk. Yet all young people have been subject to the impact of rapid social, economic and cultural change. Even those who may, from the outside, appear to be 'successful' and 'trouble free', have to face problems associated with extended periods of family dependency and transitions which are complicated and surrounded by risk. Holistic approaches must encompass the complexities involved in the transitions of all young people and not simply be driven by those who, for the moment, hold the gaze of policy-makers and practitioners.

Joined-up lives and the need for joined-up interventions

In the 1999 report of the Social Exclusion Unit *Bridging the Gap* there is an Annex B which tries to encapsulate the issues being faced by a small sample of young people. The report is strong in highlighting the 'joined-up' problems being faced by many young people. The charts cover various phases of the young people's lives, before the age of 11, between 11 and 14 and the transition years at various points between the ages of 15 and 18. The SEU report and the subsequent PAT 12 review of youth policy also attempt to chart the various kinds of support young people receive, both from formal channels (schools and careers guidance, for instance) and from family members and 'significant others' (including friends and grandparents). The SEU case studies share a common factor – that between the ages of 16 and 18 the young people described were not in any form of education, training or employment – one of the key target groups for government policy at the turn of the century. In the terms of the youth transition model they were experiencing failed and 'fractured' transitions. All those described in the Annex were also either parents, or about to be parents, in their teens – another target group for government policy – and had left home, or left foster care and experienced homelessness – a third policy area. Yet also contained within the charted biography other elements were important. Family relationships and schooling had begun to be problematic well before secondary school, with reports of bullying at school and conflict (including bullying and abuse) at home. There is an array of other issues also reported during their teenage years involving experiences of sexual abuse, drug, substance and alcohol abuse and involvement in crime and prostitution. Some of the cases also report traumatic events and illness to other family members, conflict with step-parents and truancy and school exclusions. In short, there is an attempt to come to grips with the complexities of young people's biographies, very much in line with the principles of the 'holistic' approach outlined. The chart is less hopeful when it examines patterns of intervention and support; although the report itself does make far reaching proposals about how patterns of support can be better developed and coordinated in the future.

As part of the research conducted for this book, the author met with, or was told about, similar stories, often through agencies in the voluntary or statutory sector which were trying to make a significant and lasting impact upon young people's lives. Two are, perhaps, worth telling in order to re-emphasise some of the principles of 'holistic' approaches to youth intervention outlined.

Mick's Story

Mick was brought up on a poor estate in the Midlands. He had not really seen his father for some time and he lived with his mother, a younger brother who was ill with cystic fibrosis and a younger sister with learning disabilities. His secondary school he described as 'not the best'; as falling to bits and full of graffiti, which meant he didn't feel like going very much. In year nine his mother became ill and was bed-ridden for a year. He stopped going to school to look after his mother and the younger children, a commitment which was re-doubled when social workers began to hint about taking his sister into care. He went back to school in year 11, despite his teachers saying he would only achieve F grades. In the event, he did get modest grade passes in six subjects including one grade C, of which he was proud. But this didn't really help him get a job and he 'dossed around' at home drifting between short periods on youth training, a GNVQ course of social care (which he liked but dropped out of) and short periods doing fast-food-outlet jobs which he hated the most. Most of the time he was at home but not on benefits.

He was angered one day by the arrival of a white bus that parked outside his house on the estate. It was owned by Warwickshire Careers Service which was just starting 'outreach work'. He went out to remonstrate with them for giving his area a bad name, but they managed to recruit him, with some difficulty, onto their *Double Take* programme, working with the 'hard to reach' young unemployed. They didn't try to force him into training or employment but worked on 'soft outcomes' such as raising his self esteem and self confidence. At first he went with some reluctance, ashamed to be seen by others going through the door and alienated by the 'pretty lights, suits and ties' and the invitation to go into the 'conference room'. He persuaded them to move the project somewhere else, somewhere more 'grotty and beat-up' where they would feel more comfortable. Eventually, through the scheme, and through activities such as team-building exercises and discussion, he had turned into an advocate for young people like himself. Five years on he was working as a 'peer educator' with the programme which had helped him.

Several lessons can be drawn from Mick's story. Firstly, it illustrates the 'joined-up problems' in young people's lives: how educational disadvantage can lead to educational disaffection, and how issues being addressed within the family can impinge upon educational success. Some of these are related to the three strands identified by the youth transition model; others are not. Secondly, it is sometimes tempting to read uniqueness into the detail of individual biographies. But it is also important to recognise that such factors as inequalities of health and illness, disability, and the likelihood of experiencing accidents, serious illness, premature death or other traumatic events are all socially patterned and more likely in poor neighbourhoods and poor families (Acheson, 1998). Even the Micks of this world – 'ordinary kids with mild ambitions' – have a habit (in the words of Roddy Doyle) to 'keep on walking into doors' which often knock them sideways (or downwards). They need to be taken seriously and be the subject of careful and sensitive support. The third thing of note is that Mick 'hit lucky'. Warwickshire Careers Service (WCS) was just starting an outreach programme. But it was highly unusual at the time to have a Careers Service doing such work. It would have been much more likely to have found such outreach work being undertaken by detached youth workers, as was the case in other projects covered by the research undertaken for this book. WCS would be the first to admit that they were on a steep and difficult learning curve in embarking upon such work; in developing a 'suitable sensitive service' and in resisting attempts to reach too early for 'hard outcomes' such as training, education or employment placements. Their success was in recognising that the most effective interventions need to be both sensitive and realistic. But such interventions need not be the property of statutory services, whether a careers service or the youth service.

A second story may help illustrate further lessons and the role of partnership between agencies.

Dave's Story

Dave lived on a poor estate in North Wales with a male adult unemployment rate of over 20 per cent. Locally the estate had a poor reputation. Over half the children on the estate were eligible for free school meals (although of course they don't get these at weekends or in school holidays, or if they don't go to school). Lots of young people on the estate didn't go to school, sometimes because they were excluded, and often it was suspected there was open collusion between young people and school staff. The project manager of an estate based project suspected that if young people didn't comply with the wishes of the teachers for a young person not to attend, 'flash points' were engineered to formalise exclusion. There was a pupil referral unit in the town and a visiting teacher scheme in operation for excluded pupils. Dave was described as 'pretty disturbed' and coming from a 'troubled family' with 'a bit of a reputation'.

One day Dave visited the estate project with some of his friends. His friends tried to get him to tell the project leader what he had just done. A 'visiting teacher' had called at his house that morning and Dave had welcomed him with a bucket of cold water poured on him from an upstairs window. The project leader asked 'Why!?' with some exasperation. Dave thought for a little and then explained. 'They' had been 'getting at him' at school. 'They' were always 'getting at him' in town. 'They' were 'getting at him on the streets'. His home was the only place which was his and where he felt safe. Now they were sending a teacher in there!

> The community project eventually provided a room for 'home tuition' in more neutral space – although they received no payment for this as there wasn't an appropriate budget heading.

Dave's story is told partly to re-emphasise the importance of interventions and attempted solutions to 'joined-up' problems which are sensitive to young people's needs and work in partnership with them rather than simply imposing services, no matter how well-meaning or well-intentioned. It also illustrates that many partnerships are not particularly well planned and suffer from bureaucratic and funding straightjackets which seem to prevent suitable and sensitive partnerships and 'joined-up' solutions. And of course some will get 'bucket of water' responses, or worse. Some will fail, and fail spectacularly. But we must continue to search for solutions and be prepared sometimes to fail in the short-term, and try, try and try again. The cost of failure is too great.

The remainder of this book will review a range of youth policies and youth intervention projects designed to implement them. In that one of the main aims of the volume is to review holistic approaches to youth policy, planning how to organise the chapters presented something of a problem. Whilst it is possible to sub-divide youth policies into different topic areas, holistic approaches necessarily span topic areas. Each chapter, therefore, will include some cross-referencing to others and at the end of each, we will make an assessment of the degree to which policy and practice are embracing the main principles of a holistic approach outlined in this one. The main focus of the book is with patterns of disadvantage and disaffection and with youth policies and intervention projects which target the most disadvantaged and vulnerable. The review starts in chapter two, with attempts to tackle youth unemployment. Chapter three examines educational disadvantage and disaffection. Employment and education are clearly crucial issues for many vulnerable groups. Chapter four examines domestic and housing transitions focusing on young people and homelessness and those who become parents in their teenage years. Chapter five examines the particular problems faced by young people 'looked after'. Chapter six examines a range of issues concerning health and health promotion. It also covers vulnerable groups whose youth transitions are affected by either their own or others' health and includes a discussion of drug use. Chapter seven examines youth crime and the youth justice system. In chapters eight and nine we return to issues concerning holistic approaches. Chapter eight will examine what we can learn from attempts to promote holistic intervention at a local level, through individual youth projects. In the final chapter we will review how national government has been attempting to 'join up' youth policy and offer a critical review of the new structures and services it plans to introduce for the 21st century.

Chapter two

Tackling youth unemployment – the legacy of the past and new beginnings?

The election of a New Labour Government in 1997 was achieved, at least in part, by a commitment to tackle youth unemployment and put educational achievement at the heart of government policy. Well before the 1997 election, on all measures, unemployment was falling from the three million plus of the mid 1980s to under one and a half million in 1997 (Unemployment Unit, 1997b). Nevertheless, there was still widespread concern about the waste of unemployment and before the 1997 election New Labour made clear its intention to address this in a new and radical way. It announced its intention to levy a 'windfall tax' on the profits of public utilities and use this to fund a 'New Deal' for the unemployed, with unemployed 18 to 24-year-olds a priority group (Unemployment Unit, 1997a). The New Deal for Young People (NDYP) was launched in pathfinder districts in January 1998 and rolled out into a comprehensive national programme the following April. Policy for 16 to 18-year-olds was less clear in 1997 and slower to emerge. But as we see towards the end of this chapter these policies are also radical, with proposals to develop a new profession of personal advisers and new structures to better manage the school-to-work transition.

Many of the problems the new profession will have to address have their origins in patterns of disaffection and disadvantage established well before the end of compulsory schooling. It is perhaps important to distinguish between disaffection and disadvantage (Chatrik, 1999). Disadvantage refers to the circumstances (personal, family and community) in which young people live, are brought up and are educated and trained that result in levels of achievement which significantly underestimate their potential. Disadvantage can, therefore, have as its roots a wide variety of factors which may or may not be recognised by schools, colleges and support services. It may be associated with attributes of the individual but it may also result from difficulties occurring at home, in the family or in the labour market. Unemployment especially may be the result of the lack of local labour demand rather than any deficiency of the individual. Persistently high unemployment, however, can also impact upon the motivation of young people to take their education and training seriously or to search actively for jobs. Patterns of disadvantage are, therefore, potentially linked to disaffection. Disaffection refers not so much to circumstances as to the hostile attitudes that a young person has developed towards the value of education, training or job search, no matter the reasons for this. This chapter examines evidence on the characteristics of the young unemployed and policies which are designed to build more secure bridges from school to work and ways back into education, training and work for those who become unemployed.

Youth unemployment and the development of youth training

Ever since the late 1970s, one response to youth unemployment has been to develop training schemes. In the mid 1970s there were a number of 'special measures' developed, in the main, for a small minority of unqualified young people who left school at minimum school leaving age and did not find work. These 'special measures' were short 12 week courses, some of which involved work experience or work on community projects and sometimes involved subsidies to employers to take on the young unemployed (Finn, 1987; Rees and Atkinson, 1982). In this sense it was the beginning of what is now described as an 'intermediate labour market'. As we will see, this is now properly reserved for jobs that, although subsidised, pay workers at a rate equivalent to that in the unsubsidised sector. This was not what happened in the sorry history of youth training over the last quarter of a century.

As youth unemployment among 16-year-old school leavers continued to rise in the late 1970s, the then Labour Government initiated an enquiry which, when published, became known as the Holland Report (Manpower Services Commission, 1977) This recommended a rationalisation of youth training under a Youth Opportunities Programme (YOP) to cater for up to half a million school leavers. The schemes provided in this programme were characteristically six months in length. It was hoped that this would help stagger the entry into the labour force of the age cohort, which at the time was increasing in size. The programme content was a mixture of work experience, off-the-job skills training and courses in 'social and life skills'. The Holland report recognised that such an extensive programme required the cooperation and partnership of employers, local authorities and further education providers, the voluntary sector and community groups. A whole sector of FE was devoted to servicing the schemes. Employer-led schemes of Work Experience on Employers Premises (WEEP) were the most popular and sought after, with the least qualified and most difficult to place young people on schemes run by local authorities, voluntary and community groups (Furlong and Cartmel, 1997; Roberts, 1995).

Yet youth unemployment continued to rise and did so ever more steeply after 1979 under the first Thatcher Conservative Government. Following another White Paper in 1981, YOP was replaced with a 12 month youth training scheme (YTS) which was extended to a 24 month scheme in 1985. A year later, when recruitment to YTS was at its peak, it catered for more than a quarter of the age group and covered not only the poorly qualified, but a significant number with five or more good passes in national 16-year-old school qualifications (Ashton, 1986; Banks et al., 1992). By the mid 1980s, not only were the numbers of young people involved in YTS large, but the length of training schemes had been increased by nearly nine-fold in less than ten years. Yet youth unemployment continued to rise and YTS gained a similar reputation to its predecessors as 'slave labour', accompanied by poor training, and was for many, an insecure bridge between school and work (Craig, 1991; Finn, 1987; Hollands, 1990). YTS was replaced by Youth Training (YT) in 1991. This was intended to be more focused towards the attainment of National Vocational Qualifications (NVQs). Many were run under private company brand names as if to disguise the fact they were government-supported youth training schemes at all. Under YT, attention was also given to the development of schemes which would train young people beyond the basic level of NVQ2 offered by YT, and towards NVQ3, more akin to technician grade qualifications.

The poor reputation of youth training arose from a number of factors. One was the level of training allowances young people were paid. In the late 1970s and early 1980s, allowances were regularly up-rated and stood at only £23.50 in 1981. Throughout the 1980s and early 1990s up-rating fell markedly behind inflation or rises in wages. Indeed there was no increase at all between 1988 and 1997 when the training allowance was finally raised from £29.50 by 50 pence per week. Under YT, employers were encouraged to top up training allowances but, even so, on average trainees had a take home pay-packet of £39 for young men and £37.70 for young women. Had training allowances been up-rated annually in line with wages, they would have been twice that amount. Young people taking part in youth training could, therefore, be receiving a training allowance for a forty hour week which was less than their contemporaries would receive for part-time work whilst continuing with their full-time education. This was one of the factors which led to the eclipsing of youth training in the 1990s by the growth of post-16 education. By the late 1990s, youth training recruited only 10 per cent of 16-year-olds whereas during the 1990s post-compulsory education had raised its market share by 20 per cent to over 70 per cent of the age group.

The second reason for the persistently poor reputation of training schemes was the relatively poor progression from scheme to employment. Throughout the 1980s those moving from scheme to employment rarely rose above 60 per cent and during the early 1990s was falling back to 40 per cent (Roberts, 1995). Furthermore, under new regimes of management which tied funding to positive outcomes, those for whom youth training had been initially designed (the unqualified and the most vulnerable) had been squeezed out of training altogether. Training and Enterprise Councils (TECs and LECs in Scotland) showed a lack of willingness to fully fund those with special training needs who were instead directed towards forms of special further education in colleges (Baldwin *et al.*, 1997; Mitchell, 1998; Roberts, 1995).

Thirdly, those who had the poorest outcomes at the end of youth training have persistently been those who have been disadvantaged at the start. In the course of its development, youth training had developed its own stratification system in which, on the one hand, those with the better qualifications and home backgrounds got the best placements with the best chance of employment at the end (McClagan, 1993). On the other hand, the most disadvantaged were placed on schemes with poor outcomes (Raffe, 1987; Roberts, 1995). Analysis of the Youth Cohort Studies have shown that young people taking part in youth training who come from disadvantaged backgrounds, including lone parent families, large families, and those with parents who are unemployed or in low level occupations, are much more likely to become unemployed at the end of the scheme (Dalton *et al.*, 1999). Young people from middle class backgrounds were much more likely to get on the best schemes, whereas those from working class backgrounds were allocated to the least prestigious schemes with the poorest outcomes (Roberts, 1993). Progression rates have also been persistently poorer in the north where unemployment rates were higher and where youth training recruited in greater numbers. Asian young people have also been shown to have less chance of progression into employment (Dalton *et al.*, 1999) as have young men from African and Caribbean heritage. One study in the 1980s suggested that the Careers Service was at best 'colour blind' in its approach to young people and sometimes engaged in 'protective channelling' – avoiding sending minority ethnic young people to employer placements known to be racist (Crook, 1990; YETRU, 1994; Wrench, 1990). Another study which reported on the economic activity of young people in their 20s showed that, whilst unemployment rates amongst the white population were 9 per cent, amongst those who were Pakistani or Bangladeshi rates were 29 per cent, rates for those of African descent 25 per cent and those of African-Caribbean descent 20 per cent (Berthoud, 1999)

Fourthly, youth training has persistently operated only in certain restricted labour market segments and in a way that is linked to gender stratified labour markets. Four fifths of young women taking part in YTS or YT were trained in clerical, cleaning, catering and selling jobs, whereas young men had a slightly wider mix, with a half clustered in construction, mining and manufacturing training, where jobs were highly vulnerable (Courtney and McAleese, 1993).

Fifthly, the success in recruiting young people into training has persistently been linked to the lack of jobs in local labour markets (Banks *et al.*, 1992). Even though youth training has, recently and on average, lost its 'market share', participation rates vary significantly between areas from 18 per cent in the north-east to only 3 per cent in west and north London. New Labour made a manifesto commitment to 'replace the failed youth training programme'. However, since the election, youth training has continued to be targeted at the achievement of NVQ2 under 'National Traineeships' and NVQ3 under 'Modern Apprenticeships'. It has been claimed that there is now a concerted attempt to make training available across a wider range of industrial sectors (claimed to be as many as 47 in 1999), to underpin all training with information technology and communication skills, and to ensure that trainees have employment status and wages from the start of their training (Unemployment Unit, July 1999). However, until the turn of the century, many TECs and LECs continued to pay a minimum of £30 per week for 16-year-olds and £35 for 17-year-olds. Some paid substantially more (£40 and £50 in Leeds, and £50 for both 16 and 17-year-olds in Northamptonshire) (Chatrik and Convery, 1999) although participation rates in both Leeds and Northampton were below the national average. Late in 1999, the Government finally announced the first substantial increase in the basic allowance in two decades but this still left 'wages rates' at £40 for 16-year-olds.

Young adults and (un)employment and training

One of the legacies of the failure of youth training to provide an effective bridge from school to work has been the growth of unemployment in the older age group. YOP and YTS may have succeeded in taking school leavers off the unemployment register but when training failed to provide young people with secure employment, YOP merely returned many of those it recruited to unemployment at the age of 17 or 18. In the 1970s adult training schemes were provided through the Community Programme, often through jobs involving forms of community service or environmental work. They were developed by the Manpower Services Commission which had initially strong trades union representation on it, and which made an attempt to make rates of pay commensurate with those in the unsubsidised labour market. The pattern of development in the 1980s, however, saw a close linkage of training allowances to social security benefits and made entitlement to benefit dependent on taking part in training. Under Employment Training (ET) introduced in 1988 and later Training for Work (TfW), recruitment was closely tied to the 'Restart Programme'. Under Restart, those who had claimed benefit for six months were 'called in' and had their eligibility for benefits closely scrutinised, in particular to determine whether they were available for work and taking steps actively to seek it. If they were, then they were referred on to a Personal Adviser who would assess their aspirations and then refer them to either a Training Provider or to a Job Club at which personal effectiveness training and active job search was required.

Since the 1997 election, unemployed young people between the ages of 18 and 24 have been offered the 'New Deal for Young People' (NDYP), although usually only if they have been unemployed and in receipt of benefit for six months. Yet critical questions must be asked about what is 'new' about New Deal and what are its chances of success where other schemes have failed. NDYP lies at the heart of the Government's 'Welfare to Work' strategy and is now to be funded from general taxation rather than the windfall tax on public utilities through which it was initially financed. Obtaining employment is seen as the road back from social exclusion and poverty for a whole range of different groups. One danger, however, is that, as more and more different groups attempt to move from welfare to work, they will be in competition with each other unless more jobs are created. Nearly a million new jobs have been created since 1997, yet in some regions job growth is weak and many of them are precarious. New Deal can only work in a growing labour market and one in which the jobs created can be sustained. There is, however, a recognition by Government that there is a need to address issues of labour demand as well as deficiencies in labour supply. New Deal had the advantage of coming on-stream during a period in which unemployment rates were falling rather than rising. This does, however, raise the question as to whether young people moving to employment after New Deal might have obtained work anyway and despite it rather than because of it. There is, however, a new commitment within Government to returning to full employment and the creation of new jobs through various initiatives, such as New Deal for Communities. The claim of Government is that it is recognising and addressing the problems faced by the long-term unemployed, even those living adjacent to labour markets with high unemployment rates. Employment Zones (EZs), for instance are being given additional funds and support to do this, over and above the funding of New Deal. One of the design features of the prototype EZs created before May 2000 is the development and use of intermediate labour markets in which employment is both subsidised and supported, as well as integrated packages of education and training. Later EZs are focusing more on the development of the Personal Job Account.

Glasgow (prototype) Employment Zone

Glasgow has been the centre of a number of innovative programmes to help the long-term unemployed, in particular the intermediate labour market work of the WISE group and Glasgow Works. Glasgow has a large number of job opportunities available simply through its size; over 100,000 jobs turnover annually and new 'industries' such as call centres are being developed rapidly. However, Glasgow has similar problems to London in that these jobs rarely go to local long-term unemployed people. There is competition for jobs from people commuting from outside Glasgow who take 42 per cent of the jobs in the city.

The focus of the Employment Zone will be households where nobody is in employment and it aims to offer 2,500 Employment Zone places over two years. The target for employment is 65 per cent of this figure with at least 50 per cent in employment after 12 months. During the caseload process, priority will be given to those with greatest need, a multiplicity of needs and those who would benefit most from the flexibility of Employment Zone provision. Employment Zone advisers will attempt to sift out those who could be helped by existing provision.

Learning for Work provision is central to all Employment Zone clients' experience. Clients will receive approximately £200 in an individual Employment Zone learning account to pursue an 'area of personal development'. Emphasis will be on non-traditional methods of learning and attempts to increase accessibility. Intermediate Labour Market provision is already substantially in place through the WISE group and Glasgow Works. Employment Zone participants will have access to these jobs as they become available and it is expected there will be approximately twenty jobs per month. The Employment Zone will also be looking to develop new ILM projects under the Neighbourhood Match option. The Business Enterprise option is likely to include an 'enterprise taster' module in addition to similar provision to that in Plymouth and Tees South. Glasgow Employment Zone is also looking at establishing a Mentors Pool to run in conjunction with New Deal. This may be set up on an ILM model with staff potentially coming from the Employment Zone provision themselves.

Based on material from the Unemployment Unit & Youthaid website (quoted with permission)

The New Deal for Young People was the first of a series of 'New Deals' now extended to older age groups and lone parents. NDYP is the most heavily funded (£2.6 billion) and is a political 'high risk' strategy. The target group is young people who are in receipt of Jobseeker's Allowance for at least six months. Certain groups can apply for early entry if, for instance, they need help with basic skills in reading, writing or numeracy, if they have been out of the labour market for domestic reasons for two years or more, if they have left local authority care within the past three years or have been made redundant in a large-scale redundancy. Twelve 'pathfinder' areas started to recruit in January 1998, although the programme did not start nationally until April. As we have seen, New Deal was launched in the wake of a series of youth and adult training schemes largely considered by its potential target group as failing them. If youth training had been experienced as 'exploitation', 'slave labour' and full of 'broken promises' as many reports suggest, why should young people believe that New Deal would be any different? As might be expected, New Deal is also the subject of a major research and evaluation programme and, at the time of writing, a number of research reports are in the public domain. These provide an important source of information on the characteristics of the young people who are being recruited on to the different programmes within NDYP, their early experiences of it and their progress towards employment. But before examining this, some of the basic features of the programme will be explained briefly.

New Deal has three main stages: 'Gateway'; the four 'Options'; and 'follow through'. As we have seen, previous adult training schemes started with some sort of preliminary assessment of the aims, aspirations and needs of the unemployed. Barriers to employment were identified and an 'action plan' developed through which these would be addressed, and training and job search arranged (DE, 1988). But all this was largely accomplished in a short, one day session with staff who were paid *pro rata* for each Action Plan completed. Gateway can claim to be 'new' in that assessment and planning can take up to four months, during which young people work with a Personal Adviser, for the most part, specially-trained Employment Service staff. Assessment is intended to be much more holistic than under previous schemes. It does not only address issues of job skills, qualifications and aspirations but might also cover problems associated with drug dependency, debt, homelessness or other aspects of housing and lifestyle. The Gateway approach also recognised that there will be considerable diversity between young people taking part and a need for a package of support to be tailored to individual needs, ambitions and potential. Gateway also offers the opportunity for young people to take part in short, basic skills training, work tasters and work trials (of up to three weeks). The overall aim of Gateway is to make young people 'job ready' before either seeking open employment or embarking upon one of the four 'options'.

This more holistic approach seems vindicated by early survey results of entrants to New Deal (Bryson *et al.*, 2000). This shows that a fifth of the sample reported a health problem or a disability, expected to last for a year or more; a fifth reported basic skills problems since the age of 16; and a quarter had no formal qualifications. The vast majority of those recruited to NDYP were male (71 per cent) and white (83 per cent) although Pakistani and Bangladeshi women were over-represented among female participants at 9 per cent of the total. This is broadly in line with those entitled to join the programme rather than a programme bias. Almost a half (48 per cent) were living in social housing with the same proportion living with parents who were responsible for their housing costs. One in seven, however, were living with a partner, only a quarter of whom were in employment. One in ten had children of their own. However, participant New Dealers regarded the main barriers to employment as being the lack of jobs in the areas in which they lived, although lack of personal transport was also seen as a major barrier by a quarter of those surveyed. From the start of New Deal there has been pressure on Gateway providers to move their clients through the process as quickly as possible. Yet early research found that a quarter of those surveyed had remained on Gateway for longer than the prescribed period of four months, indicating the range and severity of the issues being addressed (Bryson *et al.*, 2000).

The intention of Gateway is to prepare young people for employment. Up to September 1999, of the 226,940 who had left New Deal, 96,760 (27 per cent) left to take unsubsidised jobs. However, where open unsubsidised employment is not achieved as a result of job search activities within Gateway, or participants are not sufficiently job-ready, young people are offered one of four 'options': full-time education and/or training; subsidised employment; placement on an environment task force (ETF); or placement in the voluntary sector. What has been emphasised throughout by Government is that 'there is no fifth option'- simply returning to benefits. In order to qualify for the right to benefit young people are required to illustrate that they are fulfilling their responsibilities to be educated and trained and to look for work. Those who refuse to take part three times are now sanctioned through the benefits system.

The education and training option is intended for young people who have not yet obtained a national vocational qualification at level two (NVQ2). Initially it was anticipated that this would account for around a quarter of all placements and would be covered by a training plan signed within two weeks of starting Gateway (extended to four weeks in mid-1999). Under this option training and education can last for at least 30 hours per week and for up to 52 weeks. Those participants with children can receive childcare costs of £100 for an only child and up to £150 for two or more children. The take-up of the education and training option has been much greater than planned. Of those starting New Deal before September 1999 and moving on to options, more than a third (37 per cent) were following this route (Bivand, 2000a).

The employment option was anticipated to be the most popular route covering around 45 per cent of those leaving Gateway and moving on to options. A lot of time and effort was spent immediately after the 1997 election in recruiting major companies to take part in the programme. Placement with an established employer has traditionally always been the most popular with trainees and the most likely to lead to employment. Under NDYP, employers receive up to £60 for each New Deal participant they take on for 30 hours or more per week, with less subsidy when the employment is part-time. Participants must receive a wage covered by the statutory minimum wage and be covered by a contract of employment. Employers must also provide at least the equivalent of one day a week training during the first six months (for which they receive a £750 training grant), and the training provided

Tackling youth unemployment – the legacy of the past and new beginnings?

25

must be directed towards a recognised qualification. Compared with the education and training route which had over-recruited, the employer options had under-recruited, taking just 27 per cent of those on options in September 1999, significantly less that the 45 per cent planning had anticipated (Bivand, 2000a).

The Environment Task Force (ETF) option was designed to enable young people to take part in projects directed at a range of outcomes such as reclaiming derelict land, conserving energy and water, improving air quality, encouraging waste reduction and re-cycling, greening or promoting cleaner and safer urban areas and encouraging rural regeneration. The voluntary sector option was directed at projects run by voluntary organisations and projects that aimed to produce 'community benefits' in areas such as reducing the risk of re-offending among ex-offenders, reducing drug-misuse or more generally improving the capacity of voluntary organisations to develop community services. For both these options it was expected that participants would have spent three or more months on Gateway developing skills. The placements are intended to provide a maximum of six months of work experience although, in some areas, European Social Fund monies have provided the means through which wages can be paid for up to 12 months. Providers are asked to have a clear Personal Development Plan for participants covering at least 30 hours per week of supervised work which should take account of any issues concerning health or disability. The equivalent of at least one day a week of off-the-job training should also be provided by participating organisations and New Dealers must be provided with time, support and guidance in further job-search activities. Payment for this comes in either a wage from the ETF or the voluntary organisation, or in the form of 'benefits-plus' a staged grant of £400 paid over the six month period (equivalent to benefits plus £15.38 per week). New Dealers can choose between any offered wages and the benefits-plus alternative. Under the 'benefits-plus' option, child-care costs can be paid for the care of children under the age of 15 at the start of New Deal, and other benefits such as Housing Benefit and free prescriptions can be retained. At the end of the six months, participants are entitled to a certificate and work reference. During the period in which New Deal was being developed, voluntary sector organisations were strongly encouraged to join, even though the efforts involved in setting up and monitoring placements, and the paperwork necessary to demonstrate that they could comply with New Deal were considerable. Young People taking part in the environmental and voluntary sector options have not been as numerous as those taking part in education, training or jobs with other employers. However, up to September 1999 more than fifteen thousand young people had taken either the ETF or voluntary sector option, with slightly more taking placements in the voluntary sector than with the ETF. At the time of writing it is still too early in the programme to evaluate the success of each option in moving participants from New Deal to work. Early signs from official evaluation surveys indicate that those who have now left the environmental task force are more likely to be unemployed than those leaving from the voluntary sector (Bryson et al., 2000).

The third phase of involvement in New Deal is referred to as 'follow-through', a period of 13 weeks in which further support and guidance is offered. One month before the end of any of the four options, a young person must attend a mandatory interview with their

Personal Adviser. At this stage, providing no agreement has been reached with the provider for taking on the participant into permanent unsubsidised employment, information about jobs and help in applying for them is provided. This is not confined to the first 'follow-through' interview and may take the form of six further intensive sessions with their Personal Adviser on job search. If, however, no job is forthcoming, the young person may return to benefit and will be entitled to claim Jobseeker's Allowance from the day they complete New Deal. Unless they are part of an 'early access' group, they may not be re-called for New Deal until they have claimed JSA for a further six months, although they may be able to take part in other Government Programmes such as Jobclubs.

Several issues have become apparent during the early years of New Deal and may go some way to answering the question about what is 'new' about it. Firstly, as we have seen, the processing of young people through Gateway has been a longer process for more young people than had been anticipated. This illustrates the complexity of the problems being addressed and the fact that often there are no quick and easy solutions to them. Indeed the four month ceiling for time on Gateway has *de facto* had to be extended although the ES refer to these as 'over-stayers'. Those who have been unemployed for six months or more between the ages of 18 and 24 are an extremely disparate group. Some are highly qualified and 'job ready' whilst others have no qualifications or no, or very little, work experience. Often the lifestyle they have developed whilst unemployed means that they have great difficulties in meeting the stringent demands of employers for punctuality, reliability and hard work. Others have ongoing personal, domestic and housing problems that need to be addressed and solved simultaneously with preparation for work. Gateway is, therefore, a move towards a holistic approach.

Secondly, a number of commentators have drawn attention to a new role being created for 'intermediate labour markets' – forms of paid (albeit subsidised) work which are different from those offered by ordinary employers in the private or public sectors. Other things being equal, it would seem reasonable for young people who are the least 'job ready' to make use of one of the four options whilst those who are 'job ready' are targeted towards unsubsidised employment. Unfortunately, other things are rarely equal and the use of intermediate labour markets by New Deal seems more related to the state of the local labour market – whether 'real jobs' are available or not. In one study comparing the relatively buoyant labour market of Cambridge with high unemployment areas in Liverpool and Glasgow, the latter two schemes were making much more use of the intermediate labour market and taking longer to process young people through Gateway (Theodore and Peck, 1999). The Unemployment Unit and Youthaid, however, report that many of the worst-performing 'Delivery Units' are in areas of very marked job growth. This suggests that the level of local labour demand is only one of the critical factors in determining how New Deal operates and the training needs of the client group may well be another.

The labour market context of New Deal was always going to be a critical factor in determining its effect. Many of the failures of previous training programmes were because they largely attempted to remedy the supply of labour rather than stimulate demand. New Deal is only part of an overall economic strategy of a government that has repeatedly stated its aspiration to move to an economy supporting full employment. New Deal thus has to be seen alongside a number of measures intended to stimulate employment demand, such as New Deal for Communities, Employment Zones and Employment Action Zones. Yet in reviewing New Deal, one of its long standing supporters, the Unemployment Unit and Youthaid, is critical of the ways in which these and other projects are linked into New Deal. They call for new contracts to be offered in April 2001, specifically to intermediary organisations that really understand their local labour market and have established links to employers. They also call for the next phase to be more closely targeted in areas of high unemployment and to aim to establish links to other job-creation initiatives (Unemployment Unit and Youthaid, 2000).

With such a high political profile, debate about the success of New Deal was inevitable, as was disagreement about the best criteria for its evaluation. By the end of 1999 Government was claiming that 155,000 had moved from welfare and into work. The Unemployment Unit, however, claimed that of these, 41,000 had not obtained 'sustainable' jobs and only 57 per cent had kept their jobs for more than 13 weeks before returning to benefit (Bivand, 2000b). Taking job entry on leaving New Deal as the sole indicator of success does make it harder for NDYP to be defined as a success story. The latest available statistics at the time of writing indicate that of all 436,430 NDYP entrants across Britain, on average around a third of participants obtained sustained employment (Bivand, 2000a). Only one area (Lochaber in Scotland, which only had 91 New Deal starts) reported more than 50 per cent moving to employment. More worrying is that some of the areas with the lowest rates are in inner city London where job vacancies are high and public transport easily available. This raises the question as to whether the programme is working as well as it should in matching labour demand and supply. The Unemployment Unit and Youthaid suggests that much more could and should be done to create packages of education, training and work experience in preparing the young unemployed for employment. It also suggests that, in making certain that jobs are sustained, more could also be done in follow-through support for both young workers and employers.

The other remaining worry about all forms of training is its association with the withdrawal of benefit for those who refuse it. When benefit levels are low, young people may be driven to seek alternative forms of remunerative activity rather than endure the hassles involved in keeping in touch with agencies designed to help them. This is certainly true of 16 and 17-year-olds from whom benefits were withdrawn in 1988.

Status Zer0 and the disappeared

In the late 1980s and early 1990s sociologists in South Wales began reporting that a significant number of 16 and 17-year-olds were detached from all forms of education, employment and training. Status Zer0 was initially a technical term derived from Careers Service statistics; some young people were not in education (status 1), in training (status 2) or in employment (status 3). But the term also provided 'a powerful metaphor' that such young people seemed to count for nothing and were going nowhere (Williamson, 1997). What is more, they were not entitled to benefit and had not, as had been hoped, been discouraged from doing nothing by having their benefit entitlement taken away (since the implementation of the 1986 Social Security Act in 1988). Associated with this change was the introduction of a government 'guarantee'. This policy shift was designed to ensure that all young people started their careers with some positive prospects for at least the first two years after school leaving. Survey evidence at the time suggested that around 10 per cent of the age group had left school and were not in education, work or training (Courtney, 1989). It was hoped that the numbers in this group would diminish as the importance and value of training became recognised. In fact the evidence suggests that, despite changes in the benefit system, the size of the category has not been reduced. Some would argue it has grown (Chatrik *et al.*, 2000).

There has been unease since the late 1980s that there might be categories of young people who would be adversely affected by the changes (Social Security Advisory Committee Group, 1989 and 1992). Provision was made (and gradually extended) for some groups to receive Income Support under Severe Hardship (SH) provision (Maclagan, 1993). Throughout the 1990s the numbers of applications for Severe Hardship payments increased, reaching a peak of 140,000 in 1996. Although the vast majority of these applications are successful, there is a growing recognition that claimants may represent only the tip of the iceberg. Indeed, the Unemployment Unit and Youthaid suggested that only around 15 per cent of unemployed 16 and 17-year-olds receive any form of state income (Chatrik and Convery, 1997). Many more may be 'status zero' but not claiming benefit because they don't meet the criteria for benefit, don't understand their entitlement or how to claim it, are deterred by the need to reveal intimate personal details, or simply because the small allowance is not thought to be worth the bother. Youthaid and others have also found that many young people are turned away from benefit offices, sometimes by frontline staff who are unaware of complicated regulations but who simply assert that 16 and 17-year-olds have no benefit entitlement, despite the fact that SH regulations for this group have existed for nine years (Castle, 1997; Maclagan, 1998).

The growth of this category of 'status zero' has been documented by a number of different sources. The research undertaken by both South Glamorgan and Mid Glamorgan Training and Enterprise Councils (TECs) attempted to estimate the destination of age cohorts leaving school in their areas (Instance *et al.*, 1994; Mid-Glamorgan TEC, 1996). On the basis of these calculations, Mid-Glamorgan TEC estimated that between 16 per cent and 20 per cent of 16 and 17-year-olds in their area were 'status zero'. This is a higher estimate than one done by Wilkinson in a study in Sunderland but broadly in line with other calculations (Wilkinson, 1995). Based upon analysis of the Labour Force Survey, the Unemployment Unit and Youthaid estimate that 135,500 16 and 17-year-olds across the UK are not in any form of education, employment or training, 9.5 per cent of the age group. Of these, 108,000 want to work yet only around 14,000 receive benefits (Bivand, 2000c). The Survey of English Housing data also indicates that within households containing this age group, 17 per cent of 16 and 17-year-olds were either unemployed or unavailable for work. This same survey also indicates that 'status zer0' young people are clustered in particular types of housing tenure, with over 28 per cent of the age group living in housing association property being unemployed (Coles *et al.*, 1998). Other significant clustering is in particular minority ethnic groups. The official rate of unemployed 16 and 17-year-olds is 37 per cent with the Black Institute of Employment claiming that their calculations suggest it may be as high as 55 per cent (Modood *et al.*, 1997; Shire, 1996).

The research done in South Wales provides some limited information about the social characteristics of this group (Williamson, 1997). Only a few had been excluded from school but a quarter had had little contact with education after the age of 13 (and some much earlier). Some did take examinations but the majority had few, if any, qualifications. Four out of ten did have some involvement with youth training but most gave up on it when it failed to offer a realistic route to secure employment, or when some more lucrative (even if short term) opportunity presented itself. Training and employment careers were often complicated by a disruptive or turbulent family life, especially for 'status zer0' young women, a third of whom became mothers themselves. Two thirds of the men in the sample were living at home with both parents. There was also some evidence of involvement in crime and drug and substance abuse. The research carried out in South Wales and later replicated in Northern Ireland was locally based and not particularly high profile research and it was something of a surprise to youth researchers when the Social Exclusion Unit announced that disaffected 16 and 17-year-olds would be the subject of investigation. Government recoiled at the term 'status zer0', however, and replaced it with NEET, not in employment, education or training.

Policy initiatives and the *Bridging the Gap* report

The Social Exclusion Unit report was published in July 1999. In preparing the report the SEU asked the Department for Education and Employment to commission a review of statistical evidence on the number of people covered by NEET and the known characteristics of the group (Payne, 2000). This was based on a special analysis of the Youth Cohort Studies (YCS), a large questionnaire survey of young people. Yet, by the time young people are surveyed for the YCS at age 18, just over 40 per cent of the initial sample frame respond and there are reasons to suspect that those who are disengaged are heavily over-represented within those who do not. Young people in special schools are not even in the sample frame. Furthermore, the 'diary question' on which identification of 'status zer0' is made is not specifically designed to identify the group. It fails to distinguish between those who are genuinely 'status zer0' and those who are simply on holiday or constructively taking 'time out'. Despite this, the SEU attempted to summarise what the best available evidence can tell us about the group.

The SEU concluded that only around one in five of those identified as being NEET became non-participants immediately upon leaving school. The evidence it had suggested that the majority have tried some form of education, training or employment after minimum school leaving age before dropping out. A third of those not participating did so after dropping out of further education, with a further 40 per cent dropping out of a job or training. Drop-out from employment (27 per cent) was nearly twice as common as drop-out from government-sponsored training (15 per cent). Non-participation also varied in the length of time involved. The average time young people spent disengaged was just under six months. However, based on longitudinal cohort studies, the SEU also pointed out that many young people went on to experience further bouts of inactivity later in their lives. Those unemployed at 16 were likely to suffer the same fate, on average, between seven or eight times before they reach the age of 23. Forty per cent of those out of work and education at 16 were also not in education or work at age 18 and were highly likely to be unqualified, untrained and unemployed at the age of 21. Indeed, they concluded that non-participation aged 16 is the single most powerful predictor of later unemployment, something which underlined the importance of acting early to re-engage this group. More than two-thirds of young women who experienced non-participation of six months or more had at least one child by the age of 21, with more than a third having two or more children (SEU, 1999b).

A number of other different factors were associated with non-participation. The SEU reported a clear correlation between educational disadvantage and disaffection pre-16 and later disengagement. A quarter of those who truanted persistently in Year 11 were not in employment, education or training the year after. Those permanently excluded from school in years 10 and 11 were two and a half times more likely than their peers to be non-participants later and those with fixed term exclusions twice as likely. A quarter of those with no reported qualifications and nearly one in four of those with only 1 to 4 passes below C grade became non-participants. The SEU also reported on spatial concentrations. Regions with a history of high unemployment, and deprived areas in all regions, had much higher rates. Young people whose parents were unemployed were also reported to be over-represented (SEU, 1999b). Young people from African Caribbean, Pakistani and Bangladeshi minority ethnic groups were also over-represented. One in six young people from Pakistani and Bangladeshi communities experienced spells of non-participation of four or more months during the two years following the end of compulsory schooling (SEU, 1999b).

Young carers who looked after other family members (to be discussed in chapter six) were also over-represented. So too were young people with statements of special educational need, despite the expansion of special further education provision during the 1990s. At the age of 16 and 17 young people reporting a health or disability problem were more likely not to participate; with a quarter not participating in education, employment or training by the age of 18. Those with mental health problems too were also found to be over-represented with four out of ten reporting that they were non-participants. Those 'looked after' or leaving care will be reported upon in greater detail in chapter five. As we see, this group is associated with other patterns of disadvantage and disaffection, including drifting into being 'status zer0'. Three-quarters of male 16 to 17-year-olds who are charged with an offence and appear before the Youth Court have no involvement with education, training or paid employment. More than seven out of ten 'status zer0' young people report having used drugs compared with under half of their peers. Among those also excluded from school,

Tackling youth unemployment – the legacy of the past and new beginnings?

31

over a third reported using drugs other than cannabis, 9 per cent had used cocaine and 5 per cent crack cocaine (Powis *et al.*, 1998). 'Status zer0' has all the characteristics of being a complex, multi-faceted and joined-up problem.

The media coverage of the SEU report *Bridging the Gap* was couched in terms of 'rescuing a lost generation' of young people caught up in bureaucratic 'red tape' and 'confusion' (*The Times, Guardian, Daily Express, Independent* 14. 7. 99). Some of this was undoubtedly justified. Page 62 of the report provided a startling diagram that portrayed the planning and funding of initiatives covering the 16 to 18 age group. Patterns of provision spanned 14 different government departments and agencies at a national, regional and local level and drew from an even larger plethora of professions and other voluntary sector workers all 'involved in the education and broader welfare of young people in the 16 to 18 age group'. It reported that financial support for young people could be paid by at least eight different agencies, all with complex rules, and many with a reputation for being very user-unfriendly. The report proposed a far-reaching series of policies to address these issues.

The SEU report provided a long-term agenda for change in a number of policy areas and set up four working groups to address its 25 point 'action plan'. The DfEE White Paper *Learning to Succeed,* published shortly before the report, also signalled a wide-ranging series of reforms including:

- greater choice at Key Stage 4 and a Learning Gateway of options at age 16;
- a Graduation Certificate for all at the age of 19;
- a new Youth Support Service, Connexions and a Youth Card;
- a single Learning and Skills Council with local Learning and Skills Councils to coordinate post-16 education and training; and
- the extension of Education Maintenance Allowances for those wishing to participate but whose family circumstances mean they cannot afford to do so (DfEE, 1999f).

Each of these policy initiatives will be described in turn.

Modification of the curriculum at Key Stage 4 and a Learning Gateway at 16
As we have seen, the SEU highlighted the fact that disaffection at age 16 and 17 is linked to earlier disaffection in school and especially during the end of compulsory schooling. It argued that, if education is to engage all young people in the final years of compulsory schooling, there must be some flexibility in the restricted academic diet of the national curriculum. Firstly, following pressure from a number of well placed sources, (Bentley and Gurumerthy, 1999; Pearce and Hillman, 1998), Government announced a series of measures designed to allow vocational options at key stage 4 (covering 14 to 16-year-olds). At the time of writing, a national curriculum review is being undertaken to increase flexibility in dis-applying the curriculum to increase vocational qualifications for this age group (including a new Part 1 GNVQ) and to experiment more with work-based approaches to learning. Extra funding is being made available to enable this to happen. Some of these, including New Start, will be reviewed in the next chapter.

Secondly, the report called for more sensitive approaches to teaching and learning. The

Teacher Training Agency is being asked to incorporate into both initial and in-service training, material on the factors involved in disadvantage and some means of recognising excellence in teaching such groups. Thirdly, the SEU proposed that there was a need for more coherent help and advice about options at 16, especially for those groups most at risk of dropping out. This would be done by the development of a new youth support service Connexions as outlined below.

The New Youth Support Service – Connexions

Under the Connexions Strategy, there will be a range of measures to support progression at the age of 16, including: outreach and personal support; improved curriculum and range of qualifications; improved standards of delivery; and financial support for those who need it most. Included under 'outreach' and personal support, is the introduction of a 'Learning Card' to make young people more aware of their entitlements to education and training and a 'Learning Gateway' for all those not yet ready to access Level 2 learning, including access to personal advisers for those who need special help (also see below).

It has been recognised for some time that careers guidance and advice comes 'too little and too late' into schools with much of the work of Careers Services being regarded as ineffective, particularly with young people at risk of dropping out (Killeen *et al.*, 1992; Tan, 1997). Throughout the 1990s the Careers Service has been subjected to widespread re-organisation and change, including privatisation and changes to its work through 're-focusing'. The latter required careers companies to pay particular attention to vulnerable groups and those at risk of disengaging from all forms of education, training and employment. There is now a more general acceptance of the fact that leaving school is a 'life episode' where things can go badly wrong and where accessing suitable public services can be difficult. However, whilst there has been some successful innovatory practice developed by some careers companies and the voluntary sector (see Box below) until recently, this was far from common practice.

Warwickshire Careers Service Double Take project

The Double Take Project is a Careers Service initiative which uses strategies including outreach, inter-agency working and client centred approaches to re-engage young people who have not been able to access or sustain learning or employment. (Dave, whose biography was covered in chapter one, was involved in this scheme). It is principally funded by Warwickshire Careers Service and Warwickshire Chamber of Commerce Training and Enterprise, and also utilises European and Charitable Trust funding for different aspects of the work.

From the start of the project in 1994, the direction taken has reflected a fundamental tenet – to listen to young people and respond to what they say, and to network with appropriate agencies to maximise resources and expertise. Over a period of four and a half years, the project has utilised Careers Service records and resources to reach out to 'missing' young people. Over 900 have been contacted by outreach teams using a range of approaches which have included:

- visiting young people at home, whose post-statutory education destination was unknown to the Careers Service and who had not responded to telephone calls or mailouts;
- the provision of mobile offices on isolated housing estates and villages;
- the introduction of a menu of challenging individual and group activities to engage young people, using a range of educational and recreational activities; and
- the establishment of drop-in 'one-stop' centres where young people get advice on a range of issues including health, housing benefits, education, training and employment.

Working closely with local providers of education and training, the initiative provides access to progression in terms of pre-vocational qualifications and accreditation of key skills. Drop-in 'one-stop shops' have been established and these provide advice and guidance in an informal setting as part of a structured programme to improve self-image and motivation. In addition, mentoring and advocacy services have been introduced, together with respite provision for young people in danger of not sustaining an education, training or employment opportunity.

Project development has included the appointment of mentors to facilitate transition to mainstream programmes and designated outreach workers to focus on young people involved in drug or substance misuse, particularly in rural areas. Another specialist mentor is working with people over the age of 18 who are referred by the Probation Service. Trainers have been appointed, not only to offer basic skills training but to build in accreditation for the progress and achievements demonstrated by Double Take clients and all Double Take workers are encouraged to achieve D32, 33 and 36 trainer qualifications.

The direction of the project has been determined by young people and by policy-makers and practitioners from a range of statutory and voluntary agencies. The team of dedicated Double Take workers, crucially backed up by mainstream careers team expertise, has facilitated delivery of the services by using a non-judgmental but consistent approach to young people.

Of paramount importance has been the involvement of the clients in all stages of project design and delivery. This commitment to a client-centred service aims to ensure that the initiative is user-friendly and relevant to their needs.
Focusing Advice and Guidance Services: a Resource Pack DfEE, 1999

The SEU report points out that in most areas outreach careers work is often not well integrated into other mainstream provision and is dependent upon short-term funding and unrealistic outcome performance measures. The report proposed a further period of consultation before the setting up of a new professional body of advisers. The profession now being proposed is something of a hybrid of the Careers and Youth Service and voluntary sector projects and is intended to build on the best practice of all who have been involved in carrying out various forms of outreach and detached youth work. It is highly likely, therefore, that Connexions will involve teams of workers with different skills and competences. What is vital is that it is not merely a re-branding of old-style Careers Services and that those involved in the service are appropriately trained and managed. This might be helped by the close relationship between Connexions and the new Learning and Skills Councils (see below). The 47 LSCs cover areas which are larger than those in which Careers Companies and TECs have operated in the past.

The new service is intended to be comprehensive and cover all young people but give priority attention to the most vulnerable groups. This more comprehensive approach to the disadvantaged and disaffected is also expected to be linked to much better systems of 'mapping' and 'tracking' whereby all (and especially the vulnerable and at risk) can be identified, engaged, take an active part in career planning and have their progress monitored. With notable exceptions, the routine 'careers destination' statistics collected and published by Careers Services and companies have been both static and short term, often merely recording what young people's status is three months or so after minimum school leaving age, or three months after sixth form or further education. Under the proposals of the SEU, all young people would be systematically tracked between the ages of 13 and 19. Given that some of the major routes into non-involvement involve dropping out of employment, education or training after the age of 16, this longer-term tracking is obviously a vital part of any solution designed to prevent young people from simply disappearing from official records. One way in which this may be made easier is through the use of a new Youth Card already being piloted in a number of areas. This card often gives access to free public transport and discounts in some youth consumer markets. It can also be used as a swipe card to monitor attendance in post-16 provision. It is hoped that the combination of the card and the responsibilities of the Connexions Service should precipitate prompt action in offering support at the most critical times.

The Connexions Strategy document had a foreword with a quotation from the Prime Minister which makes clear that, 'the youth support service will be our frontline policy for young people' (DfEE, 2000b). The foreword is also signed by no less than seven members of the cabinet, covering Social Security, Culture, the Media and Arts, the Home Office, the DETR and deputy Prime Minister, Education and Employment, Health and the Cabinet Office. It pledges:

> 'our commitment to tackle this ambitious enterprise jointly, both across government and across existing agencies, is key. Statutory agencies, the voluntary sector and specialist private sector businesses will work together to provide every young person with access to a personal adviser (to) provide a wide range of support to needs (and) help (young people) reach their full potential.'

The new service will be available to all and can be accessed by parents as well as young people. It aims to build on examples of 'what works' from the Careers Service, public and voluntary youth services, voluntary and community groups out-reach, health and education, social work and those engaging in sporting, cultural and other leisure activities. It will have

Tackling youth unemployment – the legacy of the past and new beginnings?

35

a three tier structure: a national unit responsible for strategy and reporting to the partner government departments; a Connexions partnership parallel to new Learning and Skills Councils throughout England; and a local management committee operating at local authority levels (or multiples) and drawing from local partners. The service will be based on the key principles of:

- raising aspirations – setting high expectations for every individual;
- meeting individual need – overcoming barriers to learning;
- taking account of the views of young people, individually and collectively as the service is developed and operated locally;
- inclusion – keeping young people in mainstream education and training;
- partnership – agencies working collaboratively;
- extending opportunity and equality of opportunity; and
- evidence-based practice – basing interventions on rigorous research and evaluation about what works.

The service will also have 'targets' for year-by-year improvements in participation, accepting as it does that participation is an important key to other aspects of wellbeing. Further targets are expected for participation in post-16 education and training and for the achievements of minority ethnic groups; for those living in communities with low achievements; for teenage mothers; and young people with disabilities. For 2002 the targets are:

- 33 per cent reduction in time lost through truancy;
- 33 per cent reduction in permanent school exclusions;
- to raise the achievement of those 'looked after' in the 17th year to at least 60 per cent of the levels achieved by others in the same area;
- to reduce the proportion of 13 to 19-year-olds using illegal drugs (and especially heroin and cocaine) by 50 per cent by 2008;
- to reduce the propensity of young people to commit crime by 5 per cent by 2002–03 and reduce recorded crime by 1 per cent; and
- to reduce teenage conceptions among under 18-year-olds by 50 per cent by 2010.

Although the new service will, like the old Careers Services, have a 'shop-front' presence, the key role within the service will be a network of personal advisers. These will operate through a variety of different institutions and settings: schools (with learning mentors); further education, training and employment (with personal advisers operating through Learning Gateway); Youth Offending Teams (with personal advisers); social service departments (personal advisers working with 'looked-after' children and care leavers); community and voluntary provision (personal advisers working with community leaders and voluntary sector project staff).

Learning and skills councils

As youth training and forms of post-16 education expanded in the 1980s and 1990s, so too did a somewhat chaotic system for funding, managing and overseeing local provision. The intention was to create quasi-markets in which different sectors of education and training would compete. Prior to the introduction of Learning and Skills Councils, there were three main bodies to fund different kinds of post-16 provision, with hugely different funding methodologies and wide differences in the ways in which these were tied to outputs – whether qualifications are attained at the end of a course. For instance, school sixth forms were funded through local authorities according to a local management of schools formula. This was based on the number of students registered on a course and took no account of outcomes – whether students achieved their aims. Further education and sixth form colleges received funding from the Further Education Funding Council (FEFC). The FEFC funding formula was immensely complex and gave little recognition of the differential cost of putting on different courses (engineering or sociology, for instance). There was some weighting given for attempts to 'widen participation' to students from deprived backgrounds as identified by their home postcodes, and some premiums paid for special educational provision. There was also a small element (8 per cent) related to outputs. TECs and LECs were responsible for funding a variety of different youth training programmes aimed mainly at achieving NVQ qualifications (mainly through National Traineeships (Now Foundation Modern Apprenticeships) and Modern Apprenticeships). The funding of training was on the basis of the number of 'starts', numbers in training and outcomes (broadly in line with the formula for FE). Government supported training, however, had a much higher output related element – 30 per cent of funding. As we have seen, this pattern provided a significant disincentive to training providers to offer training to disadvantaged or potentially disaffected groups because, if trainees did not obtain their target qualifications, this would not trigger outcome-related funding.

The Government is now determined to promote a more level playing field for funding and more cooperation and joint planning between the different sectors. To do this a new Learning and Skills Council for England is being made responsible for delivering all post-16 education and training (outside HE) with local Learning and Skills Councils to plan and coordinate provision locally. The councils will supersede TECs in April 2001 and promote Learning Partnerships across all sectors and for all age groups. Learning Partnerships are expected to coordinate local action to raise standards, identify and address gaps in provisions, eliminate duplication and ensure that education and training meets local needs. The councils will have both a Young People's Learning Committee and one devoted to adult learning.

At the time of writing the Scottish and Welsh Assemblies are considering their own proposals. Scotland spends much more on Higher Education than anywhere else in the UK but it compares poorly on routes into further education and training. Current proposals suggest that Scotland will attempt to integrate education and training across a much wider age band than is envisaged by Learning and Skills Councils in England. In Wales too there is to be a new body to oversee lifelong learning (The Council for Education and Training in Wales). The Welsh Office is proposing a new national credit-based qualification and quality assurance framework and an all-age guidance service 'Career Wales' (Boyer, 1999). Some issues raised by these different national patterns of working will be further discussed in the final chapter.

Tackling youth unemployment – the legacy of the past and new beginnings?

37

Graduation at age 19

Both the DfEE White Paper and the SEU report proposed the introduction of a single 'Graduation Certificate' for all young people. This has been on the policy agenda for some time and was included in the Labour Party Manifesto for the 1992 General Election. The aim is to address the damaging divisions between different forms of academic and vocational qualifications whereby academic A-levels are seen by young people, their parents and employers as superior to other forms of vocational education or work-based training. Government recognises that all the different forms of post-16 education and training contain significant weaknesses. The traditional diet within academic education of three A-levels is perceived to be too narrow, does not continue the systematic development of numeracy, literacy and information technology skills, and is devoid of any basic citizenship education. 'Curriculum 2000' was introduced for many following academic courses in Year 12 to facilitate a widening of the academic curriculum and encourage a wider range of AS-level subjects to be studied. National Vocational Qualifications, one of the main alternatives to academic A-levels have had a mixed reputation. Some critics are very doubtful about whether the standards obtained are genuinely equivalent to those following the A-level route or whether a sufficiently wide range of key skills are accredited in ways which are credible to young people, learning providers and employers (Smithers, 1993). Following the SEU report, the Government asked the Qualifications and Curricula Authority (QCA) to develop a certificate available to all young people who attain records of achievement (to at least level 2) across a range of different activities. These include: formal qualifications (GCSEs and NVQs); key skills in communication; application of numbers and information technology; community participation and other 'curriculum enrichment' activities, such as involvement in sports, the arts and skills gained through work; other areas of personal development and achievement which might feature in National Records of Achievement.

Financial support for 16 and 17-year-olds

Of the estimated 160,000 young people not involved in employment, education or training, only about 15 per cent are in receipt of any financial benefits (Chatrik and Convery, 1998). The Coalition on Young People and Social Security (COYPSS) was set up in 1990 to campaign against the withdrawal of benefits from 16 and 17-year-olds implemented in 1988. Since 1990 it has produced a number of reports on inadequacies in the system, including a briefing for the Social Exclusion Unit in January 1999, *Sort it Out!* (COYPSS, 1999). The SEU accepted that there was confusion with financial support paid for by at least eight different routes by eight different agencies on behalf of two government departments. In 1999, if a young person was in full-time education and living at home with unemployed parents, parents may receive £30.95 as part of their own Income Support or dependant's allowance through income-based Jobseeker's Allowance. A young person in full-time training received a £39.50 minimum training allowance, or if waiting for a training place, a £15 'bridging allowance' for a maximum of eight weeks. This has not been upgraded since 1988. Some young people may be eligible for Social Fund payments, in the form of loans, although young people are rarely a priority group and loans have to be repaid out of other sources of income. Community Care Grants could also be paid to care leavers, or those leaving hostels, or detention centres. Where young people could not work or go on a training course, (if they are single parents, carers, sick or disabled), they can claim Income Support. If they could not live at home because they are genuinely estranged from their parents, and/or had just left being 'looked after' by the local authority or left custody, they may receive Severe Hardship Payment through Jobseeker's Allowance, usually payable for eight weeks only before re-application is necessary. In 1999, the payment for JSA/Income Support was £30.30 for those living at home and £39.85 for those living away from home. Those living in deprived circumstances and continuing in post-16 education may be eligible to receive some financial support from school or college 'access funds' made available through support from the DfEE. Those living away from home are also eligible for Housing Benefit. (Also see chapter 4 for a discussion of this.)

Parallel to the SEU inquiry resulting in *Bridging the Gap*, there was a series of Department of Health inquiries into support for young people in, and leaving, care. This culminated in a consultative paper issued in June 1999, *Me, Survive, Out There?* (DOH, 1999). Care leavers will be examined in more detail in chapter five. But the new proposed arrangements for them are introduced here in order to highlight important differences (as well as similarities) of approach. Similarities include proposals for a 'Young Person's Adviser' service. These are being recommended as part of a wide-ranging review of the care system. Also fundamental to the proposals on improving support for young people leaving care is a proposal to make it a statutory 'duty' of local authorities to 'assess and meet the needs of care leavers' up to the age of 21. This support and assistance is to include both personal and financial support for accommodation, food and domestic bills, pocket money, transport and other costs associated with education, training and finding work. Prior to the review, care leavers had to access two main sources of support; from local authorities and from the benefits systems. This gave a perverse incentive to local authorities to move young people 'looked after' into some form of independent living at the earliest possible moment, so that financial responsibility was displaced from scarce LA funds and onto benefits systems. The DOH review proposes merging the two forms of support and 'ring fencing' resources in a Children's Social Services Special Grant, to provide funding. Care leavers would thus not be eligible to claim benefits (except wages for work or training allowances). But resources from benefit savings would thus be transferred, via the DOH, to local authorities. The only exceptions to this would include teenage parents and certain disabled groups who would remain eligible for Income Support. Care leavers would thus be provided, by local authorities with a statutory duty, with an integrated system of social and financial support based upon an assessment of their needs.

These new arrangements are primarily intended to cover young people who have been 'looked after', continually or in aggregate, for three months prior to the age of 16. However, the DOH consultative paper suggests that other groups should be covered by the same arrangements, including an estimated 2,500 16 to 18-year-olds who are unaccompanied asylum seekers. It would be hard to disagree with the inclusion of this group. They are likely to experience the same difficulties as those leaving care. Yet other young people, born in the UK, who have not been 'looked after' for three months or more before the age of 16, often experience similar crises in their lives after their 16th birthday. They become estranged from their families and other forms of support. They often find themselves homeless and confronting the same tangle of confusion, misunderstanding and maladministration that led the DOH to want to design a safer and more sensitive welfare safety net for care leavers. Indeed many of the projects dealing with the young homeless to be reviewed in chapter four, were set up deliberately to try to combine services and support for care leavers with other vulnerable groups, including the young homeless and those estranged from their families, precisely because the problems they face are so similar. Yet unless these young people have been 'looked after' for an aggregate of three months before the age of 16, they are not entitled to the new integrated assessment and benefits support system being proposed by the Department of Health.

The SEU report accepts that 'there is a case for and against wider rationalisation, to make a coherent framework out of EMAs and other financial support systems' and that exploratory policy development work needs to be carried out before the end of the EMA pilots. It suggests that this should include an assessment of a system of the Single Youth Allowance which has operated in Australia since 1998. This system is means-tested according to parental income for young people living at home. There is also a series of complex 'disregard rules' about the earnings a young person can make without reductions in benefit, including the earnings of students who work part-time or during vacation time. The Australian system gives young people living at home a means-tested, fortnightly, allowance of approximately $58 (under £30 per week). Although under the Australian allowance a higher rate is payable for those living independently or with children, it is hoped that the UK review will explore the real costs of living independently including studies conducted by the Family Budget Unit. These suggest that even low cost independent living may be three or four times higher than the allowances being discussed.

Conclusions

This chapter has reviewed policy and practice on youth unemployment and training and the impact this has had on the school-to-work transition. It has concentrated mainly on issues of disaffection and disadvantage and ways in which these can be addressed. One of the main interests of this book is to examine whether there is a new approach and new policy agenda to address problems and whether this meets the criteria of a more 'holistic' approach as outlined in the first chapter.

One clear theme to have emerged in this chapter is the way in which disaffection and disadvantage after the end of compulsory schooling is linked to what happens before. In this sense, there is a recognition that, in better managing youth transitions we must not simply focus on the school-to-work transition, but widen the age range of our concern. This chapter has described the new agenda including New Deal for Young People which is

Work with pupils is both with groups and on a one-to-one basis. Work with individual pupils was on the basis of 'self-referral' (around a half) and others referred by teachers, year-heads or agencies from outside the school. Self-referral arose because young people had got themselves involved in 'incidents' and knew they must do something to help avoid or better handle these in the future. Self-referral was also more common amongst girls, although overall the project worked with twice as many boys as girls on a one-to-one basis. The case-load had, at its height, been as high as 70 pupils overall, although contact with them varied according to the issues being dealt with. All these had case files and were subject to case review by the team, although one member of the team often acted as a key worker.

Issues being addressed often changed throughout the year (the autumn term being the busiest). There was a marked tendency for serious issues concerning child protection to suddenly surface before school holidays. Many of the issues being addressed were much wider than classroom behaviour, special needs or emotional and behavioural development. Also commonly addressed were issues including those surrounding bullying, friendships and relationships between pupils (and with teachers and parents) study skills etc. Sometimes issues became highlighted by virtue of a high profile event in the news or on TV soaps. Princess Diana's death, for instance, brought out a whole plethora of issues concerning death and bereavement – 'from grandmothers to goldfish'.

Another important strand to their work was to work with teachers and school managers in a number of different ways. Sometimes this took the form of sitting in on class and advising on behaviour management and different approaches to learning and teaching. The overall profile and presence of the project within the school was enhanced by the involvement of the staff in Personal, Social and Health Education (PSHE) sessions within the curriculum which allowed them to develop and promote different strategies of learning not common in national curriculum teaching. The project also figured in the induction to the school for prospective pupils and their parents. It also explained its work in school assemblies each term.

From the beginning the project involved the development of a Student Advisory Group. This worked through five representatives from each year group who researched and developed the ideas and feelings of students on topics that were of importance to both pupils and school management. Initially developed as a form of school council, this became the basis of a number of changes to policy and practice within the school and within the project itself. It has also become the means through which the young people involved have been empowered and had their own self esteem enhanced through promoting the welfare of their peers.

The project had developed a series of protocols to deal with confidentiality and disclosures so that year heads and the school child protection manager could know of ongoing issues that were serious whilst keeping some issues confidential between the worker and young person. These protocols had been developed throughout the five years of the project on the basis of experience and discussions with school staff and management.

Work with parents was always based on the consent of the pupil, although no pupil had refused to have their parents involved. Parents mostly came into school for consultation, although some outreach work was also done, especially when there were issues around phobia about school itself.

The team had both male and female workers who had a range of different ethnic backgrounds and a variety of different professional and training experiences including training in counselling and psychotherapy. Throughout the team, there was a strong youth work presence.

The project also had an exit strategy to which it worked from September 1998. Group work was taken on by school staff, whilst one-to-one work was gradually being wound down. At the time of the visit, Genesis was exploring both expanding and diversifying its activities, working with a number of different local authorities within London and drawing upon other sources of funding, including the DfEE. Under revised plans it hoped to have both a school and community base.

School-community links

Shortly after the 1997 General Election, the Joseph Rowntree Foundation (JRF) commissioned a review of links between the school, the family and community (Ball, 1998). The report highlighted a wide range of current practice, together with different ways in which a number of different projects and initiatives were developing links to better support the education of those most at risk of under-achievement. The report covered a wide age range, from work with children in their early years and in primary schools through to a range of services that are being successfully delivered through community schools for older pupils and adults. It revealed a large number of different initiatives aiming to address educational disadvantage in its various forms, as well as a strong coordinating role of the voluntary sector, often involved in multi-agency partnerships. The report emphasises the importance of schools looking outwards towards the family and the community as well as inwards towards school management, teaching and learning. Yet the report also recognises the tensions between the two. The pressures of the National Curriculum, the testing of children and the publication of league tables has led many teachers and school managers to believe that, without extra resources, schools have little opportunity to embrace more holistic approaches to child welfare. Through partnership with other agencies and special funding regimes, however, schools do have an important potential to be non-stigmatising means of support, especially when initiatives are developed with families and communities rather than merely for them (Ball, 1997).

The JRF report proved to be widely influential and clearly had resonance with a number of initiatives planned by government. The 1998 School Standards Act required local education authorities to draw up early years development plans for pre-school children drawing on a mixture of provision involving schools, nurseries and playgroups run by the public, private and voluntary sectors (FPSC, 1998). Immediately following the General Election a series of Ministerial Conferences were held to review pre-school provision closely followed in January 1999 by the announcement of a new Sure Start programme with a budget of £452 million to develop 250 programmes across England. The Comprehensive Spending Review in July 2000 announced a further expansion of the programme from £184 million per year to almost £500 million in 2003–04. 'Sure Start' is partially based on evidence from High/Scope, a project first developed in Michigan in the US in the 1960s. Longitudinal research suggested that, when participants were compared with those in a control group, those receiving pre-school support were much more likely to complete their education and be employed, and be less likely to be arrested for drug or other offences, and be less likely (if female) to become pregnant in their teens (Schweinhart et al., 1993). Also persuasive (especially to the Treasury) was the fact that for each $1 invested in the programme there was an eventual (later) saving of $7 on welfare (Barnett, 1996; Communities that Care, 2000). High/Scope now operates in the UK under the High/Scope Institute UK, working mainly with 3 to 5-year-olds. The Sure Start programme is targeted in areas of disadvantage intended to be 'a glue to bind together a range of services for families and children'. Sure Start projects are intended to build on existing services, involve joint working and coordination, promote the participation of local families in the design and working of the programme and be 'culturally appropriate and sensitive to particular needs'. As Ball points out, however, the most comprehensive support for families and pre-school children still comes through 'family centres', many of which are run by voluntary sector organisations such as Barnardo's, the Children's Society or NCH Action for Children. Whilst these sometimes are approached by primary schools to help with difficult behaviour in the classroom, they are rarely based in, or attached to, schools (Ball, 1998).

As well as commissioning the School Inclusion review, JRF has also been investing in the Communities that Care (CtC) programme, which will be reviewed in chapter eight. Like many recent government initiatives, CtC seeks to promote patterns of intervention that have a proven track record of being successful and have had that success put to the test through independent research and evaluation. In reviewing 'promising approaches' for those participating in CtC, a distinction is made between different age groups: 0–2, 3–5, 6–10, 11–14 and 15–18 (Utting, 2000). Yet the projects it reviews are targeted at a whole range of different risk and resilience factors, some of which are connected to patterns of disadvantage, others at educational disaffection and many a mixture of the two.

Educational special needs

The area of special educational needs is fraught with conceptual confusion and highly contentious policy debate. Since 1981, pupils in schools in England and Wales with significant special educational needs should have those needs assessed and recorded in a 'statement' of special needs (called a record in Scotland). This identification of special need was linked to specific forms of extra support and special provision. The 1981 Act followed the 1978 Warnock Report which recommended that the old 11-fold classification of 'disabilities' should be replaced with a single 'statement' of need. The old categories included 'physical disabilities' such as being blind and partially blind, or deaf and partially deaf. But also covered within the old 1944 Act were those deemed to be 'maladjusted' or severely or moderately 'educationally sub-normal' (ESN). These latter categories covered more than three-quarters of those receiving special education prior to the 1981 Act (Tomlinson, 1982). It might be thought that this vocabulary of the mid-20th century has long since been swept away. However, despite the Warnock Report, some special schools still retain some of these distinctions, perhaps not helped by the same abbreviation ESN now standing for educational special need.

It has become commonplace in literature on disability to distinguish between 'impairment', 'disability' and 'handicap' (Fulcher, 1989). Impairment refers to a condition of the mind or body, sight or hearing impairment, for instance. Disability and handicap result from an interaction between impairment and the environment in which those with the impairment must function and are, therefore, partially a product of inadequate facilities. In the case of those who are partially deaf or blind, for instance, it is the facilities provided which determine how well they can hear, read or write. Mobility impairments too can be turned into a disability or handicap if appropriate access and/or support is not provided. Perceptual or cognitive impairments, such as dyslexia, learning disabilities, and emotional and behavioural difficulties (EBD) add to the complexities of defining special educational needs. Some of these needs may remain undetected and undiagnosed and poor work or problematic behaviour may be regarded as the result of a lack of skills, poor motivation or wilful indiscipline. There are a variety of different tests for dyslexia and EBD, some of which are relatively simple and quick to carry out (Buchanan, 1999). Yet, often these impairments remain undetected throughout a young person's educational career. For instance, one study amongst prisoners in a young offenders' institution in Scotland found that over a third could be identified as having previously undiagnosed dyslexia (Reid, 1999). In such cases the failure to identify and respond to disadvantage can result in long-term damage, at huge cost to individual lives and the public purse.

The Warnock Report assumed that around one in five children and young people would have special educational needs at some stage in their life. Some 'needs' may be temporary and may, at least in part, be the result of home circumstances. Warnock argued that, for the vast majority, having a special need should not lead to educational provision outside mainstream schools. Being excluded from mainstream education, even because of identified special educational needs, can itself become a disadvantage. Being educated in a special schools is highly correlated with attaining few, if any, qualifications at the age of 16. School league tables indicate that only very few special schools have any pupils attaining A-C grades at GCSE. This does not mean that the work done in such schools is necessarily poor. Indeed, in many cases, completely the opposite is the case. But special schools are often small, unlikely to have teachers who are specialists in National Curricula subjects, and many have to cope with young people with severe and debilitating medical conditions as well as special educational needs. Despite the best intentions of education policy since Warnock, however, there has been a continuing danger that 'statementing' procedures become a form of 'exclusion' from mainstream schools and that this becomes inevitably linked to further forms of educational disadvantage. Some of the correlates of having a 'statement' of special educational need are linked to other forms of educational disadvantage. African-Caribbean boys, for instance, are three times more likely than their white contemporaries to be 'statemented' for reasons of emotional and behavioural difficulties and more likely than their white peers to be educated outside mainstream schools.

Following Warnock, identifying SEN should be based upon a thorough diagnosis of the problem being confronted and the resources and help needed to do so as identified in the 'statement' or 'record'. Warnock was an advocate of integration of special needs pupils into mainstream schools wherever possible. Yet, following the 1981 Act, educational provision for many of those with a 'statement' continued to be made through special schools and the numbers in special schools did not decline. Following the 1988 Education Act there were very significant increases in the number of pupils put forward for 'statements'. Part of the reason for this is that the 1988 Education Act made schools largely responsible for their own budgets but LEAs responsible for meeting the cost of special needs provision. The 1993 Education Act heralded a new Code of Practice on Special Educational Need, in part as an attempt to stem the flow of 'statemented' pupils (DfEE, 1994). Following the Act all schools must have a policy on special needs and a special needs coordinator (a SENCO). However, the number of pupils with 'statements' continued to rise. In 1998 in England there were over 1.6 million pupils in some form of special education (nearly 20 per cent of the school population). Around a quarter of a million of these had 'statements' (3 per cent of the total school population) with nearly 90,000 being educated in special schools (DfEE 1999d).

A number of studies in the 1980s documented the impact of special educational needs (including young people with disabilities) on the major dimensions of youth transitions (Fish, 1986; Thomson and Ward, 1994; Hirst and Baldwin, 1994). Taking part in some form of post-16 education is now the norm, particularly since the expansion of FE in the 1990s (Bradley *et al.*, 1994). The Tomlinson report, for instance, estimated that 131,000 young people with learning disabilities were attending college (FEFC, Tomlinson report, 1996). Post-16 education was often part of the 'transition plans' promoted by the 1994 Code of Practice. There is, however, considerable unease about whether such planning is effective; whether it involves young people as active partners; or whether it is sufficiently long-term (Tisdale, 1996; Mitchell, 1998; Mitchell, 1999). Often planning is restricted to 'what next' and provision is in specialist courses or in specialist colleges, including residential colleges. The latter have been argued to offer only a brief interregnum of independence and social participation before returning home to inactivity and social isolation from friends (Sinson, 1995; Mitchell, 1999).

Emotional and behavioural problems

There has been increasing interest in recent years in the emotional and behavioural difficulties (EBD) manifest in children and young people. This is in part because EBD is often also related to school exclusion, truancy and other factors such as involvement in crime, drug and substance abuse, mental illness, suicide and self-harm. Buchanan has argued, there is a continuum between 'normal behaviour' at one extreme and 'mental disorders' at the other with EBD somewhere in the middle of the continuum (Buchanan, 1999). Yet the means through which EBD is defined and identified is contentious. When children are disturbed they may respond by internalising their distress. This may result in them being prone to anxiety and depression. Other children, however, externalise the troubles they feel; acting out tensions in the form of tantrums, aggression and other challenging behaviours. This can result in behaviour in the child that is obvious to those in daily contact with them, such as teachers and parents. Less easy to identify are the causes of this distress and how it can be addressed. Root causes of EBD may lie in relationships with parents, with friends or with teachers. Thus work may be required with the family, or within the community in which a child lives as well as work in school.

Since the 1970s there have been attempts to provide health and behaviour checklists through which parents, teachers and other professionals can identify children with EBD. Rutter, who developed some of the early checklists, concluded that whilst most children would manifest one or two problematic behaviours, those who scored 13 or more should be regarded as having a significant level of disturbance. More popular now is the short 'Strengths/Difficulties' Questionnaire developed by Goodman which takes only around ten minutes to complete and can be done by parents and teachers (Buchanan, 1999; Goodman, 1997). This has the advantage of being able to identify what a child is good at as well as the problems being confronted. Rutter's initial work was in the Isle of Wight where he found that around 7 per cent of 10 and 11-year-olds had significant behavioural problems. However, when the scales were applied in London, the numbers categorised as disturbed were more than double and a gender division became apparent. In London, a quarter of boys and 13 per cent of girls were found to be significantly disturbed (Rutter et al., 1975). Buchanan and others report that externalised disorders are more common in younger children and especially amongst boys. Internalised disorders are less common in younger children but are common in adolescence and especially amongst girls.

There are some signs that EBD has been increasing in recent years with some estimates suggesting that as many as 45 per cent of children and young people have moderate to severe psychological problems during their childhood and adolescence. The locus of these problems varies, with Buchanan concluding that EBD is associated with 'socio-economic conditions; relationships between parents and children and relationships within families; events at school and factors within the individual' (Buchanan, 1999). Clearly this requires a holistic approach and Buchanan's work indicates that much can be done by frontline workers with no specialist mental health training. Her review suggests many promising approaches. Yet, all too often, schools and teachers are reluctant to take on what many regard to be the province of social work.

Policy development on special educational needs

Recent policy for Special Educational Needs (SEN) since the 1997 election, was set out in the 1997 consultative Green Paper *Excellence for all Children: Meeting Special Educational Needs*. The results of the consultation were published as *Meeting Special Educational Need: a programme for action*. One theme, reminiscent of many previous White Papers, was the need for more integration of SEN pupils into mainstream schools wherever possible and the development of closer links between mainstream and special schools. One practical means through which this might occur is through making mainstream schools more accessible to 'disabled' children and £20 million was made available to promote this through the Schools Access Initiative. A further £8 million was also provided through the Standards Fund to promote inclusion. All LEAs now also have to provide an annual review of inclusion policy in their Education Development Plans (DfEE, 1998).

All schools and LEAs are now required to provide information on what special needs support they can provide and more regional and multi-agency collaboration has been promoted. The 1994 Code of Practice remains the main framework for identifying SEN although this is due to be 'simplified' in a new code to take effect from September 2001. The draft of this runs to over one hundred pages and is accompanied by a fifty page *SEN Thresholds* document (DfEE, 2000e, DfEE, 2000f). These documents provide guidance on providing a more inclusive curriculum for all children based on three principles:

- setting suitable learning challenges;
- responding to pupils diverse learning needs; and
- overcoming potential barriers to learning.

As with the previous 1994 Code of Practice, the new Code makes clear that, in defining, and responding to, diverse needs there are different 'tiers'. It is anticipated that most needs can be identified and responded to by individual teachers. Beyond that, additional action may be required by the school – 'School Action', and within its budget. Sometimes it might be necessary to identify other resources and external expertise – 'School Action Plus'. 'In a few case', the Code suggests that action will depend on resources that can only be accessed through a 'statement of special educational need.'

The new SEN Code of Practice sets out five fundamental principles and nine factors critical to success. The fundamental principles reassert: the rights of all children to have their needs met; within mainstream schools and settings wherever possible; that all children have a right to a broad, balanced and relevant curriculum; and the rights of children and parents to be consulted. Factors critical to success include: early identification; engaging in a partnership with parents; adopting multi-disciplinary approaches to issues; having regular reviews of interventions; and meeting prescribed time limits.

Although accepting that some pupils have multiple and complex needs, both documents discuss the identification of, and appropriate response to, need under four main headings:

- communication and interaction;
- cognition and learning;

- behaviour, emotion and social development; and
- sensory and/or physical.

The focus of the *Thresholds* document is on the provision of support within mainstream schools and trying to establish a common approach across LEAs and across all schools. All teacher training now includes a special educational needs component with extra funding provided for the training of special support assistants as well as teachers.

A further theme of the consultation paper and programme of action is better support for parents. Since 1999, all LEAs have been required to have a parent–partnership scheme through which advice can be given to the parents of children with SEN from an independent parent supporter. This was again supported by extra funding from central government. Parent supporters can also help in any conciliation process where there is dispute between parents and LEAs on the type of provision being offered.

Emotional and behavioural difficulties

The 1997 Green Paper gave special attention to children with EBD recognising that the roots of this form of SEN are complex, often lying in family breakdown or relationships with parents as well as poor experiences of school. It also signalled an intention of government policy to develop preventative work rather than merely waiting until a child or young person had a full educational 'statement' and was in need of specialist support or a special school placement. It also pointed to the ways in which EBD was linked to educational disaffection, including that which resulted in school exclusion and long term and widespread social costs. It called for action in schools and by LEAs to develop 'behaviour support plans' and better coordination between the education service and a range of different agencies. More specific proposals included:

- early identification and intervention to work with families and other agencies;
- effective behaviour policies in schools and LEAs;
- strengthening the skills of all staff working with EBD;
- using a range of specialist support; and
- wider dissemination of best practice.

In her review of what works with troubled children, Buchanan outlines a number of initiatives which help children with EBD at different stages in their school careers. The Health Advisory Service advocates that mental health services should be provided in three tiers with tier one involving the collaboration of social workers, health visitors, GPs, teachers and voluntary workers. Psychiatrists and psychotherapists are not involved in assessment and intervention until tier two or above. Level one intervention with young pupils can often involve offering a simple retreat for young children into somewhere safe where they will be listened to and supported.

Place2Be

This has been running in a number of schools in London since 1994. The aim is to promote positive mental health and wellbeing amongst primary school children. Most children are referred by teachers because of EBD or social reasons. It involves a mixture of group work, individual sessions and a drop-in facility called 'A Place to Talk'. Work is also carried out with parents and with special educational needs coordinators. Nearly three quarters of the children going to individual sessions were later rated as 'a good outcome' by their teachers.

(Based on Buchanan, 1999)

Buchanan also emphasises a number of principles of good practice in working with parents, as summarised in the box below.

Strategies for working with dispirited parents

- *Dealing with feelings of parental failure.* Parents need to be reminded that children come in different shapes, sizes and with different personalities. Some children are easy to manage, others require more skill. It is a question of learning how best to manage a particular child and this does not always come naturally.
- *Validating what they have achieved to date.* Many parents are coping with high levels of family adversity. Acknowledgment needs to be given for their resilience and overall coping skills.
- *Giving practical help first.* Help with day care, dealing with pressing concerns.
- *Giving hope that things can be different* and demonstrating faith that the parent can change things.
- *Discussing the daily routine.* Finding out what in an ideal world the mother/father would like to change.
- *Explaining that getting cross with a child can be like giving a child a bag of sweets and saying 'do that again'.* Children need attention like they need food, sleep, warmth, and if they cannot get attention by being good they will find a way of getting it by being bad.
- *Where a parent is being undermined by a critical parent or grandparent.* Meeting with them and professionally validating the efforts they are making.
- *Helping a mother recognise that she is nearing the end of her tether.* Ask the mother to hold out her hand straight in front of her. The hands of highly stressed mothers shake visibly. This can be used to demonstrate to partners and parents that more help is needed. (This also applies to fathers).
- *Acknowledging that children can make you feel very angry.* Give parents a strategy to deal with themselves when they feel out of control . . . 'you have every reason to feel angry but you don't want to hurt your kid . . . so you get yourself out of the situation . . . give yourself a break, get your Mum over . . . if necessary lock yourself in the toilet, you are safer there than lashing out at the kid'.
- *Helping parents plan.* Some child problems can be tough to overcome. Parents will

---

have to plan a time when they are feeling strong enough to be consistent and to see things through. This is especially important with bedtime problems.

● *Using children to change parents' behaviour.* Picture contracts with 'smiley' faces for undertaking particular tasks can be very effective, not only in changing the child's behaviour but for helping parents learn new ways of managing a child's problems. These need to be monitored weekly by the professional. The parent and the child have the credit for any success.

From: *What Works for Troubled Children.*

A similar list may be helpful in all school staff rooms. Interventions with older pupils also often involve multi-skilled teams and working with parents and teachers as well as young people themselves. Many of the principles discussed so far were found in one project, part-funded by the Standards Fund, visited as part of this project. This is briefly described in the box below.

Dorking: Learning Space

The Learning Space project started in April 1997. It arose from a multi-agency group determined to work together to better meet the needs of vulnerable young people. The management group has representation from education, social services, health, youth services and the police. The project team is also interdisciplinary and involves one member of staff who is social work trained and seconded from social services and three staff seconded from education, including one with experience in working with learning disabilities. There is regular liaison with the child and adolescent psychiatrist who also sits on the management group. The team itself is all female but occasional support is also drawn from a male detached youth worker.

The project works with two, very different, secondary schools, one a diocesan school that had been on the edge of closure in the recent past and the other a popular and successful state comprehensive school. The project also did some work with feeder primary schools with children approaching school transfer at the end of year 6. As well as working with individual cases, the project also does group work with groups of pupils (especially in year 7). It has also been involved in helping use year 9 pupils who are trained to act as 'peer mentors' on a one-to-one basis with those in the first year of secondary school.

Pupils are referred to the project by the two schools, in the main when they have reached stage 3 on the *Code of Practice*, often because they have emotional and behavioural difficulties (EBD). (Stage 3 involves the school working with outside support). It was reported that many schools regarded EBD pupils as 'troubled' or 'troublesome' kids and sometimes not in the same light as other special needs students. The project takes around five new referrals per term although it does not have a strict ceiling as different referrals need different levels of support.

Contact with the project can vary from a single meeting to varying levels of support for up to two years. Overall, of those involved with the project, boys have outnumbered girls by around 2:1, although amongst those referred because of non-attendance at school, the proportion is reversed – explained by a different 'flight and fight' response of girls and boys to the problems they face. Referrals have also included a small number of Asian pupils and children 'looked after'.

The project works to three main principles: approaching children holistically; working at prevention rather than crisis management; and inclusion – keeping children in school wherever possible. HM Inspectors, who had visited the project, were keen that the project should focus on years 7 and 8, rather than the most vulnerable who were recognised to be an older age group. The 'holistic' approach implied trying to see 'learning' and 'behaviour' as very much related. Social work involvement also meant being able to relate issues within the school to issues at home and within the peer group. When a child is referred, there is an initial profiling which is carried out with school staff and parents and also involves interviews with the child. Pupil assessment includes issues of bullying (both as victim and perpetrator) and family assessment includes issues of marital conflict, separation and domestic violence. Pupil interviews also explore what works well in school as well as what doesn't and what could be done to improve things. Work with parents concentrates on emphasising positive achievements.

Listening to children and the main carer is seen to be a key factor in the success of the project, with emphasis on looking at the child at home and in school holistically. Stress is also given to emphasising the positive and 'what works' in the lives of parents and children.

The main outcome being sought is to avoid school exclusion, including self exclusion. However, the project also claims other 'hard outcomes', including avoiding inpatient admission to child and adolescent psychiatric units and being accommodated by social services. DfEE also provides its own 'hard outcomes' checklist. But the project leader also sees issues of personal development and 'emotional wellbeing' as crucial to success. During work with the project, pupils report benefits such as: feeling more in control over their lives; being able to articulate this; being able to negotiate with staff; as well as improvements in self esteem.

At the time the project was visited, however, there was tension between the project, the schools and the LEA concerning pupils being excluded from school and provision for those who are excluded.

Its financial support comes in part from the DfEE (through the Standards Fund) and locally from health and social service budgets.

One important issue which is raised by the Learning Space project is the inter-relation of disadvantage and disaffection and this is especially so in the case of emotional and behavioural difficulties. The parents of children with disabilities or special educational needs often face a multitude of problems in supporting their children, and the voluntary sector is an important means through which needs are being met. Sometimes this involves support for children outside school hours, and expanding the range of activities in which they are involved. As we saw earlier, sometimes education in special schools can mean social isolation from friendship networks and leisure activities unless special support is offered. One project trying to address this issue is briefly described below.

Play Plus, Stirling

Play Plus is a voluntary organisation, with charitable status, which works with children and young people aged 5 to 19 who have various forms of disabilities and are at risk of experiencing isolation. Children with disabilities are explicitly mentioned in the Scottish Children Act as 'children in need' and the lion's share of the funding of this project is from a service agreement between Play Plus and Stirling Council Education Services Department. Initially its services were developed for Central Region, but following re-organisation of the authorities its work now focuses on the Stirling area. It is also involved in a partnership for the provision of Play and Out of School Services, as part of a wider initiative of Children's Services in Education for Stirling Council. This wider confederation offers over 200 places per day through six different childcare projects. Some of these projects are spatially concentrated in outlying villages. Others make use of mobile facilities such as Play Plus play vans and other portable locations for play. The Play Plus project has a management group made up of the project leader, representatives from Education (including Community Education – responsible for the youth service), parents of users and other activists.

The age range covered by this project is very wide, and funding priorities mean it has, through time, had to concentrate the bulk of its efforts on the 5 to 12 age group. Here the attempt is to integrate children into mainstream provision and to make play workers sensitive to the needs of disabled children. It has also involved setting up a 'befriending' scheme. This involves suitably vetted and police checked volunteers helping children attending mainstream services such as the Brownies and Guides. This involves them transporting children to and from meetings and supporting them during and after the session. Overall the project deals with around 100 children and young people, with over a third in the over-12 age group. Many have multiple disabilities. For the vast majority, this includes learning disabilities and communication difficulties. Some of the funding (additional to the service agreement with education) comes through offering training to other organisations and authorities. This has enabled the project to continue to work with the over-12s.

Activity with this organisation has changed significantly over time and it now works with seven different groups according to age, interests, activities and needs. One group, for instance, is offering after school support for young people with working parents. Another much larger group is working with Stirling Youth

---

Theatre on a wide range of theatrical productions, much involving directed improvisation rather than simply learning scripts. Other groups are organised along gender lines or by age, although others are mixed age or gender groups. By the time young people reach the over-12 groups, the staff of the project think they know them sufficiently to arrange small groups who will work well and support each other.

Educational disaffection pre-16

In discussing disadvantage and disaffection in the last chapter, key indicators were relatively easy to identify, even though there was also a clear connection between them. Similarly, in pre-16 education, some indicators of disaffection seem obvious, even though firm data has proved elusive until recently. One simple indicator of disaffection is when children and young people do not attend school – they truant. Another is when their behaviour in school is sufficiently unacceptable to school authorities that they are excluded either permanently or for a fixed term. The DfEE collects data on reported absences from school yet recognises that this hugely underestimates the size of the problem. Statistics on permanent exclusions from school were not systematically collected until the 1990s and there are grounds for considering these as somewhat unreliable (Parsons, 1998). The Audit Commission estimate that, of the eight million children of school age in England and Wales, 400,000 are not in school (Audit Commission, 1999b). Yet the social patterning of school exclusions and truancy is clearly important if better targeting of systems of support is to be achieved.

Exclusions from school

It is only since 1993 that local education authorities have been required to keep records of the numbers of pupils excluded from school. This requirement is, at least in part, due to the very significant increases in school exclusions taking place in the 1990s. There is also a widespread concern over the impact of exclusions from school upon levels of crime, upon the communities in which excluded children live, and upon young people's later achievements (Graham and Bowling, 1995). Parsons has estimated that there was a 450 per cent increase in permanent exclusions between 1990–97, from less than 3,000 to in excess of 13,000 (Parsons, 1998). Fixed term exclusions are estimated to be at least eight times this level, at 100,000 as estimated by Ofsted in 1996. Some more recent estimates suggest the real figure may be even higher. The figures on school exclusions peaked in the mid-1990s but, nevertheless, were sufficiently serious to ensure that exclusions and truancy was one of the first topics to be investigated by the Social Exclusion Unit (SEU, 1998b). Since the SEU report a number of measures have been introduced to monitor exclusions, to try to avoid them wherever possible, and to ensure that those who are excluded continue to receive education and training. However, an Audit Commission report suggests that the data which exists is not being used properly or effectively by local authorities (Audit Commission, 1999b).

The DfEE reported a slight reduction of 3 per cent in permanent exclusions in England between 1997–8, although the groups most at risk of exclusion remain the same (DfEE, 1999c). Most exclusions (83 per cent) take place from secondary schools and are most common in pupils aged 13 to 15 and at the start of the year. However, the SEU also reported that exclusions from primary schools had increased by 18 per cent between 1995–96 (SEU, 1999). In 1997–98, the vast majority of school exclusions (84 per cent) were boys. Black Caribbean exclusions were still nearly five times more likely than for their white counterparts who were, in turn, more likely to be excluded than those from Pakistani, Bangladeshi and Indian communities. However, where local authorities had introduced ethnic monitoring of exclusions, alongside other measures offering support to 'at risk' groups, the reduction in exclusions was very marked. In Birmingham in the late 1990s, for instance, exclusions of Afro-Carribean boys were reduced by 40 per cent in four years (Birmingham Education Service, 1999).

Pupils with a statement of special educational need are seven times more likely to be excluded and, according to one survey, young people 'looked after' are ten times more likely to be excluded (SEU, 1998). Some schools and some local authorities are reported to be more prone to exclude than others, with a quarter of secondary schools responsible for two-thirds of all permanent exclusions. Some research has pointed to the correlation of exclusions with high levels of family stress, family disruption, poverty and unemployment and an Ofsted report pointed to other factors such as poverty and poor relationships with parents, teacher and other pupils as well as poor acquisition of basic skills and limited aspirations (Brodie and Berridge, 1997; Ofsted, 1996).

The reasons for exclusion are less clear, although the SEU report some relatively minor offences such as not wearing a uniform from the nominated supplier, wearing a nose stud, or breaking a school rule about where to cross the road (SEU, 1999b). Where local authorities have been systematic in recording reasons, bullying, fighting and assault on peers were top of the list, covering nearly a third of all exclusions. Abuse and assaults on staff, often used to justify exclusions by teacher unions, accounted for only slightly over 1 per cent of the incidents leading to exclusion (Imich, 1994). The SEU report, however, suggests the possibility that much of the increase in permanent exclusions in the 1990s was connected to changes in educational climate and policy rather than simply to an increase in the bad behaviour of pupils. It was for this reason that the report suggested changes in the procedures governing exclusion and targets for its reduction. When young people are excluded from school, severe disadvantage results. Ideally, they should be immediately re-integrated into other forms of schooling, but in the mid-1990s this happened in only a third of cases. For others, teachers set school work to be done at home, especially when exclusion is for a fixed term. Otherwise they may be required to attend a Pupil Referral Unit (PRU), although until action following the SEU report, this often was only for a few hours a week. What did they do with the rest of their time? There is some evidence that they turned to crime (Graham and Bowling, 1995).

Self exclusion and truancy

Official figures quoted by the Social Exclusion Unit suggest that schools report that only around 1 per cent of secondary school pupils and under a half of a per cent of primary school pupils are absent from school without a legitimate reason. However, this is accepted to be a huge underestimate (SEU, 1998a). A slightly better source of evidence on those who do not attend school is obtained through large questionnaire surveys of young people, either those in state maintained schools or those aged 16 and over covered by the Youth Cohort Studies Study (O'Keefe, 1994; Casey and Smith, 1995; SEU, 1998b). According to one survey, one third of pupils truant at some time during their school career. Over 8 per cent truant at least once a week, including around 10 per cent who do so in their final year of compulsory schooling. When the questionnaire was administered, however, 17 per cent of the potential sample was absent (O'Keefe, 1994). The Youth Cohort Study suggests that around 5 per cent of year 11 pupils do not attend school for 'days or weeks at a time' with half of these missing weeks at a time. This suggests that the minimum size of the 'hardcore' non-attenders in year 11 alone is between 11,000 and 28,000 (Newburn, 1999).

It is noteworthy that, given the over-representation of boys amongst those excluded from school, around the same number of boys and girls report that they truant. The children of travellers are reported to have an attendance record of less than 50 per cent, with many others unlikely to be registered with school authorities. Young people 'looked after' also have a poor attendance record. A joint report by Ofsted and the Social Service Inspectorate in 1995 reported that 12 per cent of those of statutory school age were not in school, rising to more than a quarter (26 per cent) of 14 to 16-year-olds who should have been studying for the GCSE examinations (Ofsted/SSI, 1995). For boys, living in a single parent family appears to be a risk factor, and for boys and girls, so is living in social housing and in a household in which the parent(s) is unskilled. Some studies suggest that truancy is more common in inner cities and that there are some local authority areas and some schools where it is more common. For instance, unauthorised absence in Manchester is reported as four and a half times higher than in South Tyneside and nine times higher than in Oxfordshire (SEU, 1998b).

The reasons and explanations for truancy include a mixture of family circumstances, and school and community factors. Some parents may not know about the failure of their child to attend school and nearly half of those who said they did not truant were apparently held back by a fear of their parents finding out. Others who do truant think their parent(s) knows about it and condones their behaviour; they often have parents who collude in order to arrange out of school activities, including caring for other family members. In one truancy sweep in the north-east, 80 per cent of the truants stopped by education welfare officers and police were with a parent (DfEE, 1999b). Other factors are related to anxiety about being bullied – the most commonly cited factor. A third of girls and a quarter of boys worried about bullying (Balding, 1996). Other factors include dislike of particular teachers or particular subjects, and a fear of being humiliated because of being a weak reader, for instance (Carlen et al., 1998; Kinder, 1996). Home Office research also indicates a strong correlation between truancy and having a strong attachment to siblings or friends who are in trouble with the police (Graham and Bowling, 1995).

Policy and practice on disaffection, school inclusion and pupil support pre-16

There are similarities of approach within government policies covering a range of youth issues. These often involve a combination of plans and targets, new structures (including systems of financial incentives and penalties), support for specific projects, with better means of monitoring progress and the dissemination of good practice and knowledge of 'what works'.

Plans, targets and partnerships

Since 1998, all local education authorities have been required to submit Education Development Plans (EDPs) to the DfEE. Contained within these are policies and initiatives dealing with disaffection and targets for improvement. On both truancy and school exclusions, for instance, the Government has set itself a target of reducing both by a third by the year 2003 and LEAs are expected to focus their efforts on achieving this. The DfEE also wishes to reverse the situation whereby those excluded from school are left largely to their own (often criminal) devices. They have set as a target that by September 2002 all LEAs must have a programme to ensure that all pupils excluded from school for more than 15 days receive suitable full-time education. The 1997 Education Act included an amendment to previous legislation withdrawing the possibility of providing only part-time education. To facilitate what would be a significant and sizeable reversal of trends, LEAs and schools must develop Behaviour Support Plans and Pastoral Support Programmes in schools designed to support those most at risk. This comes on top of, but in line with, encouragement to develop other partnership arrangements between different groups within the education service and with other professional groups. The 1998 Crime and Disorder Act, for instance, set up Youth Offending Teams (YOTs) and requires local authorities to develop local crime and disorder strategies. Because young people who truant, or who are excluded from school, are more likely to be involved in criminal activity, schools are encouraged to take part in the development of such strategies. Educational Welfare Officers are expected to work closely with schools, to a service level agreement with them, and in clearly defined roles. School Attendance and Educational Supervision Orders (SAOs and ESOs), together with Parenting Orders, were all introduced under the 1996 Education Act to strengthen the powers of intervention, although LEAs are expected to make careful judgments about whether to proceed to prosecution on a case-by-case basis.

The 1999 DfEE circulars on truancy and school exclusion

In July 1999 the DfEE issued two circulars (10/99 and 11/99) directed at schools and LEAs respectively. These were intended to clarify policy and practice with regard to both school exclusions and attendance at school. The circulars draw attention to the specific groups of young people at risk of being excluded (or self excluding) from school broadly as outlined in this chapter. They are hard-hitting and admit that too little has been done in the past to prevent, monitor and deal with disaffection, thus allowing things to escalate out of control. School exclusions, it reports, have been allowed too often for trivial, isolated offences rather than as a tool of last resort. Circular 99/10 makes clear to schools that pregnancy is not an appropriate ground for exclusion; nor is truancy or lateness, or breaches of the school uniform policy (including hairstyle or wearing jewellery). There seemed to be some softening of this stance in August 2000 when new guidance was given. This indicated that appeals panels should not normally reinstate a pupil permanently excluded where this was for serious actual or threatened violence against another pupil or member of staff, sexual abuse, selling illegal drugs, or persistent and malicious disruptive behaviour (including refusal to conform to school policies, including dress code). The National Association of Head Teachers regarded this move as meaning that the target to reduce permanent exclusions by a third by 2002 was now a 'dead duck' (*Times Educational Supplement*, 4 August 2000).

Circular 99/10 also notes that schools should have procedures whereby parents are notified immediately (the same day) about any absence and, where problem behaviour is identified, parents should be involved in both discussions with school staff and in a written plan drawn up to address misbehaviour. Pupils who are not diverted from truancy by early (same day) intervention or are at risk of exclusion from school must now be identified and an individual Pastoral Support Programme (PSP) developed for them. DfEE guidance suggests that this should be done with LEA support and the involvement of other agencies such as social service, housing departments, the Careers Service, minority ethnic community groups, voluntary organisations and the Youth Service. Given that SEN children are known to be at greater risk, the guidance makes it clear that PSPs should not be a replacement for any special education needs assessment. The programme may, however, involve placing the young person with a Learning Support Unit located within the school. The programme may also consider: moving the child to another school as part of a planned 'fresh start'; joint registration with a Pupil Referral Unit; or disapplying the national curriculum (especially at key stage 4) so as to allow other forms of work-based learning. Other actions might involve the use of 'mentoring' whether this be with other pupils, non-teaching assistants (sometimes volunteer university students) or other 'successful adults' drawn from the local community.

All pupils who are excluded from school or PRUs must also have an Individual Re-integration Plan drawn up within a month. This must specify how and where continued full-time education will be provided. When young people are re-integrated into mainstream schools, LEAs should provide resources to offer intensive support for an initial period after admission, sometimes referred to as 'dowries' to encourage schools to cooperate. Schools excluding pupils also have the trouble and expense of the exclusion process on top of losing financially through formula funding. However, in the course of researching this book, the author was told of more than one head teacher who considered this a price worth paying.

Being seen locally as being tough on discipline by excluding troublesome pupils was thought by some head teachers to pay dividends in encouraging other parents in the catchment area to choose the school for their children.

Many schools are now expected to have Learning Support Units within school, or in the case of small primary schools, to share such a unit with others. Local education authorities are responsible for the establishment and maintenance of Pupil Referral Units (PRUs) and must notify the Secretary of State whenever they set up or close one. Members of the Management Committees of PRUs are expected to be drawn from a wide range of relevant other professional groups including the Careers and Youth Service, head teachers from schools and FE colleges within the LEA, the police and SEN coordinators. Other guidance covers admission and attendance, staffing, the curriculum and assessment, reporting and inspection. Where exclusion from PRUs are being considered, the LEA is asked specifically to consider whether an SEN assessment should be made and makes clear that the authority still has a responsibility to continue to provide full-time education.

LEAs have a responsibility under the 1996 Education Act for full-time provision of all education outside school whether the pupils concerned are ill, excluded, have behavioural problems or are pregnant or are a parent. One option to be considered is the use of crèche facilities at colleges so young mothers can continue with their education. The circular also indicates that education should normally continue up to the age of 18 especially where, because of circumstances, young parents are a 'year behind' others in their schooling.

As we have seen, the DfEE 'standards fund' has encouraged, and financially supported, work with young people truanting and/or at risk of exclusion for a number of years whilst others have been supported by a range of voluntary organisations. Spending on the standards fund grew from £17 million in 1996–97 to £140 million in 1999–2000. Based upon the evaluation of previous programmes, DfEE has outlined key principles of good practice in chapter 2 of DfEE circular 11/99. These include: an emphasis on early intervention; rewarding achievement; involving parents and pupils in a whole range of partnerships and home-school agreements; 'whole school' policies and practices on bullying and racial and sexual harassment, and engaging other pupils in supporting behaviour management programmes. Also recognised as important are commitments to equal opportunities policies and the monitoring of how and why some groups become over-represented in measures of disadvantage and disaffection.

New Start

Following the 1997 election, the Government announced a New Start programme, with the aim of motivating and re-engaging 14 to 17-year-olds who had either dropped out or who were in danger of doing so. First round projects ran in 17 pilot projects from the autumn of 1997, until the summer of 1999. Second round projects were aimed at post-16 young people and involved the piloting of Personal Advisers and Learning Gateway (covered in the last chapter). The first of the New Start pilots were intended to be diverse, shaped by local research and priorities and to build upon already existing patterns of provision. The vast majority had some form of 'gatekeeper', outreach method or other means of establishing and maintaining contact with a difficult-to-reach group (DfEE, November, 1998). Other key features included the use of mentoring schemes, an alternative curriculum at Key Stage 4, and home-school liaison. Also being promoted were patterns of multi-agency working and partnerships, including systems for tracking vulnerable groups. This too involved outreach work involving LEAs, social services, the Careers and Youth Services and youth justice systems (Craig et al., 1998; Craig and Kelsey, 2000). The evaluation of the first New Start projects comments that there are many problems of joint working and sharing confidential information which still have to be solved, not least in overcoming some of the difficulties posed by data protection legislation. The New Start pilots are, however, important in piloting closer and more coherent systems of support for vulnerable groups approaching the school-to-work transition.

Conclusions

This chapter has reviewed a wide range of research, policy and practice on educational disadvantage and disaffection amongst pupils under the age of 16. This is a huge topic and, to do full justice to the wide variety of different projects, would require (at least one) book in its own right. The main purpose of this review has been to assess whether policies and practices on educational disadvantage and disaffection do add up to a new approach and new agenda for change. Further, and in line with the main focus of this book, we should now also be in a position to assess the degree to which this provides a more 'holistic' perspective. This chapter has shown that, increasingly, policy and practice is focusing on critical points in the life course throughout childhood and youth. Certainly, much more is being done throughout young people's careers within education, rather than merely addressing problems at school leaving age, although the evenness and continuity of support is still open to serious question. Secondly, there is also evidence that some attempt is being made to relate educational issues to problems being faced within the family and community and to form a more rounded assessment of children and young people's needs. This too is in line with the principles of 'holism' outlined in chapter one. Thirdly, however, despite these positive developments, many of the initiatives and projects described are dependent upon short-term funding. Whilst some tracking systems are being tried out, worries also still remain about the ways in which information is shared between agencies. Some short-term, intensive work may be carried out with children, young people and families, but less attention is being given to continuity of support. Valuable lessons gained at one point in time may, therefore, be lost to those working with the same young person later in their careers.

Fourthly, there are some signs that different agencies providing services for children and young people have their own institutional agendas and that these are sometimes directly in conflict with each other. Successful projects aiming to promote school inclusion, for instance, can be hugely frustrated by changes of head teacher and new regimes, often driven by funding criteria, and designed to show that the school is tough on indiscipline, no matter what the consequences for the long term welfare of the individual child. Finally, many projects are being evaluated only against 'hard outcomes' even though practitioners are all too aware that 'soft outcomes' such as improvements in self esteem and 'efficacy' are vital to eventual and sustainable success. In tackling disaffection and disadvantage in education, much progress has been made, but some major problems still remain to be adequately addressed.

Chapter four

Vulnerability and the domestic and housing transitions: Teenage pregnancy and youth homelessness

This chapter focuses on domestic and housing transitions and more especially on those young people who experience either homelessness or become parents in their teenage years. Research evidence reviewed in chapter one showed that the majority of young people now experience 'extended youth transitions', mainly because of changes in education and the labour market. Because many do not complete their education or training until their late teens or early 20s, they are dependent upon their parents for longer periods of time. In chapter one it was also noted that the average age at which young women and men now have their first child is 26 and 28 respectively. The average age at which young people first leave home is 22 (Department of Health, 1999) and this includes young people who first leave to study and who may return when the course is completed. A third of young men and one in six young women are still living at home at the age of 25.

Chapter one also drew attention to the fact that whilst 'extended transitions' were now the experience of the majority of young people, there was some polarisation of experience. Buried within aggregate statistics is a significant minority of young people who leave home (or care) much earlier and others who become parents in their teens. For some, parenting and leaving home may be planned, positive and result in successful transitions. But for many, leaving home early is for negative reasons and often results in insecure tenancies and homelessness. This chapter reviews research, policies and intervention projects designed to offer support to young people during early domestic and housing careers and focusing on both teenage pregnancy and youth homelessness.

Two things should be recognised at the outset. Firstly, the twin foci of this chapter are narrow compared with all the issues that are involved in the domestic and housing transitions of young people. As was briefly outlined in chapter one, the growth of extended transitions has brought with it ever more complex patterns of intimacy, partnering, parenting, marriage and household formation (Heath, 1999; Rugg, 1999). No attempt is made within this chapter to discuss the problems faced by the huge majority of young people as they attempt domestic and housing transitions. This does not mean that these transitions are trouble-free. We know, for instance, that the housing transitions of young people in rural areas are particularly problematic (Cartmel and Furlong, 2000; Ford *et al.*, 1996; Pavis *et al.*, 2000; Rugg and Jones, 1999). But, as yet, domestic transitions, especially, remain less prominent within research and the policy agenda. Some discussion of 'housing careers' and housing policy will be covered in the second half of the chapter.

Secondly, neither teenage pregnancy nor youth homelessness should be considered as unitary phenomena, although sometimes the literature is not as careful as perhaps it should be in distinguishing differences. There is surely the world of difference between a couple in a stable relationship, appropriately housed and employed, becoming parents in their late teens and children of school age becoming parents by accident. Some of the literature on teenage pregnancy, therefore, runs the risk of lumping together incommensurate circumstances and producing moral panic based on distorted evidence. As will be seen later in this chapter, youth homelessness is a hugely complex phenomena to define, which is why there are so many wildly differing estimates of the size of the problem. Policy-makers in particular are reluctant to take seriously hidden homelessness, where young people are living in unstable, unsuitable or over-crowded accommodation. So much of the spotlight reaches only the street homeless or those in hostel or other temporary accommodation.

Unplanned pregnancy (especially in the early or mid teenage years) and homelessness do present the most acute problems. As indicated in chapter one, teenage parenting is beset with disadvantage, such as the disruption of education or training. Whilst teenage mothers may gain access to various forms of housing provision, they may be also socially isolated and poorly supported. They, and their children, are also more likely to suffer from poor health and their children often under-achieve in school. The homeless often become locked into a 'no-home-and-no-job' spiral of disadvantage. But we would do well to consider these acute problems within the context of others being faced by the majority of young people, rather than assuming that the domestic and housing transitions of the majority do not also require vigilance in the future.

Teenage pregnancy

The UK has the highest rate of teenage pregnancy in Western Europe and this was the subject of the fourth enquiry by the Social Exclusion Unit (SEU, 1999a). The rate of teenage pregnancy in the UK is twice that in Germany, three times that in France and six times that in Holland. Rates in most of Europe were about the same as they were in the UK in the mid-1970s but in other countries there were significant declines, in the 1970s and 1980s especially, during which period rates in the UK increased (in the 1980s especially). Here an attempt will be made to summarise the main correlates of teenage pregnancy, what qualitative social research can tell us about it, and how policies which might impact upon it are being developed.

In 1997, 90,000 teenagers became pregnant, including 7,700 under the age of 16 and 2,200 under the age of 14. Around half of the conceptions of those under 16 end in abortion but two-thirds of all teenage pregnancies (56,000) result in births. Rates in the UK declined a little in the early 1990s only to rise again in 1996, possibly as a result of a scare in 1995 of the effects of taking contraceptive pills. The rate of pregnancies for under 16-year-olds in 1997 was also 10 per cent higher than in 1993.

A number of factors are correlated with teenage pregnancy. The SEU outlines eight main factors:

- poverty and living in poor neighbourhoods;
- children in care or leaving care;
- having a mother who was a teenage parent;
- low educational achievement and educational disaffection;
- no involvement in post-16 employment, education and training;
- being the victim of sexual abuse;
- having mental health problems; and
- being in trouble with the police.

Those whose parents are in unskilled manual jobs (or if unemployed, had been previously in unskilled jobs) are ten times more likely to become a teenage parent than those in professional occupations. Those living in social housing are three times more likely than those living in owner occupied properties to become parents in their teens. Half of young women who have been 'looked after' (in care) are likely to be mothers of at least one child by the age of 18. Daughters of mothers who gave birth in their teens are also one and a half times more likely to become pregnant in their teens than the daughters of older mothers. Young women with low educational achievements at 16, and those whose achievements declined between the ages of 7 and 16, are most at risk. There is also an association between teenage pregnancy and truanting from, or being excluded from, school. As reported in chapter two, there is also an association between not being in any form of employment, education or training at age 16 and 17 and pregnancy; with one study reporting a third of young women in this group becoming pregnant (SEU, 1999a).

The SEU report on a number of studies that indicate that three minority ethnic groups are also over-represented amongst teenage parents: Bangladeshi; Pakistani; and African Caribbean. For some groups, this may be related to traditions of early childbirth within marriage, as in the case of the former two groups. On the one hand members of both these groups are also reported to be less likely to have had sex before the age of 16. On the other hand, there is a link between membership of these groups and other forms of disadvantage related to early pregnancy, such as living in poor neighbourhoods, poorer than average educational achievement and various forms of disaffection.

The SEU also produced analysis of the spatial clustering of teenage pregnancies in local authority districts. This enabled it to examine further the relationship between indices of local deprivation and high rates of pregnancies. There is indeed some similarity of pattern, with those districts scoring highly on deprivation having teenage pregnancy rates over six times higher than the most affluent areas. Hackney and Southwark are in the top ten for both teenage pregnancies and area deprivation. Those also in the top 20 for both include the London boroughs of Lambeth, Lewisham and Greenwich, and Sandwell and Nottingham in the Midlands. Other areas with high teenage pregnancy rates but lower in the league table of deprivation include Wansbeck, Wear Valley, Easington, Hartlepool and Middlesbrough in the north-east and Burnley and Barrow in the north-west. Many are traditional working class areas. However, there are also odd clusters which cannot be explained in this way. For instance, Shropshire's rate for teenage conceptions is 70 per cent higher than the rates in Cambridge and Huntingdon. Yet, teenage pregnancy is caused not by poverty. It is caused by young people having sex either without contraception or with contraceptive failure.

A number of studies also report a relationship between teenage pregnancy and child sexual abuse. The SEU report that of the 7,000 calls to ChildLine about teenage pregnancy in 1996–97, 5 per cent were also about sexual abuse. Relatively small scale studies have also found that a quarter of those who become pregnant in their teens had a probable psychiatric disorder (Maskey, 1991; Zoccolillo and Rogers, 1991). The SEU reports on one project for young parents run by Barnardo's in Skelmersdale. This indicated that, of those young women involved in the project, 40 per cent had been in care, 70 per cent had lived with family breakdown, 40 per cent were themselves daughters of teenage mothers and all lived in poverty and were educationally disadvantaged or disaffected. Large scale longitudinal surveys also suggest that girls and boys who have some involvement with the police are twice as likely to become teenage parents. Around a third of those in one young offenders institution were estimated to be fathers.

Problems also continue after the birth of their child. Teenage pregnancy is related to a number of negative outcomes for the welfare of both the young mother and her child. Three-quarters of teenage pregnancies are reported not to have been planned and teenagers go to their doctors much later in pregnancy than older mothers-to-be. They thus miss out on early pre-conception health measures because they are not planning to be pregnant and also often miss ante-natal planning because of the turmoil their pregnancy causes with families, relationships and their education. Nearly two-thirds are regular smokers before they are pregnant and almost a half continue to be during their pregnancy. All of this has negative health consequences for their child. Relationship breakdown is common. Only around a half of teenage mothers are still in a relationship with the child's father a year after the baby's birth. Nearly a third end up living alone, often having to get by as best they can on benefits. Post-natal depression is three times more common amongst teenage than older mothers. Teenage mothers are only half as likely as older mothers to breast-feed their baby. The babies of teenage mothers are also more likely to be underweight at birth and have a higher infant mortality rate (60 per cent higher than for older mothers). They are also more likely to suffer accidents, with twice as many being likely to be admitted to hospital as the result of accident or gastro-enteritis. All this suggests that in terms of 'risk factors', causes and consequences, teenage pregnancy should be addressed holistically.

The SEU report quotes a barrage of research reports which indicate that good and comprehensive education about sex and relationships can help in delaying the age at which young people engage in sexual behaviour and make them more likely to use contraceptives when they do (SEU, 1999a). The vast majority of parents (90 per cent) look to schools as the favoured source for sex education. Much research suggests that most young people think that sex education in schools gives too little information and comes too late. Boys were found to be much more critical than girls, but in the lessons that were observed, boys were seriously disruptive and dominant (Measor, 2000). Knowledge (particularly knowledge about sexual health) was more likely to come from friends and from the media.

The SEU report is strong in providing an impressive array of statistical correlations. It is less strong in making links to qualitative research that helps us understand teenage sexual behaviour, decision making about contraception use, or decisions to continue with unplanned pregnancy once it has been discovered. Clearly all this is important if teenage pregnancy is to be properly understood. Relationships between young women and their mothers, their partners and others close to them are influential in decisions about abortion (Allen *et al.*, 1998). Other research also gives clues as to the complexity of decision making about sexual behaviour and contraception use. Between 1989 and 1992 Janet Holland and colleagues conducted intensive, semi-structured interviews with a sample of 148 young women and 46 young men aged between 16 and 21 (Holland *et al.*, 1998). These were drawn from a larger questionnaire survey of 500 young women and 250 young men living in Manchester and London who were asked questions about their attitudes and behaviour. The interview samples were carefully selected to represent the wider group in terms of age, social class, education and sexual activity. Young men were more likely to report that they were sexually active at the age of 16 or 17 and many before that. Young men were also more likely to report 'casual sex' – sex outside a steady or enduring relationship.

The value of studies like this is not so much in providing statistical portraits of who does what, with whom and when, but in giving insights as to the circumstances and negotiations which take place between young people. For instance, Holland and colleagues report that 'negotiating condom use is not just a question of individuals making rational choices about personal safety.' Rather it is the outcome of an emotionally charged, social encounter between two potentially unequal partners, bounded and constrained by cultures which define masculinities and femininities. This research was conducted at the height of campaigns about AIDS and the importance of safer sex. Yet, having knowledge was not the same as being able to be open about it. In one telling remark a young woman told the researchers, 'If I don't die of ignorance I will die of embarrassment instead'. For young women, buying, carrying or asking for the use of condoms can signal a lack of sexual innocence and a negative stereotype of being 'easy', fair game, or 'a slag'. For young men, whilst embarrassment may be an issue, to buy, carry or to suggest the use of condoms is not as threatening to his masculinity. Nor do most young men expect the woman to resist the use of condoms if they suggest it. The research did find that many young women refused or resisted unprotected intercourse. Yet many others reported that young men had a range of negative responses to condom use with many hating it and thinking it spoiled the fun, the spontaneity and the pleasure – 'like picking your nose with a rubber glove'. Some young women also reported that they hated the use of condoms so that, within steady relationships especially, initial use is followed by non-use. Young women report that they are often relatively powerless in sexual encounters with things 'just happening' and sexual intercourse being the price that had to be paid for getting, or keeping, her man. This is especially important in understanding the negotiation of sexual relationships involving young women with low self esteem.

The title of the book reporting this research is *The Male in the Head*, a title chosen to reflect the dominance of men in defining what sex and good sex is about. To the young people interviewed, sex was predominantly about penetrative, vaginal sex, resulting in male orgasm. Young women living in circumstances in which teenage pregnancy is most likely to occur (poor neighbourhoods, brought up 'looked after', those who are educationally disadvantaged or disaffected, those who have been abused or have mental health problems) are also the most likely to have low self esteem. They and their older sisters are much less able to take a strong stance about safer sex with actual and potential partners. The links between the statistical measures which are predictive of high rates of pregnancy are thus to be found in the low self esteem of young women and the complex asymmetrical power relationships defined by masculine and feminine youth cultures. It is these that policy initiatives need to address as well as the need for adequate, comprehensive, sensitive and early education on sex, sexuality and relationships.

Policy and practice on teenage pregnancy

The SEU report includes an appendix outlining existing policy under four main headings:
- programmes which help prevent teenage pregnancy;
- measures which help teenage parents continue with their education;
- measures to help them prepare for work and find it; and
- measures which support pregnant teenagers and young parents.

The report also contains a 28 point action plan detailing what additional things can be done within the constraints of the Comprehensive Spending Review targets and who should be responsible for achieving what, and by when.

Prevention

The SEU summarises a number of initiatives which might already be addressing the problem. Some spatially concentrated interventions will be focused within the 26 Health Action Zones formed in 1998–99 with the overall aim of reducing health inequalities. (Also see cameo in chapter six). Reducing teenage pregnancies is one of the targets included in the *Health of the Nation* initiative. Also part of the prevention programme is Sexwise. This is a freephone, confidential advice service established by the Department of Health (DOH), offering trained advisers on sex and personal relationships and particularly targeted at the under 16s. It currently handles 2,500 calls per day. Under the Quality Protects programme (discussed in chapter five), a number of initiatives are being targeted at those looked after and leaving care, one of the most over-represented groups. On top of a government strategy on sexual health, launched early in 1999, the SEU now proposes a National Campaign to achieve clear goals in reducing teenage pregnancy. This aims to reduce conceptions by under 18-year-olds by a half by 2010 and establish a clear downward trend for those under 16. An implementation unit at the DOH will ensure that each local authority (SSDs and LEAs), together with the Health Authority appoints a local coordinator to identify the pattern of teenage pregnancies locally, and target those most at risk. Coordinators are also required to audit local provision and draw up action plans. Action plans on teenage pregnancy should be linked to the other 'plethora of plans' being developed. The DOH is responsible for making a first report on progress in March 2001. In October 2000, the DOH announced a £2 million campaign including peer education programmes and advertising in teenage magazines to help address peer pressure pushing young people into sexual activity at an early age. Predictably, the tabloid media reported this as 'meddling ministers' and the policy as 'Virgin on the rediculous', despite the programme being based on ten years research (Roberts, 2000). Special measures are also detailed in the SEU report to help parents, schools and groups known to be at risk. Young men are also to be targeted in a National Campaign to make them more aware about their responsibilities for using contraceptives and, where pregnancy results in a birth, their financial responsibilities for child support.

Educational support

Most of the already existing policy initiatives outlined by the SEU focus on more general issues of disadvantage and disaffection rather than teenage pregnancy specifically. As discussed in chapter three, these include New Start, Excellence in Cities, Educational Maintenance Allowance pilots, Access funds through FE and measures to reduce school exclusion and truancy. The importance of these measures is in ensuring that school aged children are not excluded from school because they are pregnant and that proper support for their continued education is given including better use of crèche facilities at FE colleges.

Preparation for work

A range of different New Deal initiatives (for Communities, for 18 to 24-year-olds, and for Lone Parents) offers patterns of support, although the latter really only applies to lone parents whose child has reached school age. The SEU report also draws attention to ONE (formerly Single Work Focused Gateway) which has run pilots since June 1999 to give support and help with barriers to work for all those coming on to benefits for the first time. Under the National Child Care Strategy there are plans for the provision of good quality child care for all children under the age of 4. Working Families Tax Credit also aims to help low income families.

Support for pregnant teenagers and young parents

Support is recognised to be needed at different times and for different purposes. The National Children's Bureau, funded by the DOH, has a project called Time to Decide to support young people in care making decisions about pregnancy and including advice and support about adoption, fostering and for mothers looking after a new baby. For the under 18s it is hoped that the new local coordinator will be able to arrange similar support and advice for all pregnant teenagers. The Sure Start programme aims to help families in greatest need, with a target of 250 local programmes running by 2002. The Comprehensive Spending Review in 2000 signalled a further expansion. The SEU propose the piloting of a Sure Start Plus programme to give coordinated support involving pregnancy advisers and a package of measures to give help with housing, health care, parenting skills, child care and education.

Support for teenage parents

The SEU includes within its report a number of projects specifically designed to support teenage parents. One such project, visited during the course of research for this book, is outlined below.

YMCA Training: Lone Parent's Project in Leeds

This project started in 1998 to support 16 to 24-year-olds who were either pregnant or were parents of babies of up to 45 weeks old. It was funded by Leeds Training and Enterprise Council and the European Social Fund until the end of March 2000. It sought to allow them to continue with their education, training and preparation for employment throughout their pregnancy and during the early months of their baby's life. YMCA has delivered training programmes to pregnant 16 to 18-year-olds since 1990 and this project is an extension of that work.

Recruitment to the project was through a variety of different sources, sometimes through a 'pregnancy group', the Careers Service, the Benefits Agency, training providers or occasionally other professions such as social workers or health visitors. When visited, this was the only provision in Leeds for this group. Potential recruits to the project have to apply for the Lone Parents Project and not all in the pregnancy group do so. Others prefer to stay at home. Those who wanted to continue their training were eligible for training allowances arranged through OPEX. Despite the widening of the age group to cover 16 to 24 and those who had already had their baby, most of those on the scheme were at the bottom end of the age range.

There were up to 18 young women on the scheme at any one time. There had been 34 young women starting the scheme, although 11 left early, including four who moved out of the area. Most of those on the scheme were white. At the time of interview, there was one Asian young woman on the scheme and two from Afro-Caribbean communities had left. Recruitment from minority ethnic groups was said to fairly reflect the ethnic mix in the catchment area. Five of the current 16 had been 'looked after' in residential or foster care. There was a wide range of different educational qualifications within the group. Some were extremely well qualified. Others were described as 'school phobic' and had no qualifications. Many had a moderate number of middle range grades, although around three-quarters had special training needs requiring specialist literacy or numeracy training.

There was a wide range of different vocational courses. The young women

---

completed an Individual Training Plan (ITP) and many of them did this in conjunction with a detailed appraisal of the local labour market. They often discovered, for instance, that there were very few jobs in child care or beauty therapy but there was more chance of employment if they took courses in food hygiene or computer literacy and information technology. The success of the scheme was reported by the coordinator as being largely based upon listening to young women's aspirations, giving them choices and making these realistic and realisable. In this sense, training and employment outcomes were determined by young women being empowered and supported in trying to achieve their own goals.

The project had three main phases. Phase one was a nine week programme starting during the 30th week of pregnancy and finishing shortly before the birth of the baby. Participants attended for around 15 hours per week. During this phase the ITP was researched and completed and participants given training and support on housing benefits, as well as aspects of health and welfare such as appointments with their doctor, hospital and midwife. Although the project was ostensibly concerned with training and employment, a holistic perspective on welfare was taken from the outset. Attempts were also made to work with others in the young woman's life including family members and partners. Attempting to work with fathers, however, proved difficult. Involving a male outreach worker had been tried unsuccessfully. Because of its holistic perspective the project raised issues concerning drug awareness, violence and abuse and other aspects of leisure and lifestyle that might impact upon the welfare of either the mother or her baby. (Most participants were reported to smoke and many continue to use recreational drugs and expect to continue an active social life.) Parenting skills were also covered including a 'parenting pack' from *Care in the Family*.

Phase two was equivalent to ten weeks 'maternity leave' and was designed to maintain contact and momentum. There were drop-in sessions of up to eight hours per week involving specific training modules, guest speakers from other organisations and agencies and discussion sessions. Participants brought their babies with them as the project has its own on-site 'baby room'. Mothers went in and out during their time at the centre if their baby needed them but most time was spent away from their baby in some form of training. Outreach support was also given for young women who felt they could not attend. All participants were seen either at the project or at home, once a week. Perhaps surprisingly, drop out was not common at this stage. Indeed, participants were often keen to return to more formal training well before their ten weeks 'leave' was completed.

Phase three could be 36 weeks in length and continue until the baby is 45 weeks old. Those who joined the project when they already had a baby still stayed with the project to the time the baby was 45 weeks old. Those who joined the project late still had to compress their career planning into this period. All participants attended for 15 hours a week to complete National Vocational

Qualifications as identified in the ITP. Those who completed their NVQ before their baby was 45 weeks old could finish early. During phase three, work experience with an employer for one or two days per week was also arranged. This also involved arrangements for child care, although this was sometimes expensive (as much as £25 per day). Arrangements were also sometimes made for a child minder (around half the cost) which could possibly continue (and be more affordable) after the project had finished. Places in nurseries and early years centres were reported to be extremely scarce for babies, with nearly 100 on a waiting list.

The first group to complete the project finished their training in July 1999. The project had been given outcome targets in terms of NVQ qualifications (levels 1 and 2) and employment. Participants also had their own targets in terms of employment goals. Most participants achieved a range of vocational qualifications as well as 'producing beautiful babies'. The vast majority had certificates in computer literacy and information technology as well as a certificate in parenting, St John's Emergency Aid Training and Basic Food Hygiene. Three had gone on to a Modern Apprenticeship in Business Administration and many others to further training or education.

There are also other 'soft' outcomes, such as coping skills and self esteem, and a child being well looked after by her mother rather than 'looked after' by the local authority. These were recognised by project staff as being real achievements and of huge benefit to the child and the community although they were not formally part of the evaluation of the scheme.

Like many youth intervention projects, this project had limited and short-term funding. As this book neared completion, the project closed. A further project supporting teenage parents is contained in chapter five.

Young people and housing careers

Chapter one reported that part of the pattern of 'extended transitions' was that young people remained living in the parental home for longer. Two-thirds of 21-year-olds are still living at home and a third still do so at the age of 25, although there are marked gender differences with young women more likely to move away from home earlier, and in greater numbers. Early parenting is one of the key factors influencing movements away from the parental home, but this is by no means the only influence. Leaving home to live with a partner is also important but so too are more negative factors. Analysis of the Survey of English Housing shows that at the age of 16, only 2 per cent of young women are living as a couple and a much lower proportion of young men are doing so. By the age of 21 nearly a quarter (24 per cent) of young women and 11 per cent of young men are living with a partner. At age 25, six out of ten women and nearly four out of ten men are living with partners (Rugg and Burrows, 1999).

Whether young people or couples had children is also very much linked to housing tenure, with those with children much more likely to be living in some form of social housing (accommodation rented from local authorities or housing associations). Many of those in the 16 to 25-year-old age group who are living with both a partner and child also lived in owner occupied housing (42 per cent), although this was sometimes 'nested' within another household usually headed by a relative. But the use of social housing was also a predominant tenure of this age group, with nearly four in ten families living in social housing, more than three times the proportion of childless couples (Rugg and Burrows, 1999). SEH data also indicates that in 1996–97 in England there were 167,000 (predominantly female) 16 to 25-year-olds living as young lone parents, with nearly three-quarters (74 per cent) of these living in social housing.

Jones distinguishes between 'positive' and 'negative' reasons for leaving home (Jones, 1995). Positive reasons are often associated with traditional reasons such as leaving to study, train or gain employment. Sometimes this move away from home is temporary and involves the use of 'transitional housing' such as that provided by universities or colleges. This may be followed by a return home when the period of education or training has been completed. Negative reasons for leaving home include conflict with parents, moving away because there are no jobs available locally, or simply to escape parental surveillance. Leaving home for negative reasons is also related to youth homelessness in its various forms.

Youth homelessness

A number of attempts have been made in recent years to estimate the size of the homeless population resulting in widely differing estimates. At least part of the reason for this is differences of definition. The Social Exclusion Unit reported on Rough Sleepers as one of its first tasks. This estimated that, despite a number of initiatives introduced by governments in the 1990s, 2,400 still slept rough in London alone each year, with a further 10,000 sleeping rough outside the capital at some point during the year (SEU, 1998b). This report estimated that a quarter of rough sleepers were aged between 18 and 25 although it did claim that only a few rough sleepers were under the age of 18. At the beginning of the 1990s young people, usually defined as under the age of 25, were reported to be under-represented amongst the 'street homeless' or 'rough sleepers', but over-represented amongst those living in hostels or bed and breakfast accommodation (Anderson et al., 1991; Hutson and Liddiard, 1994). At the time of the 1991 census, 16 to 24-year-olds constituted 18 per cent of the general population but 30 per cent of single homeless people living in hostels (Anderson et al., 1991; Pleace and Quilgars, 1999). Taking a broader definition of youth homelessness, a National Inquiry into youth homelessness published by CHAR in 1996 concluded that, in the previous year, just short of a quarter of a million young people (246,000) between the ages of 16 and 25 were homeless (Evans, 1996). The definition this enquiry used included those who were totally without accommodation (the street homeless) but also those who only had temporary shelter, in hostels, bed and breakfast accommodation or a squat, and those who were insecurely housed living with relatives or friends who were unable, or unwilling, to continue to accommodate them in the long term.

The last official attempt to measure youth homelessness nationally was made by a study commissioned by the Department of the Environment in 1991. This involved a survey of 1,346 people living in hostels and bed and breakfast accommodation, and smaller samples of people who were sleeping rough or making use of soup runs in which food was distributed to those assumed to be homeless. This study was not limited to young people but included all single homeless people. Young people under the age of 25 were, however, over-represented in all three samples (Anderson *et al.*, 1993). The main aim of this research was to identify the characteristics of the single homeless, examine why they remained homeless and what were their accommodation and support needs and preferences. A recent review of the evidence suggests that the homeless population is still predominantly white, middle aged and male (Fitzpatrick, 2000; Pleace and Quilgars, 1999). Women were less likely to figure amongst the homeless population than men, although the CHAR inquiry reported recent increases in the number of young women in the mid-1990s. Ethnic minority groups were also over-represented, although some of this may have been based on the areas (mainly London) where the data was collected. Minority ethnic groups represent only 5 per cent of the national population, yet 40 per cent of the single homeless living in hostels were from ethnic minority groups and under the age of 25. Those who had been 'looked after' and those who had been in custody were also heavily over-represented. Although less than 1 per cent of the age cohort, those leaving care represented around a third of all those homeless and living in hostels or bed and breakfast. Among those aged 16 and 17, 39 per cent had previously lived in a children's home and 32 per cent had experienced foster care. In the older 18 to 24 age group, care leavers were less heavily over-represented, with 18 per cent reported to have previously been in children's homes and 11 per cent foster care. Just over a third of all 16 to 24-year-olds who were homeless also reported that they had been either in prison or a young offenders institution, and a further 6 per cent had been in a drugs or alcohol unit. Another significant group were those who reported that they had left home because of conflict with parents (14 per cent), relationship breakdowns (6 per cent), violence or abuse (3 per cent) or because they experienced harassment or felt insecure in their last home (5 per cent). Only 1 per cent of the sample wanted to return home with the vast majority (95 per cent) wanting to find a house or a flat in which to live. Yet given their experience of unemployment and their entitlement to benefit, this seemed an unlikely prospect. The vast majority of the single homeless are unemployed and dependent upon benefits (Please and Quilgars, 1999). The 1991 survey found that only 12 per cent of the sample had been in work the week before. Some 44 per cent of 16 and 17-year-olds and 60 per cent of those aged between 18 and 24 were receiving Income Support. This meant that they were in receipt of average incomes of £31 and £40 respectively. Perhaps understandably, most recognised that they not only needed access to adequate and secure accommodation, but help and support with budgeting and money management.

At the time of writing, there is no national data set on the range of transitional accommodation for young people in housing need, although the London Hostels Directory produce data for London which lists 26,000 bedspaces, some of which include specialist support (RIS, 1998). Quilgars and Pleace report that this directory divides schemes into six main categories defined as 'non-specialist', although with varying degrees of support:

- *Direct access:* hostels with emergency places which can be accessed immediately;
- *Low support:* often large hostels;
- *Medium support:* hostels and shared houses where staff are available, but often not on a 24 hour basis;
- *Supportive:* hostels and shared houses with a high staff-resident ratio, usually with 24 hour support including emotional and practical support;
- *Foyers:* schemes which provide a combination of accommodation linked to training and employment services; and
- *Housing schemes:* flats, bedsits and shared houses providing good quality housing and sensitive housing management providing either permanent housing or with good links to permanent re-housing.

More than a third (34 per cent) of the beds for such schemes were targeted at young people although most of this is some form of 'transitional' housing. Yet there is continuing concern about whether the right balance of provision and support has been achieved and about how vulnerable young people move between different types.

Policy and practice on youth homelessness

Despite rough sleepers being one of the first topics of investigation for the Social Exclusion Unit, little has been done to reverse the more general housing policy agenda of the 1980s and early 1990s. Some have argued that housing policy has exacerbated the problem of homelessness amongst young people (Rugg, 1999). In England, whereas more than two-thirds of the population live in owner occupied properties, 60 per cent of young people under the age of 25 now live in the rented sector (Rugg *et al.*, 1999). During the 1980s, the availability of housing for young people was very much affected by the 'right to buy' policy which moved vast tracts of housing from the social rented to the private ownership sector. In many parts of the country, unless young couples have good, secure and well paid employment, they cannot afford to buy a house. Young people in employment are also likely to be expected to be geographically mobile during the early stages of their occupational careers, which again makes buying a house an expensive and often unsuitable option. The private rented sector, thus, is of increased importance for young people. It is more quickly available and more likely to be furnished. However, young people's eligibility for assistance with private rental costs was significantly changed during the 1980s (Rugg, 1999). First came changes in board and lodgings payments in April 1985. This set a national maximum of £50 to £60 for Housing Benefit paid under the old Supplementary Benefit scheme, with a slightly higher level in London. A further time limit (up to eight weeks) was set depending on region, with coastal areas restricted to only two weeks support before the young person had the housing element withdrawn. Even this has now been withdrawn. A 1985 Green Paper recommended that benefits should be age-related with lower payments made to those under the age of 25, no matter whether the young person was living independently or not. This came into force under the new disaggregated Housing Benefit introduced in 1988. Housing Benefit was further revised in 1996 with a 'single room rent' amendment. This meant that all single young people without dependants would only receive benefit at the local rate for the average cost of a single room, no matter what their real living arrangements. As Rugg points out, if such a young person lived in a self-contained, single person flat with a rent of £65, benefit would only be paid at the rate for a single room in a shared house with joint access to facilities, which might be as little as £35. Much of this was justified in terms of targeting limited resources on those in greatest need and an attempt to prevent perverse incentives for young people to leave home prematurely. This was despite the lack of evidence that housing benefit was an inducement to leave home (Kemp *et al.*, 1994). To be sure, many first moves away from the parental home, do make use of the private rented sector (Jones, 1995). Under the new regulations, however, housing has to be paid for by topping up any Housing Benefit from wages. For those not in employment, this is often impossible. Where a young person later became unemployed, this often resulted in them not being able to afford the rent, so tightening the connection between joblessness and homelessness.

Projects supporting young people with housing

As we have seen, there are a number of reasons why many young people face acute difficulties during their housing careers. Over the past few decades, the voluntary sector especially, has developed a number of different patterns of support for young people who become homeless, or require varying degrees of support in obtaining and maintaining tenancies. Many of the problems they face are not only related to gaining access to appropriate accommodation but being able to manage other aspects of their lives. Often, trying to find somewhere to live is associated with trying to find work or suitable training that might lead to employment. On other occasions moving away from home and trying to live independently intensifies other problems young people are trying to deal with, such as emotional distress.

Foyers

Foyers were first introduced in Britain in 1992 based upon a French model which provided young people with a mix of housing and social support, tied to employment and training. Initially started with five pilot projects, the number of Foyers in the UK increased to 70 by the summer of 1998, with a further 90 being developed or planned. They are in rural, as well as urban, areas. Critics of this development saw them as a return to large institutional style hostels with draconian rules and regulations (Gilchrist and Jeffs, 1995; Chatrik, 1994). Later developments, including rural foyers, have sometimes been based upon a dispersed model that uses a variety of different accommodation, with some central support services, including a drop-in centre and links with the Careers Service and Training and Enterprise Councils (Quilgars and Pleace, 1999). Others, such as the purpose-built foyer in Camberwell in London, have also embraced New Deal for the Young Unemployed, by offering Gateway services not only for foyer residents, but for others living within the community.

Centrepoint: Camberwell Foyer

Camberwell was the first, purpose-built, foyer in the UK, and was opened in November 1994. It houses 80 young people aged 16 to 25 and also offers employment and training advice and support. It aims to give young people the skills involved in sustaining employment and housing when they leave.

Since it was first opened, access to employment and training support has been opened up to young people from the local communities. This support involves teaching basic literacy and numeracy skills, information technology, and giving access to the internet and Career-Scope (a directory of job opportunities). Young people are also provided with access to independent legal advice on aspects of tenancy agreements and a debt counsellor. Residential courses are also offered to young people to build confidence and work on motivation and skills. Young people cannot self-refer to the project but must do so through another agency such as a homeless unit of local government. The foyer is a low support hostel and has very few referrals of those leaving care. The predominant ages are late teens and early 20s as younger age groups often need high levels of support. There are slightly more young men than young women and the client group is around 90 per cent from minority ethnic groups with most coming from Lambeth and Southwark, although with some coming from much further afield. There is counselling on issues such as drug and alcohol misuse but this support is given by outside agencies.

To be accepted, a young person must be homeless in some shape or form, and have some idea of what they want to do in terms of an occupational career, even though they may need help in developing this. Residents sign a 'licence' that commits them to developing a career action plan. This is reviewed periodically during their stay. Young people can stay for a maximum period of two years. If a young person is not fulfilling the terms of the action plan, they will be interviewed and may receive a warning about the consequences of not fulfilling this. After three warnings, they will receive a 28 day notice of eviction. This will be followed by a joint review between the employment and housing sections of the foyer to try to arrange somewhere more suitable. The resident-staff ratio is relatively low compared with other hostel accommodation, with only three project workers for 80 residents. There are 'house rules' including a restriction of the number of guests they are allowed to receive in their room. There is also a strict no drugs rule, and alcohol consumption is restricted away from communal areas. The foyer is intended to be a safe place to live and harassment or violence results in formal warnings or eviction.

This foyer also delivers the New Deal Gateway programme (see chapter two). At the time of interview, more people were coming into the programme who were not resident in the foyer than who were. Some of the residents were also going to college rather than taking part in in-house training. This balance of provision had been much affected by New Deal. There were strong links with business, including Shell International who also seconded a member of staff, and local business links had been developed in recent years.

Some follow-through evaluation takes place on both the housing and employment fronts. Follow-through evaluation on employment training includes 'soft outcomes' such as self-confidence, ability to do job search, construct CVs and ability to complete a realistic action plan. The full service, across both housing and employment training, claims to be client centred and one-to-one.

High Support Hostels

Other projects, including another run by Centrepoint, work with young people who need significant amounts of personal support. Homelessness is often either precipitated by, or associated with, a wide range of personal, emotional and mental health problems. Some projects, especially in the voluntary sector, attempt to deal with homelessness within a more 'holistic' assessment of young people's needs, as in the case of the Centrepoint project outlined below.

Centrepoint: Buffy House

When visited, Buffy House was an accommodation project for 12 young people between the ages of 16 to 25 who have high support needs. The project had a holistic, person-centred approach and aims to accommodate, support and resettle young people with mental health problems which had been brought on by emotional trauma and who were considered able to benefit from a non-clinical structured environment. Residents were also expected to have had some period of stability before they joined, have an ability to communicate, a desire to move forward and be able to maintain a level of independence. The project had been in existence for over 20 years and initially started as a high support project. It did change to being an independent living project but reverted to its role as offering high support in 1996. The project employed five project workers and a housing worker four days a week, with project workers coming from a variety of different backgrounds. Some had been volunteer workers with a variety of homelessness projects. Others had a background in mental health, or housing work, but none of the staff were social work trained. Some were continuing their training in higher education and Centrepoint itself offered in-house training on a range of issues relevant to their work.

Residents must be referred to the project from other agencies, including any social services department and specific lists of other hostels for the homeless.

Application was made in writing, giving a history of their background, including care history and any involvement with drugs or alcohol misuse, medication and a statement by the young person themselves as to why they wanted to join Buffy House. It aimed to have an equal mix of male and female residents. Although the vast majority of residents were white British, it had in the past had members of minority ethnic groups, including refugees, as long as they were entitled to benefit. Although the eligible age group was 16 to 24, residents were more usually in the 18 to 21 range. Referrals were from all over the UK and Ireland. The project operated a strict equal opportunities policy.

Because of the need for high support, by no means all residents were expected immediately to be able to re-engage with education, training or paid or voluntary work. Indeed, at the time of interview only four residents were in work or education. All the project workers had two or three residents with whom they work on a one-to-one basis through a 'key-worker' system. The first eight weeks of residence involved a period of assessment based on regular meetings (at least once a week) with the key worker and reports from other workers. The resident was expected to identify the issues they wished to address, their goals and steps through which these might be achieved. Records of this were kept on file and shared with the resident. Activities arranged within Buffy House were limited but there was some art work and music. A nurse from the local medical centre also provided support. There was a cleaning and cooking rota, with residents expected to share the day-to-day domestic tasks with staff. Staff shared with residents in buying and cooking an evening meal (including vegetarian and sometimes special diet options) on a limited budget of £30.

The building was a little short of space, especially of rooms where confidential one-to-one work with residents could take place. It had a light, well equipped, kitchen, and an interview room which had barred windows, as security for the building. The residents' lounge was not well equipped and the resource room had a single PC that was out of action at the time of the visit.

The project received funds through RSI (Rough Sleepers Initiative). Centrepoint employed five project workers and a project manager. It was line-managed by an area manager. Centrepoint also had a resettlement team that helped in arranging move-on accommodation. Residents were expected to stay with the project for no more that two years, although work towards moving on began during the initial eight week assessment period. 'Success' was regarded as a resident being able to move on to accommodation with lower levels of support, although parallel improvement in self esteem, ability to cope and come to terms with their past and look forward to a more positive future was also promoted. Of course, not everything developed positively or in a straight line and, on occasions, the project did have to evict. Violence and/or persistent threatening behaviour was challenged, with an attempt to understand and correct; but more serious offences such as arson resulted in eviction. Overall the project tried to be non-judgmental, although illegal activities, such as drug use, were not allowed on the premises. Other reasons for eviction were for a serious lack of progress and dis-engagement from the help and support offered. Referral to psychiatric services at the request of residents was not uncommon, although a significant delay of around six weeks was reported in obtaining an appointment.

The project did have occasional complaints from neighbours about noise levels, but relationships with the local police were described as being good.

A number of voluntary sector projects offered help and support for young people who were homeless, but combined this with services for young people leaving care. These will be reviewed in the next chapter. But it is important to note here that the reason that many projects combined support for care leavers and other young people who were, or were at risk of being, homeless was that many of the problems they faced were largely the same. Whether care leavers or not, they were often poorly qualified, separated from their parents and suffering deep-rooted problems associated with family breakdown. In some cases they were parents themselves. Many were also dealing with 16 and 17-year-olds, an age group with which other homelessness projects seemed reluctant to work. This was either because they were considered to be too young and immature, or because the benefits to which they might be entitled were more difficult to access. We will return to these issues in the next chapter.

Resettlement services

Resettlement services for young people were developed in the late 1980s when large hostels were scheduled for closure. By the middle of the 1990s some local authorities had a combination of a high number of voids in social housing and high numbers of young homeless people (Quilgars and Pleace, 1999). Some programmes involve a limited amount of social support for young people in maintaining their tenancies and some operate through the voluntary sector. The Capital Youth Link service, quoted by Quilgars and Pleace for instance, offers practical and emotional support for 16 and 17-year-olds as they move to independent living.

The project detailed below was unusual amongst those visited. One factor that might explain this was that it was located in a city that has a surplus number of houses in the social rented sector. The project did, however, work with young people requiring different degrees of support, including some needing high levels of support. Many of the young people it worked with were also moved into accommodation that was not simply a form of 'intermediate housing', but could, if tenancies were supported, be regarded as permanent accommodation. Compared with other projects, it also worked with a wide age range, including those who became homeless at the age of 16 or 17.

Barnardo's

Newcastle Independence Network (NIN)

This is a coordinated project, which involves a partnership between Newcastle Social Services, the city's Housing Department, Newcastle and North Tyneside Health Authority and Barnardo's. A range of different funding sources support five main projects:

- Outreach (funded by DETR);
- Support Needs Assessment;
- Start-Up Scheme: intensive 1:1 support for young tenants (Barnardo's led); and
- Community Based Support (less intensive) support for young tenants by four area based teams.

The project also linked to leaving care support managed by the social service department of the local authority.

Outreach

This project, which had been running since September 1998, worked with young people who were known to be difficult, either because of drug misuse, their behaviour, or chaotic lifestyles. Funding was through the DETR (S180), now part of the Homelessness Action Programme. Young people offered support were not necessarily 'street homeless' but often they did not have a fixed address. Their behaviour also made it difficult for them to be housed. This scheme was regarded as filling an important gap in provision for a group of highly mobile young people identified by a number of agencies. None, however, had previously felt able to work with them. The scheme used 'outreach' rather than 'detached' workers in that they worked from a venue in the community, such as a 'day centre' or another social care venue.

This scheme had dealt with around 200 young people by the end of 1999; almost exclusively white, and more often male than female. Many were ex-care leavers (four in ten of the 18 to 21-year-olds and a further two in ten aged between 16 and 18). Around 15 per cent self reported mental health problems. Many were also known users of drugs, including 'wobbly eggs' (Temazipan) and speed (amphetamines). Participants were given somewhere warm to meet during the day, a range of leisure activities and free food in the middle of the day. Whether demand will be seasonal was, at the time of the visit, unknown. It was said that the DETR hoped this group could not only be housed but turned into bright, socially and economically viable young people. In practice, simply keeping in contact and helping whenever, or wherever, possible was thought to be more realistic. Data was collected on the number of emergency bed nights arranged as well as longer-term placements.

Support needs assessment

This worked with around 150 young people aged 16 and 17-years-old each year. Nearly two-thirds of the group were female. They became homeless as a result of family disputes, often involving violence (40 per cent), pregnancy and sometimes sexual abuse. More than two-thirds of this group had no previous connection with a social care agency. They were also usually unaware of any entitlement they may have. They had no money, were often unemployed, and suddenly found themselves with nowhere to live. The assessment and support they received, however, went far beyond being told about their legal entitlements. It gave them friendship, support and help in trying to sort out their lives. Sometimes this involved simply helping them to think through their options although often it also included referring them to emergency accommodation or forms of intermediate housing. Despite the age group with which this project was working, however, there was little systematic work done in partnership with the Careers Service or training providers. The Careers Service did, however, attend multi-agency advisory meetings.

Start up scheme

This project did high intensity work, mainly one-to-one. The scheme was taken over by Barnardo's in 1997 because of involvement in successfully running Homeless North. Sixty-two young people were supported in 1999. Part of the work done involved challenging offensive behaviour. It also made referrals to a health centre specifically working with homeless people. The main aim of the project was to help maintain and sustain young people in tenancies.

Community based support

Previously called 'First Move', this project involved community-based support for young people. All young tenants were initially mailed to give details of the support available. Under the scheme, nearly all new social housing tenants under the age of 25 received a visit from the team within two weeks of moving in. Most of the work also involved setting up and running a drop-in centre and doing group work with young tenants. Other work activities was undertaken by volunteers, such as the Crocodile Mobile Crèche in which volunteer young women provided play groups for under-5 children in church halls and leisure centres, often using their own cars to transport play equipment.

The project received funding from a variety of different sources including SRB and Joint (Health and LA) funding as well as from different departments of local, and central, government and Barnardo's. Each of the funding agencies, however, had their own agenda for judging effectiveness and measuring success. Indicators of success for the housing department, for instance, were tenancies maintained and no neighbourhood disputes. Other indicators the project had to produce, however, were sometimes restricted to the numbers of the young people who used the project. Success for social services would be no care leavers turning up anywhere else. The leaving care team, however, were committed to positive outcomes in terms of education and employment. Success for NIN was regarded as being young people fulfilling their potential and minimising homelessness. The location of the project within the voluntary sector was thought to have helped in forging better cooperation between the housing and social services departments. Even facilitating regular monthly meetings helped better liaison and a joint approach to problem solving.

The project coordinator thinks the project is being successful in helping young people with their two main priorities of housing and money, but less successful in providing either constructive activities or progression possibilities. Despite their best efforts, many young people remained socially excluded and socially isolated. In this targeted work it was regarded as not yet 'holistic' in addressing problems. But it was hoped to move provision in that direction by making service providers cooperate. Improvements for the future might include having a better city centre base and being open for access for longer periods of time.

Despite Newcastle having a purpose-built foyer very few of the clients dealt with by NIN are placed there. As the project leader commented, 'they don't really like the bunnies we work with'. More common is placement in other supported housing projects, such as those run through the De Paul Trust or the Children's Society (CS). The latter project entails CS acting as legal landlord.

Conclusions

This chapter has examined teenage pregnancy and youth homelessness. It has done so within a more general context of the domestic and housing careers of young people as they move towards adult partnerships and forms of independent living. As we have seen, Government policies are premised upon the assumption that parenting and independent living are best undertaken when young people have adequate resources and means of support. Often this means both a stable adult partnership and a good income based on employment. Yet not all young people are in such a fortunate position when domestic and housing transitions occur. State support often walks a tightrope between wishing to discourage early parenting and independent living and ensuring that long-term social exclusion does not ensue when this happens.

In the first part of the chapter, we focused on teenage pregnancy, examining the correlates of early parenting and the outcomes in terms of the welfare of both the young parent and their children. Yet even here, there is a need to distinguish between early and unplanned teenage pregnancy and planned parenting in late teenage years. The Government's policy agenda is clearly both to reduce teenage conceptions and, where young people do become parents at an early age, to minimise their social exclusion. In that teenage parenting is associated with more general problems of educational disadvantage and disaffection, and poverty more generally, this requires much more than better sex and parenting education. The policy agenda thus includes raising standards in schools for all and preventing educational disaffection, as discussed in chapter three. More specifically, it now includes means through which young parents can be given better education and training support so that the many disadvantages associated with teenage pregnancy do not turn into a more permanent inability to compete for jobs when young mothers feel able to continue their occupational ambitions. This is to be welcomed. However, many projects also try to address issues of self esteem and the need for better systems of support and training beyond those simply linked to employment. Yet funding for such support remains short-term and insecure and the YMCA project described earlier has ceased to function.

The chapter has also examined youth homelessness and support for young people during their housing careers. It has been argued that both have been made more problematic because of trends in the supply of housing and housing policy more generally. Youth homelessness, especially, is linked to other forms of disadvantage and requires intervention based upon a more holistic assessment of need. Research does indicate that much youth homelessness is caused by young people leaving home because of conflict or abuse within the family, or tensions that cannot be resolved. The most common problem that has been addressed, however, is the link between homelessness and joblessness and some projects attempt support for young people on both fronts, simultaneously. Where homelessness has its roots in family conflict, however, young people may need much more in terms of emotional and social support than can be supplied through foyer-type solutions. Tenancies are unlikely to be maintained unless young people have financial and emotional security. Yet benefit levels and the conditions in which homeless people are accommodated are unlikely to provide that. In reviewing disaffection and disadvantage in education and the labour market, we saw that the Government now accepts that training schemes alone do not provide an adequate bridge from school to work. New Deal Gateway and the proposed Connexions strategy are means through which a more holistic assessment of needs is required *as well as* requiring young people to better plan their own occupational careers with appropriate levels of support. Whether this will adequately address their housing and domestic careers remains to be seen.

Chapter five

Young people 'looked after' in care and leaving care

This chapter will review research, policy and practice offering support for children and young people 'looked after'. Before embarking upon this review, however, it is important, to comment on the term 'looked after'. In England and Wales this term was introduced by the 1989 Children Act, in part as recognition of the attempt to reduce the number of formal 'care orders', and to emphasise the voluntary nature of much local authority care. However, to those not familiar with this, the terminology can be confusing. When discussing one of the cameos for this book with a project leader (and, it should be emphasised, not one covered in this chapter) she was outraged to find reference in my summary of the project to the small proportion of her clients who were 'looked after'. She thought this implied an accusation that the rest were not being properly looked after at all. To avoid confusion and clumsiness, therefore, the terms young people 'in care' and 'leaving care' will be used inter-changeably with the more technically correct terms of 'looked after' or 'accommodated' or ceasing to be so.

In March 1999 there were approximately 55,300 children and young people 'looked after' by local authorities in England (with a further 12,000 in Scotland and a further 2,000 each in Wales and Northern Ireland). In England, the numbers involved have reduced markedly in recent decades, from 96,000 in 1977, to under 60,000 in 1990, and to below 50,000 by 1994. Since then there has been a rise of around 6,000. The reasons for the rise in recent years remain unclear. There is no evidence that it is as a result of anticipating the proposed changes in the responsibilities of social service departments contained in the 1999 Leaving Care Bill. Indeed, at the time of writing, young people are still being discharged from care as soon as is legally possible (DOH, 1999c). These official statistics on the number of children and young people 'looked after' are, however, snap-shot figures as recorded at the end of each year and the 'looked after' population changes throughout each year as young people move into, and out of, care. Recent research evidence on this 'moving picture of care' suggests that, of the 11.4 million children in England and Wales, 190,000 will be referred to social service departments in any one year, 160,000 will be supported at home, and 30,000 will become 'looked after'. Half of this latter group will be 'looked after' for six weeks or less before being returned to the charge of their families, although around 4,000 of these will later have a second period of care. Of those who are 'looked after' for more than six weeks,

9,500 will be placed in foster care and a further 750 in a mixture of foster and residential care (DOH, 1998). This suggests that, of the 55,000 at the end of 1999, there were just under 11,000 new cases involving children and young people spending significant amounts of time away from their parents.

Slightly more boys (54.5 per cent) than girls are 'looked after' by local authorities and this gender difference remains broadly the same in all age groups. The ethnic composition of the care population is much more difficult to determine. The DOH accepts that it is likely that around one in ten of those 'looked after' are from minority ethnic groups and that this is probably a lower proportion than ten years ago (Department of Health, 1998). In an earlier study Bebbington and Miles concluded that no ethnic group was over-represented (Bebbington and Miles, 1989). However, gender and ethnicity are important in the distribution of the population. Girls have a greater chance of being in foster care (three in four admissions compared with one in three boys). Minority ethnic children are also over-represented amongst the small number of those 'looked after' in 'secure accommodation' (DOH, 1998).

The last chapter described the characteristics of young people who embarked upon domestic and housing transitions in their teenage years. It reported that over-represented amongst those who become parents or homeless in their teens are young people who have been 'looked after'. Chapters two and three of this book indicated that this group is also over-represented amongst those who are disaffected or who under-achieve at school and who later become unemployed or are disengaged from education, training or the labour market. Those who become 'looked after' are much more likely to have lived in deprived and disadvantaged circumstances before they are taken into care. One large scale study at the end of the 1980s, for instance, found that children living with only one adult were eight times more likely to be taken into care than children from dual parent families, and three-and-a-half times more likely to be moved to care from over-crowded accommodation. Their parents were three times more likely to be on benefit and twice as likely to be under the age of 21 (Bebbington and Miles, 1989). However, there has also been a growing recognition that many young people taken into care because they were vulnerable have their future welfare further disadvantaged, rather than enhanced by their experiences in care, and the support offered to them when they leave. The recent Children's Safeguards Review (The Utting Report, 1997) summarises some bleak 'headline statistics' based upon evidence reviewed by the Social Services Inspectorate:

- more than 75 per cent of care leavers have no academic qualifications of any kind;
- more than 50 per cent of young people leaving care after 16 years are unemployed;
- 17 per cent of young women leaving care are pregnant or already mothers;
- 10 per cent of 16 to 17-year-old claimants of DSS severe hardship payments have been in care;
- 23 per cent of adult prisoners and 38 per cent of young prisoners have been in care; and
- 30 per cent of young single homeless people have been in care (SSI, 1997).

These outcomes alone would be sufficient reason for examining in detail the circumstances of young people whose welfare is the responsibility of the state. Yet, concern for the welfare of children and young people 'looked after' has been acute in recent decades, not so much because of such poor outcomes, but because of a number of scandals concerning the systematic abuse of young people whilst they were in care. A 'Children's Safeguard Review' was commissioned shortly before the General Election, carried out by Sir William Utting, and published in 1997. One of its major concerns was continued revelations about widespread sexual, physical and emotional abuse of children in residential and foster care. Although there are significant legal and institutional differences between Scotland and England and Wales, the parallel report for Scotland came to similar conclusions (Kent, 1997). The reports recommend the development of a protective strategy designed to better root out abuse and protect children from it.

Abuse and protection from abuse

The major concern of the Children's Safeguard Review was that, despite decades of public concern, still not enough was being done by those responsible for corporate parenting to prevent serious harm being inflicted on those in their care. Initially, in the 1960s and 1970s, this concern centred on the death of children in care and the infamous cases of Jasmine Beckford and others. By the time of drafting the 1989 Children Act, it had turned to concern about child sexual abuse in the wake of allegations in Cleveland and the inquiry by Lord Justice Butler-Sloss (Butler-Sloss, 1988). The 1989 Act, and much of the detail contained in ten volumes of *Regulations and Guidance* that followed it, was intended to safeguard children and young people living away from home. Yet increasing evidence of widespread physical and sexual abuse continued after the Act and resulted in several major public inquiries. These included inquiries into Kincora boys' hostel in Belfast (1989), Pindown Regimes in Staffordshire (1991), Castle Hill School (1991), Ty Mawr former approved school in Gwent, Feltham Young Offenders Institute (1993), Leicestershire children's homes (1993) and an on-going inquiry into abuse in North Wales (Health Committee, 1998).

In the foreword to the Government Response to the Safeguards Review in 1998, the then Secretary of State for Health, Frank Dobson, accepted that the Utting Report 'painted a woeful tale of failure' and that 'the whole system failed'. Amongst the recommendations were some designed to protect young people from abuse including to:

- improve protection for children in foster and residential care, in schools and in the penal system;
- provide more effective safeguards and checks to prevent abusers from working with children;
- provide more effective avenues of complaint and increase access to independent advocates;
- provide more vigilant management;

- provide effective disciplinary and criminal procedures; and
- provide effective systems of communication between agencies about known abusers.

There is little clear evidence about the scale of abuse, although the Utting Report refers to one study on 84 children referred between March 1991 and February 1992. In this study, more than three-quarters of the victims and nearly nine out of ten (87 per cent) perpetrators were male. The peers of victims (other young people) were nearly as likely to be the abusers as staff (48 per cent compared with 42 per cent). Forty per cent of victims were also found to have had physical or learning disabilities. The Utting report also draws attention to the involvement of young people in care in forms of pornography and child prostitution, although there is no reliable evidence of its extent in the UK. Chapter one of the Utting Report includes a quotation from The Leicestershire Inquiry of 1992 in which Andre Kirkwood QC wrote the following. 'It would not be wise for anyone to approach this Report on the basis that it all happened a long time ago and that nothing like it could ever happen again.' Despite the far-reaching reforms now being implemented by government this warning deserves to be repeated.

Children and young people's rights

One key element in addressing the abuse of young people in care has been the denial of their rights, including their right to complain of abuse and have their views listened to and respected. The International Convention on the Rights of the Child had a strong influence in the drafting of the 1989 Children Act and the Regulation and Guidance on the implementation of the Act and these have clear implications for the rights of young people in care. Four different and distinct categories of rights have been identified (Coles, 1995). These are:
- *entitlements* – the right to know or have something;
- *protection rights* – the right to be protected from exploitation or abuse;
- *representational rights* – the right to be involved in decision making and to be helped and supported in this process; and
- *enabling rights* – the right to adequate resources through which rights translate into real opportunities.

Since the implementation of the 1989 Children Act, young people 'looked after' should be made aware of their rights, including their rights to play an active role in decisions made about their care and in planning for their futures. They should also be made aware of their rights to be protected from abuse (including corporal punishment), as well as their rights of privacy and association. Some attempt has been made to make these easily available to children and young people 'looked after', including through the use of video material.

There are, however, some misgivings about whether local authorities have been active in promoting the rights of young people in care. In the second report of the Health Committee in July 1998, the Department of Health was fiercely criticised for not having met its statutory duty to provide annual reports on compliance with the 1989 Act. A report on actions taken between 1995–1999 was finally published in January 2000 (DOH, 2000). Stressing the importance of listening to the voice of children and young people, the Health Committee Report further recommended that local authorities should be required to ensure that all 'looked after' children should have the option of having a recognised 'adult friend' to actively promote their best interests. It also proposed a Children's Rights Commissioner. Despite criticism of local authorities dragging their feet in implementing legislation, regulations and guidance, as Jackson and Thomas point out, 'there is clearly no going back to a time when decisions about the future of children in care were routinely made without reference to their own wishes and feelings' (Jackson and Thomas, 1999). However, their own report suggests there is some way to go.

Principles of care for 'looked after' children

Although public provision for deprived children dates back to the Elizabethan Poor Law, the more modern statutory framework is based on the 1944 Curtis Committee and an Act of Parliament that followed this in 1948. This led, for the first time, to provision for children and young people which 'would equal loving family care as nearly as possible' (Health Committee, 1998). Since the 1948 Act, there has been a general acceptance in principle that the care system should make life for children and young people as normal as possible. The debate has been about what this means and how it can be achieved. One way is by trying to ensure that families are supported so that as few as possible become 'looked after'. Much of this has been achieved as a result of a deliberate policy to work with families and parents to prevent situations in which being taken into care is necessary and to continue to work with families to ensure children become re-united with them wherever and whenever possible. There has also been a deliberate move to make being taken into care a positive and 'non-punitive' experience with criminal care orders reduced significantly even before the 1989 Act withdrew the order.

Where children and young people are living apart from their birth families there is also a widespread acceptance that the 'corporate parent' (the local authority) should provide care and support that is similar to that which natural parents would provide. The acceptance of the normal as possible principle has recently been re-emphasised in the Government's response to the Children's Safeguards Review. In its response the Government emphasised that 'the local authority must act towards the children in their care as any natural parents would act towards their child'. The Secretary of State for Health insisted, in the foreword, on standards of care and responsibility which correspond to two main tests: 'Would this have been good enough for me when I was a child?' and 'Would this be good enough for my own children?' (Department of Health, 1999a). What this means in practice is also laid out clearly in 12 specific responsibilities which are important, not only in offering clear guidance to local authorities, but also in indicating what should be required of all good parents. The 12 responsibilities are:

- provide care, a home, and access to health and education and other public services . . . according to their needs;
- provide a mixture of care and firmness to support the child's development, and be the tolerant, dependable and available partner in the adult/child relationship even in the face of disagreements;
- protect and educate the child against the perils and risks of life by encouraging constructive and appropriate friendships, and discouraging destructive and harmful relationships;
- celebrate and share their children's achievements, supporting them when they are down;
- recognise and respect their growth to independence, being tolerant and supportive of their mistakes;
- provide consistent support and be available to provide advice and practical help when needed;
- advocate their cause and troubleshoot on their behalf when necessary;
- be ambitious for them and encourage and support their efforts to get on and reach their potential, whether through education, training or employment;
- provide occasional financial support, remember birthdays and Christmas or annual celebrations within the individual child's religion and culture;
- encourage and enable contact with family members – parents, grandparents, aunts and uncles;
- help them to feel part of the local community through contact with neighbours and local groups; and
- be proactive, not passive, when there are known or suspected serious difficulties.

The importance of following the principle of normal as possible is also supported by much research evidence on the importance of stability of care in young people's lives. In a recent review, Jackson and Thomas conclude that remaining at home, or returning to it quickly, offers the best chance of stability and continuity for most children. Offering families respite care can sometimes help provide continuity. Where placements away from an immediate birth family are necessary, placement with relatives is the most stable form of foster care. However, adoption also offers by far the best chance of permanency and lifelong commitment where children and young people can no longer live with their birth families. Specialist or professional foster placements are less likely than other forms of placements to end sooner than planned and may sometimes provide opportunities for ongoing support into more stable forms of independent living. The research concludes that residential care has had only a limited success in the UK although it admits that there is some comparative evidence of its successful use elsewhere (Jackson and Thomas, 1999). Residential care is, however, still important, especially in the care of older children and young people. The latest figures from the Department of Health indicate that, of the 7,800 care leavers in 1997–98, nearly a quarter (23 per cent) had a children's home as their final placement (DOH, 2000a).

Types of placement

The reduction in care placements overall in recent decades was largely achieved by a very significant reduction in the proportion of young people 'looked after' in residential care. The proportion 'looked after' in foster care nearly doubled in 20 years, increasing from 37 per cent in 1980 to 57 per cent in 1990 to 65 per cent by March 1999 (DOH, 2000). Government now requires social service departments to provide, on an annual basis, a number of key indicators, designed to monitor progress in improving the care system. One key indicator is the proportion of those 'looked after' in residential care. This is based on an assumption that reducing the proportion of young people in residential care represents improvement. Yet, given changes in the nature of residential care, too much can be made of this. Firstly, it must be recognised that, in the 1990s, being 'looked after' in residential care has increasingly come to mean being 'looked after' in small units. Furthermore, around a half of all children and young people 'looked after' in foster care are placed alongside other children being fostered and in families in which carers have their own children. This can mean that they live with three or more children in larger than average households. In terms of household size, therefore, there may be little difference between foster and residential care. Secondly, children and young people in residential care are looked after by professional workers whose main occupation is to care for children and young people. Many, though by no means all, foster families have at least one adult who has an occupation outside the home, yet a considerable number are, in effect, professional carers. Although foster care remains, on average, a cheaper option for social service departments, this does not mean that foster care is either less 'professional' or that units of care are smaller. Many of the key differences centre on the fact that residential care may not be able to provide the continuity of one-to-one support with professional workers. Residential homes inevitably employ staff who work to rotas and shifts. Thus, continuity of care may be a more important issue than the size of household unit, although, as we will see, 'continuity' is far from a straightforward concept. The assessment of the impact of different types of care experience must, however, be careful to avoid overly simplistic classifications of different types of placement.

Careers in care and stability and continuity of placement

There is also now a recognition that being 'looked after' needs to be treated as a dynamic concept. Children and young people are likely to experience several different placements over the period in which they are growing up and these 'moves' in care can have considerable impact upon their welfare. Much research relies upon the number of moves in care as an indirect indicator of its quality (Garnett, 1992; Rowe et al., 1989). In one of the largest and most extensive studies of careers in care in the 1980s, Rowe and colleagues studied admissions into care, moves and discharges in six local authorities and followed the fortunes of more than 2,000 children over a 12 to 23 month period (Rowe *et al.*, 1989). Whilst over half of admissions (57 per cent) during this period had no moves, 26 per cent had one, 9 per cent had two and 8 per cent three or more. Although this study was extensive in its coverage it was relatively short-term as regards the period of time young people were tracked through the system. In a follow-up study of a smaller sub-sample, Garnett and colleagues found that the vast majority of their sample (74 per cent) experienced a change of placement in the final two years of being 'looked after'. A quarter of the sample had been moved three or more times during this period (Garnett, 1992). A more recent questionnaire survey of over 2,000 children found that, for those who had been looked after for more than five years, only one in ten had remained in the same placement throughout and nearly a quarter had been in 11 or more different placements. (Shaw, 1998). This suggests a form of what Brown has called 'accommodation pinball' (Brown, 1998). In a study of leaving care schemes, Biehal *et al.* studied a sample of 74 young people from three contrasting areas. Just over half of this sample had entered the care system as teenagers, with the rest at different ages from infancy upwards. More than half this sample (52 per cent) had experienced between one and three moves in care, a third had moved more than four times and one in ten had experienced more than ten different placements (Biehal *et al.*, 1995). This study correlated unsettled careers in care with patterns of instability after care.

There is some debate within research about whether things might have been getting better or worse in recent years (Jackson and Thomas, 1998). The Government accepts that there was an increase of those experiencing three or more placements between 1993–97 of between 17 and 20 per cent, with significant differences between local authorities. Some reported that no young person had three or more placements, whilst others reported that this was the experience of over a third (36 per cent) (Department of Health 1998). Following the Children's Safeguard Review, the Government initiated a Quality Protects programme aimed to fundamentally improve matters. This requires local authorities to provide data on the percentage of children and young people 'looked after' who experience more than three placements a year with a national target aimed at ensuring that less than 16 per cent of children experience more than three placements a year (DOH, 1999). There are some grounds for accepting that a large number of moves lead to a lack of coordination of effort, insecurity in those 'looked after' and poor outcomes at later stages in the life course. However, there are doubts about whether setting simple targets on the number of placements per year alone will adequately address the real issues. The concept of 'career' is potentially important in drawing attention to the ways in which decisions taken about each successive placement do impact upon a young person's welfare. Yet the discussion below also suggests that a much more complex understanding of careers in care is required, rather than simply considering the number of moves experienced.

Research indicates that some groups within the care system are more at risk of unstable and unsettled careers in care than others. Jackson and Thomas report that age has been repeatedly linked to changes in placement, with many studies reporting that the older the child, and the older the child at the time of first placement, the more likely they were to experience placement breakdown. Placements in which the carers have children of their own of about the same age are also reported as more likely to fail. However, Jackson and Thomas note the important exception of those placed with the long-standing Children's Family Trust. Placing children and young people with their brothers and sisters, rather than separating them and placing them with more than one foster family, is also thought to enhance stability. The behaviour of the child or young person is also important, although this is difficult to assess from research studies. Hurried placements and poor coordination of services are also linked to frequent breakdowns. In a multi-variate analysis of more than a thousand placements over a ten year period, Fratter and colleagues identified nine risk factors associated with placement breakdown. Age and the presence of emotional problems were the factors most correlated with failure. Others included being of mixed parentage, having a history of deprivation and abuse and having special needs (Fratter *et al.*, 1991)

The *Voice of the Child* provides a number of case studies which indicate the potential traumas involved in even a single move. One of these is quoted in Jackson and Thomas and is outlined in the box below.

Ian and Robby's Story

Ian and Robby, brothers aged 10 and 9, were admitted to a children's home after their mother died, and then moved to a foster home. They told their story three years later.

'We felt scared and angry when we were moved. But we settled in and we expected to stay here until we grew up. Our care plans said that we would stay in our foster home "with a view to permanency". We planted a tree in a local cemetery in memory of our mother. Then came THE BOMBSHELL. Our social worker told our foster carers about Social Services' plan to move us. He said he didn't agree with the plan but that he was being told he had to move us. He did explain that we had rights. This bombshell fell and it was a very difficult time.'

Ian and Robby were helped by an advocate who facilitated a financial agreement between Social Services and the fostering agency which enabled them to stay in their placement.

From *Voice of the Child*, 1998.

There are some dangers in focusing only upon negative outcomes of careers in care with the number of 'moves' taken as the key indicator of instability. Some moves are known to be temporary, planned as such, and with the temporary nature of the stay known to young people. As Rowe and colleagues pointed out in their study, it is misleading to compare these with ones which might involve a move into residential care after the breakdown of a long-term fostering relationship (Rowe *et al.*, 1989). In a recent review, Jackson and Thomas have highlighted the importance of distinguishing between 'continuity' and 'stability' (Jackson and Thomas, 1999). If a young person remains in the same placement this may be deemed to imply continuity of care. Yet the placement may be surrounded by instability if schooling is disrupted, if there are changes in their friendship network or their relationships with carers, or even if, as often happens, there is a repeated change of social worker. Jackson and Thomas recommend that we must unpack the notion of stability to focus on six different dimensions against which its value can be more properly assessed. Stability of placement is important if this continues to provide reliable and trusted support in a predictable way. Stability of relationships, however, is a much wider concept and encompasses relationships within household and kinship groups and also relationships with friends and peer groups. Stability of education implies continuity in which educational progress is assessed and planned. Stability of health care is also important if a proper balance between surveillance, treatment and responsibility is to be developed. Stability of community is important if a young person is to feel connected to a cultural reference group with which they can identify and to which they can relate. This might be a key to the sixth dimension, stability of identity, although other factors might also be important in promoting this. 'Accommodation pinball' clearly has the potential to disrupt all this. But, as Jackson and Thomas argue, we should be concerned to look more closely at indicators of good care rather than use the number of moves as a proxy measure of good and bad experience.

Education and health care

Comment was made in chapter three about the over-representation of young people 'looked after' among those who under-perform in education and/or are not in school because they have been excluded or self-exclude. In the mid-1990s more than a quarter of 14 to 16-year-olds were not in school because of exclusion or truancy, the latter sometimes in collusion with care staff (Ofsted/SSI, 1995). Only a tiny proportion of 'looked after' young people are educationally successful. The DfEE reported to the Health Committee in 1998 that only between 12 per cent and 19 per cent go on to further education compared with 68 per cent in the rest of the age group. Part of the reason for such poor performance lies in the complex difficulties and turmoil in their lives; 13 per cent have special needs and over half of this group have emotional and behavioural difficulties (Koprowska and Stein, 1999). They often have unstable care careers, with movements in care being associated, either with changes of school, or with long journeys if they stay in the same school. In evidence submitted to the Health Committee, The Who Cares? Trust associated poor achievement with poor coordination between SSDs, LEAs and schools. They often did not share information and were unclear about their respective roles. Those with day-to-day responsibility for young people in care are also reported as not valuing education sufficiently. Both schools and carers have been accused of having too low expectations. Where, because of disruption, young people fall behind in their school work, prompt and sensitive action to help them catch up is reported to be only rarely offered (Health Committee, 1998). One care scheme which has attempted both to maintain stability and in which education is valued highly is run by the Children's Family Trust. Reviewed by Jackson and Thomas, young people being 'looked after' on this scheme are reported to be much more successful.

One report suggested that all of the 15 who were tracked attended school until at least the age of 16, and 11 continued into further and higher education (Cairns and Cairns, 1989).

Evidence from the Department of Health also suggests that many young people 'looked after' have poor health including undiagnosed chronic health conditions, poor uncorrected eyesight, significant weight problems and uncompleted immunisation programmes. They are also more likely to be suffering from mental health problems, including depressive illnesses, some with serious psychiatric disorders, not all of which are detected or diagnosed (Health Committee, 1998). There is relatively little systematic evidence about the mental health of young people in care. Yet one study in Oxfordshire reported that a staggering 96 per cent of those in residential care and 57 per cent of those in foster care had some form of psychiatric disorder, a combined total of 67 per cent (McCann et al., quoted by Koprowska and Stein, 2000). Another study they report on suggested that long-term mental illness and disorders, including depression, eating disorders and phobias, were especially common amongst young women (in 87 per cent of the sample) (Saunders and Broad, 1997).

The Who Cares? Trust reported that there were significant gaps in basic health care information: little guidance given on healthy eating and eating disorders; limited access to confidential information about sexual health, contraception and drugs; and lack of contact with trusted adults to discuss personal health matters; as well as 'some alarming breaches of confidentiality'. Those who were disabled were reported to have additional problems with little regard given to their wishes and feelings (Jackson and Thomas, 1999). To be sure, some of the reported ill-health will be the result of aspects of their life before being taken into care, such as poverty, bad housing, poor diet and parental neglect. But this seems to be compounded by frequent moves within care, poor record keeping, failures to transmit records following moves in care, and an over-reliance on formal six-monthly medical examinations.

A number of surveys have pointed to the fact that many young people being looked after become parents either whilst they are in care, or shortly after leaving (Biehal et al., 1995; Botting et al., 1998; Broad, 1998; Garnett, 1992). Biehal et al. reported that one in eight young people were parents before they were legally discharged from care. Within two years of leaving care, overall one third had become parents and half of all the young women mothers of at least one child (Biehal et al., 1995). Just over half of the pregnancies were unplanned. Of those that were planned, the vast majority had been planned with their partner. Although young women had moved in with their partners, some of the relationships broke down within a short time. The SEU report on Teenage Pregnancy raised questions about the personal and social education being offered to young people in care and the lack of a trusted adult with whom the young person could talk and from whom they could receive advice.

Running away from care

A number of recent studies have commented on the disproportionate number of people within the population of young people 'looked after' by local authorities who run away. In 1989 Newman estimated that there were nearly 100,000 running away incidents per year (Newman, 1989). This is close to an estimate of 102,000 made in 1990 by Abrahams and Mungham (Abrahams and Mungham, 1992). Abrahams and Mungham claimed that much recorded running away was concentrated amongst young people 'looked after' – nearly a third of all runaways were young people running away from 'substitute' care. This was confirmed in the large scale survey of running away conducted for the Children's Society (Stein *et al.*, 1999). This found that 45 per cent of those in residential or foster care had run away and spent at least one night away from home, compared with just under 10 per cent of those living in birth families. Of those running away from care, the vast majority were running away from residential care. In a recent review of running away from care by Wade and colleagues, those running away from children's homes were also more likely to repeatedly run away. Young people running from residential care were also more likely to do so at a younger age and to stay away for longer. The same research found that girls were as likely to run away as boys and that the peak ages for running away from care are between 13 and 15, although there was a considerable minority who ran away before this age. However, this research cast doubts on previous findings that there is an over preponderance of black (mainly Afro-Caribbean) children running away from care. However, it did note that bullying (including incidents of racist abuse) were important in some cases. Young people defined as having emotional and behavioural difficulties (EBD) were also found to go missing more often, at an earlier age, stay away for longer, be more likely to be excluded from school, have past convictions and return reluctantly, than runaways without EBD. The 1997 Utting report noted that homeless children are the most vulnerable of all children and repeated his earlier call for all instances to be treated with proper seriousness and sensitivity to the issues involved (Utting, 1997). Most disturbing are instances reported when young people are running away from abusive relationships in care only to be picked up by the police and returned to those same relationships without proper investigation and enquiry.

Leaving care

By the time young people reach the age at which being formally discharged from care is being considered, they will be highly likely to have to face a labour market which increasingly demands formal certification of their abilities and skills. Yet most care leavers have few, if any, formal qualifications. They may be asked to live independently at an age when few others would even contemplate it, or their parents allow it. And often they do so with little support and with meagre financial resources available to enable them to survive. Section 24 of the 1989 Children Act made it a duty of local authorities to advise and befriend young people ceasing to be 'looked after', with a view to promoting their welfare.

Within the Act there is also a power but not a duty to assist. This assistance may be in kind or cash and includes help with their education, training and employment up to the age of 21, or where this was not yet completed, beyond that age. Given that only a tiny minority do stay in post-16 education, however, much of the support from local authorities is in the form of after-care, including various leaving care schemes and supported accommodation projects. Stein suggests that these differ according to whether they are based on 'Independence' or 'Inter-Dependence' models (Stein, 1997). The former relies on instruction in practical survival skills, or what Stein calls 'domestic combat courses'. The latter gave a higher priority to inter-personal skills, self esteem, self-confidence-building and ongoing support after young people had left care. However, a survey by Berridge in 1995 suggested that 40 per cent of young people received no support from social services after leaving care (Berridge, 1995). This figure may be open to question as many local authorities have now franchised out duties under section 24 to voluntary sector organisations, such as Barnardo's or NCH Action for Children, which may not be recognised by respondents as 'social services'. A number of such schemes were established in the late 1980s and 1990s and there is evidence that they do make a considerable contribution to assisting local authorities in fulfilling their duties and powers under the 1989 Act (Biehal *et al.*, 1995). But this research also suggests that schemes were by no means universal, not always successful in preventing negative outcomes for many care leavers, and far from comprehensive in reaching all of them (Biehal *et al.*, 1995). The main areas of continuing concern are, therefore, the early age at which young people are required to live independently, whether support is continuous, and whether it is available to all. Too often young care leavers fail to maintain tenancies often because of lack of adequate financial and social support.

At the time of writing, most young people cease to be 'looked after' shortly after they reach the age of 16. A quarter of young people 'looked after' are discharged from care at the age of 16 and two-thirds will have moved to independent accommodation before they are 18 (DOH, 1999c). Contemplating living independently at such an early age is a major anxiety and a paramount concern at the time when their peers are more concerned with other post-16 options in education and training. This goes some way to explaining why care leavers are over-represented amongst those non-participating in education training and work (SEU, 1999b). As discussed in chapter two, the benefits system for 16 and 17-year-olds is also chaotic and not user-friendly. What living independently means, therefore, is managing a budget which gives little, or no, room for error, and often whilst living alone in the hostile environment of a social housing estate. For many young people being moved to independent living also means being moved from the instability of care to the instability of after care. Biehal *et al.* report a high degree of housing mobility after young people have been discharged from care. A third of their sample reported two additional moves within a few weeks; over half, two or more moves within two years; and a sixth, five or more moves (Biehal *et al.*, 1995). More than one in five of their sample experienced homelessness at least once in the two years after leaving care and many studies have pointed to care leavers being hugely represented amongst the young homeless (Evans, 1996).

'Quality Protects': The policy agenda for care and leaving care

The Ministerial Task Force which considered the 1997 Utting Report (sometimes referred to as The Safeguards Review) considered over 130 recommendations for change and developed a radical new programme for the reform and regeneration of services for children and for those 'looked after' more particularly. The Government response to the Safeguards Review involves a three year programme called Quality Protects with a total of £380 million of funds allocated to it over three and a half years. This is to be distributed through a new Children's Services Special Grant, details of which will be discussed below. Much of the associated legislative change is contained in the Care Standards and Leaving Care Bills. The Care Standards Bill proposed a new independent body, The National Care Standards Commission. This will be responsible for the regulation and inspection of all children's homes, including for the first time, small homes catering for fewer than four children. This Bill also introduces a regulatory regime for fostering agencies and residential family centres. The Commission will have the task of appointing a Children's Rights Director who will be responsible for investigating complaints or suspicions of abuse. In addition, the Department of Health has issued new guidelines on inter-agency working (*Working Together to Safeguard Children*) to promote the welfare of children. This gives guidance to social workers, the police, teachers, health staff and others, on working together to protect children from abuse and to promote their welfare.

In common with other policy initiatives, the Quality Protects programme involves a series of targets, changes in the responsibilities of local authorities and recommended changes in practical support. In terms of targets, the Government aims at:

- reductions in all authorities of children who have three or more placements in any one year to no more than 16 per cent by 2001; and
- improvements in the educational record of those they looked after so that the proportion of 16-year-olds gaining at least 1 GCSE or GNVQ increases to 50 per cent by 2001 and to 75 per cent by 2003.

The Health Committee has already commented that, given some research evidence, the target for qualifications may already be being met before any change is introduced. Having one, low grade, qualification is also unlikely to radically improve the job prospects of young people, although it might ensure that they stay in the education system for longer. The target related to placements also seems to confuse 'stability' of placements with 'continuity of care', as discussed earlier. Without adequate independent monitoring, it is subject to manipulation by SSDs eager to meet targets. The critical questions about Quality Protects are about whether it will produce the required radical improvement in the quality and coordination of services, rather than whether crude outcome targets will be achieved. Chapter three discussed the use of gender and ethnicity monitoring within schools and illustrated how this had helped raise standards of under-achieving groups. Given the paucity of data, especially on ethnicity on careers in care and outcomes afterwards, it would be good to see more gender and ethnicity monitoring being used within the care system.

The Quality Protects reforms do call for some better systems of assessment, care planning and record-keeping, as well as better quality assurance procedures to ensure that national and local standards are met. There is a commitment to making certain that children and young people are given adequate access to the services they need from other agencies and that due consideration is given to issues specific to black and minority ethnic backgrounds. The Government is also keen to promote an increase of choice in both foster and residential placements. To achieve this the Government proposes new regional groupings of SSDs to review the placements available and targeted local campaigns to recruit more foster carers. To help improve standards and ensure the quality of care, it proposes to introduce a Code of Practice for the recruitment and training of foster carers and National Standards for foster carers. Quality assurance will also be promoted through the introduction of improved complaints procedures. Running throughout the Utting Report, and taken on board in the Government's Response, is a recognition of the important role young people can play in re-designing and monitoring better systems of care. Quality Protects is firm in its commitment to promoting the voice of the child, including mechanisms through which young people are involved locally in policy and practice development. To support young people, Government proposes that there should be an independent visitor system for those under care orders and an extension of befriending and mentoring schemes. The organisation First Key is to be supported in establishing a group to provide a national voice for children in care.

In chapter two comment was briefly made on some of the new proposals contained in the Green Paper *Me Survive, Out There?* – especially those dealing with new financial arrangements for their support. One of the major policy changes announced both in the Green Paper and in the response to the Safeguards Review, is to change the statutory responsibility of local authorities. At the time of writing, the Care Leavers Bill before parliament proposes that local authorities should have a duty (rather than the power to assist as at present) to assess and meet the needs of 16 and 17-year-olds leaving care. This was amended in the House of Commons to extend this duty until the age of 21, or when full-time education was completed, whichever was the latest. There is also a clear indication that young people should not be discharged from being 'looked after' before the age of 18 except in exceptional circumstances. Enhanced forms of personal support are also proposed so as to ensure that all 'looked after' young people are given a Young Persons' Adviser to coordinate support and assistance in accordance with a 'Pathway Plan' which they will develop with their adviser. These plans are intended to set out clearly the support and assistance the young person will receive and include a named person responsible for delivering this, as well as target dates for the achievement of particular transition milestones. The plans are to cover education, training and employment, accommodation, personal support (such as befriending or mentoring), health care, life skills and financial support. Pathway Plans are to be based upon a multi-agency assessment of need, and involve a planning process in which the young person must be a key partner. It will also involve a range of other service providers. If a young person does not agree the plan, it is proposed that an Independent Review Panel will adjudicate an appeal. It is intended that plans should be reviewed regularly and at least once every six months. As discussed in chapter two, it is proposed that financial support for care leavers will be made through a single source, social services, rather than, at present through a complex range of different agencies such as the Employment Services and the Benefits Agency. At the time of writing it is difficult to assess what impact all these policy initiatives will have. Researchers and practitioners will need to be vigilant to make certain that they are followed through diligently.

Putting policy into practice

For many years now, some voluntary organisations have been trying to develop systems of support, despite fundamental flaws in the statutory framework. This brief review of projects examines ones which are working with care leavers. Some are also working with a wider group of young people in need even though care leavers are an important constituent group. Amongst the most interesting from the overall perspective being advocated in this book are projects which are attempting to put into practice 'holistic' approaches to working with vulnerable young people. Some of these offer a one-stop-shop, together with a wide range of services that the project provides either directly or indirectly. The first example is managed by NCH Action for Children.

King's Lynn NCH Action for Children Young People's Preparation for Leaving Home

This project, developed in partnership with Norfolk Social Service Department (NSSD), describes itself as 'holistic and unique'. This meant offering a range of different services in an integrated way and from a single site base. The base was located in an old rectory on the outskirts of King's Lynn. It had kitchens, a laundry and several large rooms used for consultation and training. The project served a largely rural area. Initially funded jointly by the European Social Fund (ESF), NSSD and NCH, the project also had funding from the local TEC and the Basic Skills Agency. The fundamental commitment of the project was to work with young people, to promote their long-term welfare and to promote and protect their rights. The project started in 1996 and had three main strands:
- support for 16 to 24-year-olds leaving care;
- education and employment support (Workways); and
- accommodation support (including the provision of shared housing).

It also had a 'sister project' nearby, providing family support services working with families and children up to the age of 14.

The project worked with an assumption that there are probably no 'quick fixes' to solve all the problems in vulnerable young people's lives. Often the most effective help takes the form of a range of different supports from a number of different sources and given over a long period of time.

Supported lodgings

The project grew out of 'leaving care' provision that worked to a service agreement with NSSD with an average case load of around seventy 16 to 18-year-olds. When visited, it also worked with young people as young as 14 and as old as 24, with most, but not all, 'looked after' or leaving care. Many care leavers were keen to be discharged from care at the age of 16. Young people were told at the beginning that they can be supported until they are 25 and contact is maintained through birthday and Christmas cards. The vast majority of those joining the project were leaving foster placements. When doing so, typically, the young person would move initially into supported lodgings where they would be provided with two meals a day by their carer. The care provider was also encouraged to keep in touch with the project and notify them of any difficulties, including any significant amount of time spent away from the lodgings at night. This 'next phase fostering' costs around £70 per week inclusive of housing benefits. Those offering supported lodgings were recruited, trained and supported by NSSD.

Workways

Most of the client group had had little success in education. The expansion of the project to include 'Workways' was intended to try to prevent young people from dropping out or failing again in post-16 education and training. This part of the project was largely supported by the European Social Fund. Workways focused on 'employability' rather than simply placement in employment or training. Indeed, the project encouraged young people to join post-16 education rather than youth training as the latter was thought to offer only low grade training and poor prospects for them. There were strong links to the local college and some initial education work done at the base. Education courses at the Old Rectory involved working with young people in small groups and in non-intimidating surroundings. The focus was mainly on key skills: literacy; numeracy; working with others; ICT. Initially, recruitment to the scheme included care leavers but was later also made available to those who were 16 to 18 and who were homeless. With the encouragement and financial support of the local TEC, they also recruited other groups of young people who were considered difficult to work with. Workways also involved running New Deal Gateways and the 'volunteers' option. The latter included placements for young people as 'peer educators' with some of these later being taken on as employees at the end of their time in New Deal. Whilst the project worked with young people with little previous educational success, many of the young people were known by project staff to be bright, talented and with considerable potential. Often their under-achievement was the result of institutions underestimating their potential. Workways also linked to activities arranged for year 11 pupils who are either excluded from, or are not attending, school. This was arranged through links with the local authority Visiting Teacher Service and others involved in a multi-agency partnership.

A number of those leaving care were, or were about to become, mothers. Under a 'next steps' programme with the local TEC, attempts were made to keep them in touch with training and work opportunities, although some difficulties with employers in arranging placements were reported.

Accommodation support

The accommodation project had three large four to five bedroomed houses with on-site support from a warden who sleeps in five nights a week. One of these houses has been converted into bedsits and was also used as move-on accommodation from other supported lodgings. Other organisations also had houses and the project acted as a clearing house to access these. It also provided links to the housing department for the provision of independent housing when it is thought the young person is ready for this.

Some monitoring and evaluation was required by its various funders, although it was also thought that more could be done by way of a more systematic evaluation of the impact of the scheme in terms of raising self esteem.

Much of the impetus for the whole programme and the reasons for its success was said to stem from the enthusiasm and drive of the person who set up and directed the project and her determination for it to succeed.

The project also worked closely with Purfleet (another charitable body working with the young homeless) which has recently set up a Women's Refuge and Domestic Violence Unit. Like the NCH project, this was described as having a director who just makes certain that adequate provision is made available and multi-agency cooperation works.

The downside of all this commitment was that the project could be treated by statutory services as a 'taken for granted safety net' which will continue to provide services, whether it is funded through service agreements with the local authority or not.

Other projects visited as part of the research for this book included some linked to aspects of the leaving-care service and broadly in line with some of the proposals contained in the Leaving Care Bill. A mentoring scheme for care leavers is being developed under national guidelines drawn up by the National Children's Bureau and is still being piloted at the time of writing. One of the pilot schemes is described below.

Bristol Wings Mentoring Scheme

This was a mentoring scheme working with young people being discharged from being 'looked after' either through foster or residential care. The project was largely funded with money obtained by The Prince's Trust from Camelot (The National Lottery). The Prince's Trust commissioned the National Children's Bureau (NCB) to develop the scheme. After developing a manual of guidance and minimum standards, NCB then sought the cooperation of a number of social service departments (five) to pilot the scheme. Bristol Wings (a name chosen by young care leavers consulting with Bristol Social Services) was one of the pilots. The social service department seconded staff to run the scheme. Bristol Wings started to recruit and train mentors in June 1998. The first 23 mentoring relationships started in March 1999. At the time the project was visited they were preparing to recruit a third cohort of mentors, although they had learnt from previous experience that it was easier to work with smaller groups of around eight at a time.

The NCB-designed guidance on minimum standards gave detailed, practical advice to the partners on recruitment, selection, training, matching, supervision, monitoring and evaluation. All mentors were adult volunteers, with Bristol's first sweep pilot including mentors aged between 22 and 58. Most were in their mid to late 30s. The majority of their recruits were white (only two so far are from minority ethnic communities) and female (only two male mentors recruited so far). Mentors were asked to sign 'contracts' both with Bristol Wings and with the care leaver. This makes clear that they are expected to continue a mentoring relationship for either six or twelve months. Young people being 'looked after' have often experienced broken and failed relationships with adults. However, it was accepted that this scheme cannot seek to remedy this. Rather, the mentoring relationship sought to be issue- and problem-focused; it aimed to give young people one-to-one support from a competent and safe adult during a particularly difficult time in their lives. The expectation was that there should be a meeting at least once a week, with some mentors dealing with intensely problematic cases arranging as many as three meetings a week.

All mentors are subjected to a rigorous selection process, are police-checked, provide two references and are interviewed by the coordinator. They were asked to participate in groupwork and required to engage in searching self-assessment as part of their training. A six hours selection process was recommended, together with a further 30 hours of training. In Bristol, of the 49 information packs sent out to applicants, 42 completed applications were returned and 25 were selected for training. Two subsequently dropped out. The emphasis of the training was upon a proper understanding of the scheme, issues concerning 'adolescence' and the particular problems of young people 'looked after'. Training required reflection on the skills, competences and interests the mentors themselves bring to the scheme, and the mentoring relationship itself, as well as discussion about the 'policing of boundaries'. This latter issue was to be strictly followed. Mentors were not expected to be surrogate, unpaid, social workers or to offer advice and guidance on issues beyond their competence. They were encouraged to ask for professional advice from the leaving care team rather than give it spontaneously. Where particular problems can be anticipated, mentors were given more specialised training in the issues with which they might have to deal. Mentors and mentees were given clear guidance about what was, and was not, within the boundaries of 'confidential disclosure', and what was an appropriate topic for discussion and guidance. Issues concerning illegal behaviours, child protection and 'disclosure about others' were also subject to considered and careful supervision and monitoring by project staff.

Given the (relatively) short time span allocated to the mentoring relationship, much of the work was concerned with problem identification and 'action planning'. The young people in the scheme volunteer to take part and identify the issues they wish to address, although it was recognised that 'presenting problems' may well widen into a much wider agenda. The monitoring of the relationship also required mentors and mentees to self report on what was talked about and what actions had been decided upon. In this sense the relationship was 'task focused' rather than 'open ended' or 'holistic'.

NCB guidance was that the schemes should have a multi-agency advisory board. Bristol Wings had a board made up of Bristol Cyrenians (who have run a mentoring scheme for young homeless people), the youth justice team manager, the youth education service (which offers free literacy schemes) and NCH Solutions (job incentives for ex-care leavers), and Sandwell College. National organisations, such as The Prince's Trust and the NCB, involved in setting up the project, were also involved on the advisory board. The group helped to advise, give information and support the coordinator.

A number of projects combined a responsibility for care leavers with provision for others in similar circumstances, as was the case in the NCH project described earlier. Combining services for care leavers and the young homeless was fairly common although the pattern of support was different, as the examples below illustrate. The two projects differ significantly in that the first directly provides services for young people. The second defines itself as mainly concerned with supporting the volunteers.

Centrepoint
The Glaxo-Ealing Hostel
This hostel was developed in partnership with the local social services department. The building offered accommodation for care leavers and homeless young people for up to 18 months and was acquired by Centrepoint in 1995. It was previously a children's home and was disused for three years before being bought by Centrepoint. Some of the potential residents had been in the home previously and were reported to be not keen to return there as young adults. The building had 12 single rooms and two and three bedroomed shared flats for a further six young people. Centrepoint had a ten year service contract with the social service department for 12 placements, for which it gets a block grant, even though, at the time of the visit, the full quota had never been used. Following an adverse report by the Social Services Inspectorate, marked improvements in services and liaison with the SSD were reported, including the setting up of a specialist leaving care

team. The SSD also had one other leaving care project, which offered more by way of self-contained flats. Many of the care leavers joining this scheme were leaving residential, rather than foster, care. In addition to contact with the leaving care team, Centrepoint also attached each care leaver to an individual key worker. As well as the placements from the local SSD, some beds were filled by placements from other authorities.

Residents were a mixture of care leavers and the young single homeless. Care leavers were predominantly 16-year-olds, evenly mixed between male and female, with a maximum of 40 per cent white British and, at times, 90 per cent from a mix of minority ethnic groups. Placements also included a significant number of refugees, some of whom had English very much as a second language. Some had also suffered severe traumas before becoming refugees, having first seen their parents tortured or killed. Single homeless people were referred to the project from a range of agencies but, because of its location in outer London, predominantly not from Centrepoint itself. Often the homeless were in the same age group as care leavers and had left home within the last month because of problems within the family. The majority of residents had a history of educational disaffection, and had had little contact with school in the final year of compulsory schooling. Many had no qualifications and had difficulties in reading and writing. Occasionally there was a resident who was educationally successful, including one current resident who planned to go to university to study medicine the following year. Some students had financial support from the Buttle or Prince's Trusts. Many other residents, however, were not in education, training or employment despite the best efforts of staff.

Because of the age and, often troubled, background of the group, the project did have to tolerate some 'childish' behaviour, with workers trying to help them to adjust and take small steps towards taking on adult responsibilities and independence. Work done with young people included some basic independent living skills, such as cooking, personal hygiene, living with others and negotiating with adults and agencies. Within the group, it was reported that there were sometimes understandable tensions. A lot of time was spent talking with young people, sometimes about how their behaviour affected others in the home. Young people could stay in the hostel for between one and a half and two years. Occasionally a young person may be asked to leave, although this was usually because of violence and threatening behaviour. Young women who were pregnant were also subject to a 28-day notice and moved to other accommodation. Sometimes this was bed and breakfast accommodation for six weeks before being accommodated by the borough Homeless Unit. Links had been established with other support services including youth counselling and the Careers Service.

The project had five project workers and one housing worker and night cover through one worker (on a rota) who would 'sleep over'. Project workers had a mixture of training including both social work, residential care and youth work.

Staff too came from a mix of different ethnic backgrounds.

The hostel had a communal lounge, a kitchen and laundry facilities. However, at the time of the visit, conditions seemed cramped and run down, with communal rooms full of stacks of broken furniture donated by hotels. Many facilities seemed in need of urgent repair. The building was said to be unsuitable, not homely, and to be unwelcoming, with narrow corridors. The project planned to re-develop the property, however, to focus more on smaller units. For many young people, communal cooking and living had not been a success. The project also planned to recruit a vocational worker to deal with employment and training.

The hostel was located right on the far edge of the borough and travel to the Careers Service and local benefits agency took an hour and a half, by two buses.

One Barnardo's project visited was concentrating on providing services through volunteers rather than dealing directly with young people. This was intended to supplement the more direct work with those leaving care that was provided through the social services leaving care team.

Barnardo's: Leeds Accommodation Project

This project started in April 1996 and grew out of a leaving care project. In 1996 the project changed to become one that offered resources to the main social service-led leaving care team. The main service users were young people aged 16 to 21 but the work of the project was mainly with volunteers and resource providers. This concentration of service provision through volunteers, rather than direct work with young people, was what makes this project distinct. The main 'users' were described as being the local authority and the volunteers. Trained volunteers were used to deliver three different, but related, strands of provision:

- a befriending scheme for care leavers;
- a supported lodgings scheme for care leavers (but including some under the age 16); and
- Nightstop – emergency accommodation of 1 to 7 nights for homeless young people.

When the project recruits volunteers to work on any of the streams of activity, everyone was trained together. Training involved one full day of compulsory training and another day on child protection issues. There was also training on mental health issues, drug and alcohol misuse, sexuality and HIV/AIDS, although not all volunteers attend these sessions. Volunteers could, and did, switch between different forms of volunteering. Recruitment and training took up to three months because of police checks, health checks and training dates. At the time of the visit, the project was examining whether befriender volunteers could be 'fast-tracked' and approved by project staff rather than by the panel of adjudicators which is usually involved.

Befrienders

This was offered to care leavers when they were being prepared for leaving care after their 16th birthday (numbering around 190 in Leeds at the time of the visit). By no means all choose to have a befriender. Volunteers were recruited from a wide range of backgrounds, and in the past had been predominantly women, and either older women with children of their own, young students or volunteers who became befrienders after being involved in other forms of volunteering (such as offering supported lodging). In the early years of the project, attempts were made to recruit volunteers from minority ethnic groups by using a worker from another Barnardo's project with a regional brief. However, although some minority ethnic volunteers had been recruited, minority ethnic care leavers had never been offered by social services for the befriender service, despite attempts by the project to encourage this. The minority ethnic volunteers they had recruited were never used. The local authority did not encourage much contact between the project and the young person. However, project staff did visit the young person, and filled out a form detailing the kinds of things that might be important for them in being attached to a befriender. This was kept on file and used by the volunteer coordinator in matching the young person to the volunteer. Every volunteer also had a link worker and the scheme runs a 24 hour pager service.

The matching of the volunteer and the care leaver was done by the project team, which included the person who had seen the young person and someone who, through the training process, knew the strength of the volunteer. The two were introduced and afterwards both had an opportunity to raise any issues of concern. Befrienders signed an agreement and the relationship with the care leaver was reviewed by the project after six or twelve months. Befrienders were asked to notify the project if meetings had ceased, and were expected to keep notes of all contact with the young person. All befrienders were given a resource pack jointly developed with social services to help identify topics in which they might be able to help and some did work through this with young people. These topics included the skills that a young person may or may not have. They also covered issues concerning crime, illegal activities and what to do if these were made known to the befriender. Much of the contact, however, was informal, such as over a meal, for which the volunteer could receive expenses. Young people were given their befriender's telephone number but not their address and befrienders were advised not to take the young person to their own home.

Supported lodgings

This involved offering accommodation to young people leaving care with a volunteer householder. The householder involved usually had a spare room in their house. It was described as differing from fostering in that the young person would have their own key and, whilst they would be expected to be semi-independent and help with cooking and cleaning, they were expected to be more independent than would be expected in foster care. The provider also sometimes worked with the young person on topics included in the support pack. The scheme was intended as part of the preparation for independent living although, in effect, it was accepted to be a form of teenage fostering. Funding, however, was considerably less than that offered to foster parents, with some funds from housing benefit and the rest from social services. Referral was made to this scheme only through social services. The volunteers were all visited in their own homes by both social services and Barnardo's as well as taking part in the training programme. At the time of the visit, the young people referred to the scheme had been two-thirds male and exclusively white. All the young people involved had a 'link worker' from the leaving care team in social services. Young people stayed in this accommodation for anything from a few weeks to over a year. Afterwards, the young person was expected to move to their own, unsupported tenancy, other lodgings or into hostel accommodation. It was reported that some found difficulty in managing any of these accommodation options and moved back through supported accommodation more than once.

Nightstop

This had been running in Leeds for over ten years. It was initially set up by a religious organisation in Leeds that wanted to make a positive response to a number of reports on youth homelessness. Barnardo's became involved in assessing volunteers and this scheme was amalgamated into the other two strands in 1996. This service offered from between one and four nights accommodation with volunteers. The upper limit was the result of negotiations with housing benefit officials. Referral was from any organisation within the city and the project was a member of the Forum on Youth Homelessness. This kept it in touch with both sender organisations and other providers. Nightstop did not expect the young person to stay in the accommodation during the day. The city Housing Department was expected to have assessed the young person as being suitable before referral to the scheme. Barnardo's staff had only paperwork, or a telephone call, on which to make their own judgments about whether the young person was suitable to stay in a stranger's house. There were around 270 referrals and 130 placements a year. The prime responsibility of Barnardo's staff was for assessing and training the volunteers. Although it was known that some of those who are being referred had drug or alcohol misuse problems, they were all told firmly that they must not turn up for accommodation 'out of it', and most had respected this. Some referrals were rejected when they were known to be unreliable or untrustworthy. Only one serious incident involving the theft of a computer had occurred in the last three years.

As well as the three main strands of provision, the project also ran a young people's support group which met fortnightly. It also produced a quarterly newsletter for young people who used the service. Volunteers also received a monthly newsletter.

Funding for the project includes money from the Department of Health, under the opportunities for volunteering fund, although this is ring fenced for the Befriending part of the project. Other work was contracted from the local authority. The project provided quarterly reports for each of its funders, each to their individual specification.

In terms of the range of services it offered, this project had some similarities to both Bristol Wings and the NCH project in King's Lynn. Its use of volunteers, particularly in the befriending scheme is a form of mentoring by another name. However, there are marked differences in the length of time devoted to training volunteers. Under the NCB guidance on minimum standards, selection and training takes a minimum of 36 hours, whereas compulsory training in Leeds was reported as taking only two days, at the time of the visit. One concern about mentoring is that, especially if insufficient care is given to the training and monitoring of volunteers, it is a form of unpaid amateur social work (Jeffs, 1999; Philip, 2000). Some critics have gone so far as to describe it as 'a form of blind dating masquerading as social policy' (Freedman, 1995). In both the Bristol and Leeds schemes reviewed here, the matching of mentee and mentor was done by professionals. Both were intended to offer specific kinds of support and to be issue- and task-focused and as such were what the mentoring literature calls a form of 'secondary relationship' only (Freedman, 1993). Both schemes offered guidance on the 'policing of boundaries', record keeping on topics discussed and actions recommended, although it was impossible from the visits undertaken to assess how carefully this was being undertaken or with what degree of vigilance from project staff. It is also unclear how mentoring fits into other aspects of aftercare support from leaving care schemes, or how issues of confidentiality are dealt with. Mentoring is sometimes argued to be successful mainly because it can involve the building of relationships of trust (Philip, 2000). Yet there is clearly some conflict for mentors between the desire to build and maintain such relationships with vulnerable young people and the need to use professional advice and support in dealing with difficult issues. The relationship between mentoring support and the Personal Adviser service proposed in the Care Leavers Bill also remains a matter for concern.

The NCH, Centrepoint and Barnardo's projects so far described were also working with a combination of young people leaving care and others who were homeless and in the same 16 to 18-year-old age group. We also described in chapter four how a number of, predominantly homelessness, projects also attempted to cater for the continuing needs of care leavers. Yet many of these were reluctant to work with 16 and 17-year-olds, partly because of difficulties that occurred in their access to benefits and partly because they were considered to be too immature for the levels of support they felt able to offer. The three projects described in this chapter were more specifically targeted at this younger age group. Yet only the NCH and Centrepoint project did so in a way that could be claimed to be 'holistic'. The Centrepoint project reported less success in linking accommodation needs to education and training support, although it was working (probably) with a more disadvantaged group and from a less suitable base. Having on-site education provision and continuity of support across the age range offered distinct advantages to the NCH project. However, the Centrepoint project was the only care leaving and homelessness project working with significant numbers of young people from minority ethnic groups. The absence of such young people from the Leeds accommodation project was surprising, and despite all their efforts to recruit minority ethnic volunteers.

The NCH project also included provision and support for young parents. A second project which was visited also worked with young parents and had done so for some time.

Barnardo's

Cardiff: Marlborough Road Project

This is a long established project which was initially established in the 1970s as a leaving care project to provide 'hostel accommodation for about 20 male and female 16-year-old care leavers'. It then changed to be community accommodation (rather than a hostel) managing flats and houses owned by housing associations. There was a growing recognition of the increasing number of young mothers within this population and a range of different needs of this group which were not being catered for. The relatively small TAF Housing Association agreed to build seven flats which were incorporated into the project in December 1992 and initially earmarked for single parents aged 16 to 21, many of whom (but not all) were care leavers. Since January 1993 the project had involved both a single persons' supported accommodation project and a single young parents' project, although the senior social work practitioner had a caseload of only up to a maximum of six young mothers, their children and their partner. Initially this involved a partnership between Cardiff Social Services and Barnardo's. The recognition of the need to work with fathers and/or partners had developed relatively recently and such work with young fathers was recognised to be rare. Two of the six were now from outside of the Cardiff SSD areas (one from Bristol and the other from the valleys).

Of the current six families being worked with, three of the mothers were mixed race and one Black-Asian. Four of the six were care leavers. The social work team was also a mix of black and white and male and female workers. The support provided was via a key worker system in which the young mother would initially receive a visit once a day. With the worker, she drew up an action plan of what needed to be done to achieve greater independence. Some elements were issues common to all, such as fire and safety, benefits, or care for children. An attempt was made to address the needs of their clients as young women as well as their needs as young mothers. Thus attention was given to encouraging personal growth and maturity in the woman as well as to issues of good parenting. There was an emphasis on re-enforcement of worth and positive attributes, successes and good behaviour. Although the project also wanted to address the needs of the

---

fathers/partners/boyfriends this was found to be the most difficult issue to successfully address since many of the men regarded the project as primarily about the mother and child.

One of the problems of the scheme is the availability of suitable 'move-on' accommodation, much of which is now located on the fringes of the city, something which would cut the mothers off from forms of social support and exacerbate their social isolation.

Other attempts to provide for young parents were reviewed in the last chapter, as was Government policy both to reduce teenage pregnancy and better support teenagers who did become parents. There the problem was recognised to be multi-faceted, requiring multi-agency intervention and long-term programmes of support. Yet often individual projects offered only short-term support and were based on short-term funding.

Conclusions

This chapter has reviewed research, policy and intervention projects concerned with young people 'looked after' in care and leaving care. This and other chapters have indicated that on many criteria this group are amongst the most vulnerable of young people both in terms of the disadvantages they have experienced before being taken into care and on a number of outcome measures when they leave. Yet they are often asked to live independently at a much younger age than other groups, and in circumstances which make later homelessness and unemployment seem an almost inevitable consequence. Rather than compensating for early disadvantage, for many young people being 'looked after' seems to exacerbate this sometimes through systematic abuse and denial of their rights. Until recently, the care system seemed unable to make a proper, holistic assessment of their needs, or provide adequate 'joined-up' systems of support.

A number of the major problems young people face have been identified for some time, notably in reviews which led to the 1989 Children Act, the Regulations and Guidance which followed this, and in the 1991 and 1997 Utting Reports. There was much of value in the principles laid down in the Children Act and much to applaud in the ten volumes of Regulations and Guidance. But for the most part it was a case of 'fine words butter no parsnips' and when the implementation of the Act was reported, many local authorities were shown not to be in compliance (Department of Health 1993, 1994).

Much of the research evidence reviewed in this chapter indicates that we now have a fuller knowledge of what goes wrong and a clearer picture of the circumstances which promote better outcomes. This is also substantially in line with a more holistic approach to understanding and better managing youth transitions as outlined in chapter one. So, for instance, whilst it is clear that more can and should be done for young people during the main youth transitions, to be most effective, this must be accompanied by better assessment and response to needs earlier in the life course. Jackson and Thomas' discussion of a more holistic understanding of the continuities and stability of care helps underline this (Jackson and Thomas, 1998). Furthermore, there is now a clearer recognition of the importance of continued support throughout the transition processes rather than anticipating that, once the age of 16 is reached and a young person has left both school and care, further assistance and guidance is not either required or necessary.

Other elements of the holistic approach are also critical for care leavers, not least of which is the importance of engaging them as key participants in transition planning. The proposals contained within the Care Leavers Bill and the amendment of the Children Act should assist in this and are to be welcomed. So too should the recognition that planning and support should involve both multi-agency partnership in provision and a named person responsible for making sure that assistance, provision and support is delivered. However, in the past, similar recommendations, for instance in the transition planning for those with special needs, have not proved to be either as empowering or effective as might have been wished. Assessment, planning and provision has been shown to be short-term, lacking in comprehensive coverage and rigour, and dominated by professionals – often treating young people as objects of concern rather than equal partners (Baldwin, 1998; Mitchell, 1998; Tisdale, 1997).

Many of the policy changes announced since 1997 are to be welcomed and especially the decision to extend the period in which local authorities have a duty to look after vulnerable young people. The Government has shown a laudable recognition that a failure to invest in the welfare of young people at critical stages brings much greater long-term costs than supporting them when important needs first arise. Whether the resources it will commit to promoting the long-term welfare of care leavers will be sufficient only time will tell. But it is hard to fault the current Government in turning the spotlight on young people 'looked after', in accepting that much is wrong and that much more needs to be done. Whether this frank assessment will result in reform and resources that are adequate to such a huge task remains one of the crucial questions. The other is the ability of local authorities to deliver joined-up solutions to the problems faced by care leavers. This chapter has illustrated that some successful initiatives have been piloted by the voluntary sector, often despite the legislative and administrative framework of national and local government, rather than because of it. It is hoped that local authorities might learn from these examples.

Chapter six

Health, illness and health promotion

This chapter reviews research, policy and practice about health and illness and the ways in which this impacts upon youth transitions. With notable exceptions, issues concerning health are not well covered in the mainstream literature on youth and little attempt is made to examine the impact of health-related issues on the main youth transitions (see Furlong and Cartmel, 1997; Coleman and Hendry, 1999). The general literature on health and adolescence similarly fails to examine the wider implications for later phases of the life course, with the exception, perhaps, of young people with disabilities (Hirst and Baldwin, 1994). Hirst and Baldwin found that many young people who were disabled did have positive experiences of their transitions to adulthood. They enjoyed age-appropriate social activities, gained independence, had a good image of themselves and some sense of personal control of their lives. Not a few entered paid work. However, those who had attended segregated schools were at greatest risk of not finding constructive activities and had the lowest feelings of self esteem and control over their lives (For a fuller discussion of these issues see Coles, 1995 and Mitchell, 1998. Issues concerning special educational needs and segregated schooling were discussed in chapter three). Clearly, when young people experience chronic illness, this can have a marked impact upon their general wellbeing, upon their education and upon other factors affecting youth transitions. Similarly, when other family members suffer chronic illness, young people may be called upon to play a significant caring role within the family and this can have a comparable effect.

This chapter is organised in four main sections. The first will examine the distinctive health problems young people have. It should be noted that issues surrounding teenage conceptions and pregnancy were discussed in chapter four, even though sexual behaviour, sexual health, conception and pregnancy are often important elements of health policy and practice directed at young people. Mental health is covered in the second section. This includes a resumé of research on suicide and self-harming, even though it is highly contentious whether this should be regarded simply as a mental health issue. The third section will examine some of the main health risking behaviours of young people, including smoking, drug taking and alcohol misuse. Finally, we will examine circumstances in which young people take on the role of being a 'carer' and how their welfare is affected. It is shown that young people's careers and transitions are not just influenced by their own ill health but by those of other family members for whom they perform caring duties and responsibilities.

The distinctive health needs of children and young people

Many authors regard 'youth' and young adulthood as associated with peaks of general health and fitness, although it is now generally accepted that a minority do suffer distinctive patterns of risks. Some have argued that, in general, marked inequalities of health that occur in childhood seem to disappear during adolescence only to re-appear in adulthood (West, 1997). Yet, based upon data drawn from a large scale longitudinal study in the West of Scotland, the same author has argued that 'teenagers who become unemployed can, at an earlier stage in life, be distinguished from those with more favourable prospects (such as work or continuing education) in terms of health, lifestyle, significant events in their lives, and "social integration". Whilst still at school, they are more likely to have a longstanding illness, poorer mental health, to smoke, drink, try drugs, experience more undesirable life events and be more peer-orientated and disaffected.' (Sweeting and West, 2000) The authors speculate that the prospect of having no job or only poorly paid work, or long periods of family dependency, may lead to poor mental health and the adoption of a more risky life style. Other researchers working with large longitudinal surveys have also pointed to the accumulation of risk within childhood and the negative impact this has on youth transitions (Schoon, 2000).

There is a widespread acceptance that some health needs of children and young people are different from those of adults, although a recent review for the Child Poverty Action Group (CPAG) claimed that health researchers and statisticians have paid relatively little attention to young people. They are often assumed to be healthy and resilient. The CPAG review did draw attention to some distinctive health problems and argued that most of these were associated with poverty. These included 'accidents, respiratory problems, depression, schizophrenia, suicide, eating disorders, sexually transmitted diseases, teenage pregnancy, and tobacco, alcohol and drug abuse' (Dennehy et al., 1997). The 1997 Health Committee report also concluded that children and young people are more vulnerable to certain types of injury and accident, less able to choose and control their environment and, for children especially, more dependent upon adults for care, protection and advocacy (Health Committee, 1997).

Death amongst children and young people under the age of 20 is most likely to occur because of accidents (just under 30 per cent of all deaths), with road traffic accidents being far and away the most common cause of death in young people (Quilgars, 2000b). Accident rates increase as children get older, are higher for boys than girls in all ranges, and are more likely to occur outside the home in older children and young people. There is also a strong correlation between death by accident and social class, with the children of unskilled manual workers five times more likely to suffer a fatal accident than children of professional and managerial workers. This class differential increased during the 1980s. The CPAG review also reported that children whose parents were in manual occupations (social class five) are more than four times more likely to die as pedestrians than children whose parents were in professional or managerial jobs (class one). Children whose parents are classified as 'unoccupied' (largely economically inactive single mothers) have the worst mortality rate of all social groups, with 10 to 15-year-olds being four times more likely to die at that age than those in classes one and two. Social and economic disadvantage can be fatal; and children and young people are not exempt.

Children and young people are prone to different serious illnesses from adults. Cancers (nearly 15 per cent of all deaths) largely take different forms to those contracted by adults. These have not changed in recent decades although survival rates have improved markedly. Mortality rates are not always the best indicators of patterns of ill health in children and young people. Acute illness affects around one in ten children and young people at any one time. About the same proportion consult their GPs in any two week period, although consultancy rates are twice as high for children under the age of 5. The most common reason for visiting a doctor is because of diseases of the respiratory system (over a quarter of all consultations) including bronchitis and asthma. Especially for young people in their late teens, this is rarely a life threatening condition (only 4 per cent of all deaths) (Health Committee, 1997). It can, however, be seriously debilitating. Consultations about respiratory complaints are twice as common among children and young people as among adults and are a common cause for admission to hospital, especially amongst younger children. Diagnosis of asthma by doctors was reported amongst 23 per cent of males aged 13 to 15 and 18 per cent of females in the same age group (NSO, 2000b). Reports of 'wheezing' were of a similar proportion and thought to be related to passive smoking. Meningitis and septicaemia are also serious and life-threatening diseases that are prevalent in children and young people. Meningitis results in death in one in ten cases and is known to have been increasing in recent years, with 275 notified cases amongst 16 to 19-year-olds in 1999 (NSO, 2000b). It is most common in young children, with 16 to 19-year-olds being the next most vulnerable group, especially students in their first few weeks of college and university. Because of this, starting in the autumn of 1999, students were offered a special vaccine that offers long lasting protection. Injury is the second most common reason for hospital admission amongst all under the age of 20. For those aged 15 to 19 pregnancy is the most common cause, accounting for over 30 per cent of all admissions, far higher than accidents (17 per cent) or respiratory complaints (9 per cent). Consulting a doctor about respiratory diseases and infections is more likely in classes four and five than in classes one and two. CPAG claims that respiratory diseases are more prevalent amongst those living in inner cities and among young people from minority ethnic groups (Dennehy et al., 1997). Often this was associated with living in houses which were damp or mouldy. Other studies report on the impact of homelessness on both children's and young people's health and the use of medical services (Quilgars, 1999d).

Much of the evidence reviewed above points to the fact that ill health is socially patterned, though arguably less so during teenage years (West, 1997). What is less clear is how it impacts upon youth transitions and later stages in the life course. Clearly, chronic illness can have an adverse effect upon schooling and education. The prevalence of long standing illness or disability has also been increasing in recent years, rising from 12 per cent of 13 to 24-year-olds in 1975 to 20 per cent in 1998–99, covering slightly more young women than men. It should be remembered, however, that West and Macintyre did not find a correlation between morbidity and social class amongst 15-year-olds in western Scotland (Macintyre and West, 1992). In a later report, Sweeting and West argue that cultural factors related to family functioning do help explain many of the social inequalities of ill health amongst the young. In their West of Scotland Study, they found that the poor quality of relationships between parents and young people were associated with lower self esteem, poorer psychological well-being and, amongst young women, more physical symptoms of ill health (Sweeting and West, 1995). This suggests a much more complicated relationship between social background and factors associated with ill health and mental illness.

Health policy and health intervention projects

The Government has several policies directed at improving the health of young people as published in *The Health of the Nation* and the 1999 White Paper *Saving Lives: Our Healthier Nation* (DOH, 1999d). These include a target for reducing the death rates amongst children under the age of 15 by a third, from 6.7 per 100,000 in 1990 to 4.5 in 2005. Government has also set a target to reduce the death rate of those aged 15 to 25 by a quarter over the same period to no more than 17.4 per 100,000. A major means of achieving this is to reduce serious road traffic accidents and to promote safer routes to, and from, schools. Priority is being given to young and vulnerable road users on foot or bicycle. The 1997 House of Commons Health Committee also paid considerable attention to the incidence of respiratory diseases, especially the growth of asthma. But whilst there was much speculation as to the causes for such rises (from double glazed windows and fitted carpets in the home to pet parasites), little was suggested which would reverse the trend apart from trying to ensure reductions in passive smoking.

Health services for all age groups are often conceived as mainly concerned with dealing with 'pathological process'. This suggests that, through treatment by drug, operation or inoculation programme, clear solutions can be obtained to discrete and circumscribed medical conditions. Our outline of the main correlates of ill health in young people, however, suggests a more complex series of problems requiring equally complex solutions. If, as has been shown, the causes lie in poverty, poor housing and family circumstances, then it is not simply a matter of providing more doctors, hospital beds, or better inoculation campaigns. To be sure, part of any improvement in the health of young people may involve encouraging better take-up of what is already available. But what are also needed are new and different forms of outreach work with young people to promote healthy activities and reduce behaviours which cause ill health. Care should be taken to target places where young people are likely to be reached, and through personnel who are likely to be influential. The Department of Health and the DfEE jointly launched *The Healthy Schools Initiative* in May 1998. In 1999–2000 this had an annual budget of £2 million to raise awareness of how schools can help in improving health. The Health Education Authority is also helping to manage and develop a number of projects, producing a quarterly Healthy Schools newsletter *Targets* available on the internet, and organising regular conferences and events. One conference in March 2000, for instance, focused on young men's health. The Health Development Agency has also developed a Young People and Health Network to encourage the exchange of ideas and examples of good practice amongst a wide range of professionals.

In some parts of the country health workers have experimented with teenage clinics. Many have stressed the importance of these being easily accessible by public transport, of having specially appointed staff and a welcoming and non-judgmental atmosphere (Dennehy *et al.*, 1997). Many of the services offered were concerned with sexual health and drug abuse with some of the literature provided regarded by young people as ranging from 'brilliant' to 'absolute rubbish'. Mental health issues have also been addressed in similar ways although often this was done through self-help support groups (see below).

Health Action Zones

In recent years Health Action Zones (HAZ) are probably the most interesting means through which Government is promoting a more 'joined up' approach to identifying and meeting the health needs of children and young people. At the time of writing there are 26 of these in England and Northern Ireland. They have been set up to improve health and reduce health inequality and involve partnerships between different agencies including health trusts, local authorities and other agencies. One HAZ that has specifically committed itself to addressing the needs of children and young people is Lambeth, Southwark and Lewisham Health Action Zone.

Lambeth, Southwark and Lewisham Health Action Zone

This HAZ has a seven year programme which started in 1998–99 with a budget of £5.4 million. These London inner city boroughs have a combined population of around three quarters of a million people, a quarter of whom are from black and minority ethnic communities. From the outset the Zone has had a 'mission' of 'Children First' to improve services for children and young people on the grounds that patterns of social exclusion and inequalities of health will be carried through into later stages in the life course.

Within the services offered by the HAZ are nine main programmes of work that include:

- working with excluded young people;
- improving opportunities for disabled children and youth people with special needs;
- reducing teenage pregnancy and improving sexual health; and
- reducing youth crime; reducing substance misuse.

Across the nine themes there are also four main work-streams:

- improving information, sharing information between agencies;
- community development and listening to young people;
- evaluation and learning, including developing learning networks to share and roll out lessons and benefits; and

---

- communications and participation.

Over a hundred different projects are working within the zone at any one time. Those included below have been chosen to reflect a range of innovatory approaches in delivering health care, especially to young people.

Bronchial Boogie

This service was still in the planning stage when the HAZ was visited. Its aim was to improve the health of young asthmatics between the ages of 8 and 18. As is suggested by its title, it aims to use singing classes as a means of improving the breathing techniques of young people with asthma. However, although this is likely to be a popular means of offering support, the project also plans to reach parents and teachers to offer education and advice about the use of inhalers and to work with parents on issues surrounding damp-management in the home.

Locally based child mental health services

This project aims to provide a 'whole system' approach to Child Mental Health Provision in partnership with local agencies within the community including home-based parent counselling services and services based in general practice, health centres, schools and voluntary agencies. The aim is that these should be more user-friendly, accessible and reduce the stigma in receiving mental health services. It also plans to train, supervise and support community, primary care, education and social care professionals in core child mental health, parent counselling and communication skills.

The supply of emergency contraception by accredited community pharmacists

This project seeks to make available emergency contraception through community pharmacists, who are trained and accredited to run the service. Pharmacists display a board or poster in their shop window to indicate that they can supply emergency contraception (popularly, though wrongly, often referred to as the 'morning after pill'). Although this project seeks to address the needs of all women, it has particular relevance to young women. Indeed of those who have made use of it so far, nearly a half (46 per cent) have been under the age of 25 and 13 per cent under the age of 20. Under a strict protocol drawn up between the HAZ, the Health Authority and participating pharmacists, young women under the age of 16 may access the service as long as the pharmacist meets the legal rules about the 'competence' of the young woman in understanding the full implications of their actions. There are, of course, many other conditions laid down in the protocol and guidance and training to ensure that the service given is the same as would be offered by a health centre or family planning clinic. Clients are always advised to talk to their GP or a specialist clinic regardless of whether the contraceptive is

> supplied. Amongst the factors that make this service special are its high street presence and the hours when it is available.
>
> Through these and other projects, the Health Action Zone is experimenting with how health services can be delivered in more user-friendly ways.

Mental health and illness

The extent of mental illness amongst young people is disputed. A survey conducted by the Office of National Statistics, in partnership with the Institute of Psychiatry and the Maudsley Hospital, claimed that around 10 per cent of children and young people between the age of 5 and 15 had a mental disorder (Meltzer *et al.*, 2000). This survey was based on a large sample of children (10,438), families and teachers, with a sampling frame based on child benefit records. The survey involved lay interviewers administering a computerised structured interview after which the detailed answers were analysed by three child psychiatrists. The results indicated that 5 per cent of children had conduct disorders, 4 per cent had emotional disorders and 1 per cent had hyperkinetic (hyperactive) disorders. These findings are at odds with a two year inquiry conducted by the Mental Health Foundation and published only a year before.

The Mental Health Foundation (MHF) estimated that, of the 14.9 million children and young people under the age of 20 in the UK, one in five (20 per cent) experienced psychological problems. They quote epidemiological studies which indicate that among those aged 4 to 20 the following problems occur in the following proportions:

- 12 per cent – anxiety disorders
- 10 per cent – disruptive disorders
- 5 per cent – attention deficit disorders
- 6 per cent – enuresis and substance abuse
- 1 per cent – pervasive developmental disorders (such as autism) or psychosis

Commenting on the ONS survey, the MHF stands by its findings and stresses that, despite differing estimates of the size of the problem, both studies point to the fact that mental illness amongst the young is widespread and that much of it goes unrecognised and undiagnosed. Even the ONS survey indicates that only a third of those diagnosed are in contact with specialist services. As elsewhere in the developed world, despite problems involved with definitions and recording, rates of mental illness have been rising since the Second World War (Mental Health Foundation, 1999). Kurtz claims that nearly a half of all children and young people (49 per cent) may meet the criteria for at least one disorder at some stage in their life before the age of 20 (Kurtz, 1996). The case of 16 to 25-year-olds is particularly problematic in that responsibility for servicing their needs falls between child and adult divisions in both health and social services.

A number of studies help identify the 'risks' of mental illness or 'resilience' in avoiding it, even when living in adverse circumstances (Meltzer *et al.*, 2000; Mental Health Foundation,

1999; Rutter and Smith, 1995). Risk and resilience factors are related to characteristics of the child or young person, their family, the communities in which they live and the experiences they have. Boys before the age of puberty are more likely than girls to suffer from autism, hyperactivity and to exhibit conduct disorders. Children with a low IQ or a learning disability, a chronic illness or a 'difficult temperament', are more likely than others to develop a mental illness. Genetic factors are related to some mental illness although this may also be triggered by other factors. Young black men have been found to have more diagnoses for schizophrenia, but this has not been found to be so in the US, raising questions about the possibility of a race bias in the diagnosis (Bhugra, 1997; Smaje, 1995). Risk factors within the family include having a parent: with a mental health problem; who is violent or abusive; has problems with the law; or who has alcohol problems. Volatile or hostile family relationships, physical or sexual abuse, a lack of emotional warmth, or harsh or erratic discipline (including violent punishment) are all associated with depression and conduct disorder and personality disturbance. Parental separation and divorce, or death and loss (including loss of friendship) can also be important. The ONS survey reported that there was a strong association between unemployment and mental illness in young people, with 20 per cent of those in families where the parent(s) had never worked having a mental disorder. Children in families in manual unskilled occupations were three times more likely to have a mental health problem than the children of professional workers. CPAG also reports that poverty, unemployment and other adverse social circumstances, including the psychiatric disorder of parents and physical and emotional neglect, have an adverse impact upon children and young people's mental health. Schizophrenia is five times more likely to be diagnosed within working class families than those of other social classes (Dennehy et al., 1997).

Other significant life events are associated with 'community factors', including the experience of disadvantage and poverty, racial discrimination, a disaster, or homelessness. Attending schools with a high morale, good academic opportunities or positive sports and recreational activities, and ones with effective anti-bullying strategies, promotes resilience. So too does the development of personal characteristics such as good communication skills, an ability to reflect and a positive approach to solving problems. These are also associated with good self esteem and self confidence. Risk factors are cumulative. Where there is known to be one risk factor present, this increases the chance of developing mental illness by only 1 or 2 per cent. However, where there are three factors present this increases the likelihood by 8 per cent and when four or more by 20 per cent (Rutter, 1995).

A number of attempts have been made in recent years to examine the possible link between social class background, child poverty and mental health (Quilgars, 2000e). This review suggested that, on a series of different measures of mental health and illness, very few positive correlations could be discerned between these and parental social class. However, the 1999 survey on the mental health of children and young people aged 5 to 15 indicated that the prevalence of mental disorder was correlated with a number of background factors. A range of factors including class, income, family structure, the qualifications of parents and housing tenure were associated with doubling or trebling the prevalence of mental illness in young people (Meltzer *et al.*, 2000). This was so in the cases of:

- families in social class five compared with social class one (16 per cent compared with 5 per cent);
- families with a gross weekly income of less than £200 or more than £500 (15 per cent compared with 6 per cent);
- living in social housing compared with owner occupation (17 per cent compared with 7 per cent);
- lone parent families compared with two parent families (16 per cent compared with 8 per cent); and
- a parent with no qualifications compared with those having a degree (15 per cent compared with 6 per cent).

A number of studies in the 1990s attempted to link health indicators to the current positions occupied by young people themselves, rather than parental social class. Using data from the West of Scotland study, Glendinning and colleagues did find that young men and women on training schemes, those unemployed and young women at home, were more likely to report psychological stress (Glendinning *et al.*, 1997). West and Sweeting also found poorer health amongst 18-year-olds who were unemployed. Those unemployed were also much more likely to report attempting suicide than those in work or on training schemes, with the odds of attempting suicide increasing by a factor of six (West and Sweeting, 1996).

Research has identified some specific groups of children and young people that are at greatest risk of mental health problems. Broad estimated that of children and young people 'looked after', 17 per cent have a long term mental illness or disorder, 35 per cent have deliberately self harmed since the age of 15 or 16, 60 per cent have contemplated suicide and 40 per cent had made at least one attempt (Broad, 1999) (also see chapter five). Young offenders are also estimated to have high rates of mental illness, with 50 per cent of remanded males and 30 per cent of those sentenced having a diagnosable mental disorder (MacFarlane, 1997). Kurtz estimated in 1992 that a diagnosis of a primary mental disorder could be made for a third of young men between 16 and 18 who had been sentenced before the courts (Kurtz, 1992). The Howard League for Penal Reform has also estimated that young people on remand are three times more likely to attempt suicide than the general population in custody (Grindrod and Black, 1989).

The 1999 survey also reports that the incidence of mental illness is associated with other factors in the welfare of young people and was likely to impact upon their future life chances (Meltzer *et al.*, 2000). These included indicators related to the social functioning of the child, their families, and scholastic achievements and education. Those aged 11 to 15 with a mental disorder were reported to be more likely to drink alcohol more than once a week, smoke cigarettes and regularly use cannabis. They reported that they had a severe lack of friendship with others and were reported by parents to cause difficulties with other family members. Parents were also more likely to report ill health, including mental health problems. The young people concerned were more likely to be frequently sent to their room, and be frequently shouted at and 'grounded'. Nearly half (49 per cent) had officially recognised special educational needs, with 28 per cent having a statement of SEN. Those with emotional disorders, especially, had been absent from school for more than 11 days in the previous term and those with all disorders were four times more likely to have played truant. All this suggests that mental illnesses in young people are important mediating factors in producing low educational achievement, family friction and social isolation.

Self harm and suicide

In the UK as a whole, for young people in the 15 to 24-year-old age group, suicide is the second most common cause of death (after road accidents). There are around 19,000 suicides by 10 to 19-year-olds each year – on average around one every 30 minutes. Within the UK, Scotland has much higher rates of suicide than elsewhere and there, young men are twice as likely to kill themselves than to die in road accidents. Yet, in half the cases of suicides by young people, there was no previous classification of young people as mentally ill. Rates of suicide in young men have increased alarmingly in recent decades, from 10 per 100,000 in the late 1970s to 16 per 100,000 in the late 1980s (a 60 per cent increase). A small decrease has been reported since 1993 (Samaritans, 1998). Approximately a half of those who take their own lives have previously attempted suicide and many have shown signs of low self esteem and social withdrawal and isolation (Samaritans, 1999).

There are also marked gender differences in the methods used to commit, or attempt to commit, suicide. Young men are more likely to resort to hanging or jumping from high places, whereas young women tend to overdose on paracetamol. Many of the latter do this when there is someone else in the house, which raises questions about whether this should be regarded as a suicide attempt or a cry for help (Hill, 1995; Madge, 1996). Research on suicide attempts and self harm suggests that the gender difference consistently reported in the case of suicide is reversed for cases of attempted suicide. Amongst suicide attempts by young women, young Asian women are over-represented, something which raises questions about the cultural context in which this occurs (Coleman, 1996; NHS-HAS, 1994).

Whilst some of the social patterns involved in suicide and suicide attempts are recognised, less is known about the reasons why some young people decide to take their own life, whilst others, in apparently the same circumstances, do not. Amongst professionals dealing with those at risk of suicide, there has been more than a little temptation to pathologise it, either as a form of mental illness and/or to individualise it as something buried inside the person at risk (Hawton and Catalan, 1997). Psychologists have linked adolescent suicide to depression, anxiety and conduct disorders, although, because of poorly integrated services, these may remain undiagnosed or untreated (Kerfoot, 2000). Self harm in childhood and adolescence is also commonly reported to be linked to depression. Psychologists report feelings of hopelessness and impulsiveness, both of which mean that potential suicides are difficult to identify beforehand. (Hawton et al., 1982; Kerfoot, 2000). Those who feel that their situation is hopeless are the least likely to seek help, whilst those who act with little planning and forethought offer little chance to those around them to intervene. This also helps explain why friends and relatives are often shocked and appalled to find they were ignorant of the plight of the young person who has committed suicide (Hill, 1995).

There is also a long tradition in sociology of linking suicide rates to patterns of support in the family, the community and in faith communities, and patterns of risk and isolation induced by socio-economic change (Durkheim, 1952; Giddens, 1971). More recently, in-depth studies have been carried out about the growth of unemployment, particularly youth unemployment, and suicides and parasuicides amongst young men (Platt, 1986). A number of studies have pointed to the other social and psychological consequences of unemployment, including poor health and depression, which make their correlation to steep rises in suicide amongst young men in the 1980s 'understandable' (Pritchard, 1992). Another, socially structured, 'at risk' group is young offenders, particularly once they have been caught, convicted and incarcerated (Lloyd, 1990). In 1996–97 the chief inspector's *Thematic Review of Younger Prisoners* reported a doubling of suicides on the previous year (Macfarlane, 1997). The sociological study of suicides is also plagued by methodological difficulties. The very factors sociologists see as connected to suicide are also those that determine whether the death is recorded as suicide or as something else. Madge and Harvey have recently suggested that the statistics on suicides by children may be vastly underestimating the size of the problem because coroners are reluctant to assign suicide to a death without the clearest of corroborating evidence (Madge and Harvey, 1999).

Research is unable to give clear answers about the causes of suicide amongst children and young people. We know something about the social correlates of suicide and this should make us aware that it is socially patterned and may have social, as well as psychological, causes. Psychologists can tell us about the states of mind which appear to be correlated with young suicides. A third simply express a wish to die. Others want to escape from a stressful situation or to express hostility towards, or gain the attention of, someone around them. Sometimes these studies can help to identify means through which intervention projects can help build up protection from circumstances that make some young people particularly 'at risk'. Some projects, for instance, encourage children to express their emotions. Yet, if the ability to cope with emotions and externalise them is least common among the sociologically most at risk groups – for instance, poorly educated, young men, with poor social skills in prison – then different strategies may be required in such circumstances.

Policies for promoting better mental health

The 1999 Audit Commission report, *Children in Mind,* reported widespread variation in the services available through the Child and Adolescent Health Service, with resources allocated varying by a factor of seven. It called for more consistency of service and better links to the activities of other agencies (Audit Commission, 1999c). The review in this chapter of young people and mental health also suggests that policies and practices need to be targeted in several different ways. Firstly, because mental illness is so widespread amongst the young, there is a need for generic services through which it can be recognised and support given for those in need. Some of this may be achieved through already existing generic health services. However, schools can also be important locations in which mental health can be monitored and fostered and patterns of support delivered. Chapter three reviewed the introduction of Behaviour Support Plans drawn up by LEAs and described a number of school-based projects working with 'troubled children'. Secondly, because some groups are known to be particularly at risk, special support can be targeted through agencies dealing with them. The Mental Health Foundation has recently reviewed a number of projects working specifically with young people on mental health issues through the youth service (MHF, 1999). Thirdly, there are other agencies, often in the voluntary sector, which can offer important and non-stigmatising forms of outreach, advice and support. Some of these projects are also described in the MHF review. Such projects also need to have clear mechanisms of referral and support from specialised professional services.

The MHF stresses the importance of early interventions and especially support for parents both before the birth of a child and during its early years. In that good parent-child relationships are of critical importance to mental health, this is understandable. A strong emphasis can also be found within government policy in supporting early years initiatives in children's services, including the introduction of Children's Service Plans and the Sure Start programme (Utting, 1998a). Research conducted by the MHF suggests that the main supports in children and young people's lives come from family and friends. Anxieties and depressions are, however, often linked to conflict and loss in family and peer relationships and there remains a considerable stigma about individuals or families asking for help with emotional problems. Keeping problems repressed is also known to be one of the reasons why young people, particularly young men, 'act out' forms of aggressive behaviour.

Some institutions that could, and should, act as important agencies of support, such as schools and the youth service, have themselves been either significantly under-resourced or subject to competing pressures. In schools, for instance, the National Curricula, testing and league tables have sometimes emphasised the importance of academic standards at the expense of systems of pastoral support and the promotion of emotional wellbeing. In many areas of the country, the potential role of the youth service is not being used, either because of cuts in a service or because it was low down a list of priorities. The MHF suggests that there is considerable room for improvement in both school and community-based services. The development of Behavioural Support Plans requires LEAs to identify ways in which they work with other agencies such as social services and the child and adolescent mental health services. This may lead to more 'holistic' approaches to child development services. However, in many authorities, the school psychological service is overstretched, with staffing levels far lower than those recommended by Warnock in 1981. As a result, the service is almost solely used to address issues of special educational needs and help in the development of 'statements', with little support given to more generic work and support for schools. The MHF recommends that staffing levels must be improved so that schools can be given more, and a wider range of, support. It also recommends that all schools should have a mental health coordinator to develop whole school policies on mental health. As with measures designed to support pupils at risk of exclusion (see chapter three), they commend the development of 'peer support' systems, such as 'circles of friends' together with the better training for all teachers on the sources of mental health difficulties.

Within the community, the emphasis is upon the need to provide 'young people friendly' services. The research undertaken by the MHF suggested that some general practitioners were too often unsympathetic, and specialist services difficult to access. Better training for doctors on mental health issues and in listening to, and communicating with, young people is still required. Voluntary sector projects, such as 42nd Street in Manchester and The Base in Whitley Bay (see box below) provide other means through which the vulnerable can be reached and given a voice. Often this support takes the form of counselling and befriending. The 42nd Street project in Manchester, however, has also been instrumental in developing education programmes in schools and with youth clubs, including the development of a mental health education pack (MHF, 1999). However, there remains a serious problem in coordinating peer group support and facilitating proper access to professional services. Youth Access Services can often provide confidential and unstigmatising counselling and support but this has to be recognised as being only a very limited service.

Barnardo's:

The 'reach-out' group at The Base, Whitley Bay

The Base was initially set up in 1985 as a drop-in and support centre, largely focused on young unemployed people aged 16 to 25, and on young people coming to the end of their period of youth training. It was set up with the support of the local council and with additional funding from the European Anti-Poverty Programme. The Base provides a menu of activities and practical resources including a café, condoms, free use of telephone, a laundry, a play room and advice and information. One of the guiding principles from the outset has been to 'start from where young people are at'. The approach is 'holistic', based on a voluntary relationship, in a welcoming environment. It also has a strong tradition in responding to youth homelessness but gained a reputation in the town as being a general 'first aid' point offering a range of different forms of support.

Since 1996 it has offered support for young people with mental health problems. Research in 1995 suggested that 30 per cent of their users had significant mental health problems. It also found that there were few services for this group and some were inaccessible. Some services were hospital based and did not offer a proactive service for young people whose lives were sometimes in chaos. Initially there was a 'closed project' for young people who were using mental health services. This lasted for about six months. The group later produced a book of poetry for Mental Health Day. The group was then opened up to others using The Base, by either staff, or other users, suggesting that they might benefit from joining the group. The group is now self-selecting. There is a little stigma attached to membership of the group but members often both joke and are serious about its benefits. One member described it to a new recruit as 'a group for psychopaths' but then added 'you won't get laughed at if you cry in here' and explained more about what they did.

One of the reports includes an example. 'Kate spent most of her life in and out of care. Since then she has been involved in a number of abusive relationships, has a major drug problem and in a six month period had 15 admissions to hospital, onto eight different wards and in four different hospitals for mental health, medical and surgical needs. Attendance at casualty was an almost daily occurrence. Although she has had much contact with mental health and medical professions, Kate and the staff see it as problematic and negative. She is, however, one of the most positive and influential of the Reach-Out Group members.' The group has not solved all her problems. She was still in and out of hospital and self harming. She has lost her baby, but learned to express her emotions herself and is influential in helping others to do the same. Other members were similarly described as having serious problems but didn't get the support they needed from statutory services because they don't engage readily and often 'kick-off' if they feel they are not being helped. Others are described as being 'on the borderline of personality disorders' as well as more traditional mental health problems such as depression.

One of the main aims of the project was that young people should have major control over the process and the product. More formally the project aims:

- to develop effective ways of consulting with young people who are experiencing mental health problems or issues of mental health;
- to ensure that young people's voices are heard and influence the provision of services;
- to empower young people via this process to have confidence to share their views;
- to increase young people's knowledge base and skills in personal coping strategies;
- to gain experience of developing and advocating for services to meet their needs; and
- to ensure that their message will get somewhere (to be decided by the group).

Evaluation of its success is difficult. Young people will say that they enjoy the meetings and value them and continue to attend. Membership of the group may result in a reduction in their visits to casualty. But hard performance indicators are difficult to attain. The main achievement of the group is providing a supportive environment and sometimes helping a young person get through a difficult period of their lives. Sometimes it might prevent them being hospitalised or provide a link to the community.

This, and four other projects, were evaluated by Sophie Laws of the Mental Health Foundation.

The MHF report *Bright Futures* contains a number of other cameos of interesting projects working with young people with mental health problems. It also summarises what young people want from a modernised mental health service. This includes:

- somewhere for young people to go during the day. This might include a drop-in centre, talking treatments, art or drama therapy, or other therapies instead of drugs and more drugs;

- a 24 hour mental health help line with someone experienced and qualified to help;
- support groups in all towns and cities; and
- mental health advocates for young people.

The overall conclusion of the MHF inquiry was that government should legislate to establish a statutory duty for local authorities (including education and social services) and health authorities to establish a National Framework for children and young people's mental health, similar to that developed for adult services Within this, the report argues that there should be a strategy on the mental health needs of young people. This would address a number of different issues including:

- the gap between children's and adults' services;
- the funding and location of preventive work ensuring that innovative models gain access to long-term funding;
- ways and settings which young people find acceptable; and
- access to specialist support for community-based services and specialist services for those dealing with eating disorders and self harm.

The recommendations also suggest that urgent attention should be given to groups known to be especially at risk, including those 'looked after' and leaving care and those in the criminal justice system. The Mental Health Foundation supports the recommendations made by the *Thematic Review of Young Prisoners* for full assessments to be carried out on all young people with warnings issued to staff concerning any who exhibit signs of vulnerability. The review also recommended that all young prisoners should have access to the full range of services of trained mental health nurses, clinical psychologists and occupational therapists and others who form the normal mental health care teams within the NHS. The MHF further recommends that the operators of YOIs should be required to work to clear standards of provision. This should be in line with both the 1989 Children Act and the UN Convention on the Rights of the Child and regular inspections should be carried out by appropriately trained groups of professionals to ensure that service provision is appropriate (MHF, 1999).

Risk behaviours; smoking, and alcohol and drug use and abuse

In Britain, there have been significant increases over recent years in young people engaging in a number of behaviours that are thought to aggravate or cause ill health. Much of the research concentrates upon smoking, drinking alcohol and drug misuse. But other behaviours are also important to healthy living. Regular physical activity, for instance, can reduce obesity, increase psychological wellbeing, including self esteem, and be generally advantageous for health and growth. Health guidelines for adults suggest we should carry out at least 30 minutes exercise on five days a week. The Health Education Monitoring Survey indicates that only around a half of 16 to 24-year-old young men and less than a third of young women are doing the recommended amount of exercise. Furthermore, when young people complete compulsory schooling, the exercise they get through compulsory physical education, including games, declines, and the survey suggests that physical activity among young people significantly declines after the end of their teenage years (NSO, 2000b).

Eating a balanced diet is another important means of reducing health risks. Eating fresh fruit and vegetables is particularly important. The Health Monitoring Survey indicates that young women aged 16 to 24 have much healthier diets than young men of the same age. Yet according to the 1998 survey, less than two thirds of young women (63 per cent) ate fruit, vegetables or salad daily and less than a half (44 per cent) of young men did so. Unhealthy eating, such as eating chips more than once a week, was also more common amongst young men than young women. Whilst some healthy eating (fruit and vegetables) habits increased in the late 1990s, unhealthy eating had not shown any marked decline (NSO, 2000B).

Our knowledge of young people's risk-taking behaviours has also increased substantially because of a number of large-scale surveys (Aldridge et al., 1999; Goddard and Higgins, 1999; HEA/BMRB, 1996; ISDD, 1996; Leitner et al., 1993; Parker et al., 1998; POST, 1996; Ramsey and Percy, 1996; Ramsey and Partridge, 1999). Particularly important for this summary are longitudinal surveys conducted with cohorts of young people, first in North-West England between 1991 and 1996 (Parker et al., 1998) and more recently in Northumbria and West Yorkshire (Aldridge et al., 1999). Similar studies have been carried out in the West of Scotland (West and Sweeting, 1996). These surveys concentrate upon smoking, drinking and drug use and give information on 'prevalence' (ever having used), as well as 'current use' of tobacco, alcohol and illegal drugs. They also provide insight into at what age, and under what circumstances, young people start smoking, drinking alcohol and using drugs and how this relates to other aspects of their lifestyles. This allows researchers to examine the patterns through which risk behaviours are taken up, discarded for something else, or associated with other future behaviours (ONS, 2000).

This kind of research covers behaviours which are legal for adults but illegal for children and young people, as well as other behaviours which are illegal at all ages. Smoking rates amongst 11 to 15-year-olds have risen during the same period in which they have fallen for adults. Smoking amongst 14 and 15-year-old girls is more common in the UK than anywhere else in Europe apart from Denmark. Rates for boys are at about the average of other European countries. Rates in Scotland are known to be especially high (Plant and Plant, 1992). A Department of Health Survey reports that nearly one in five 15-year-old young men were regular smokers and nearly a third (29 per cent) of young women were regular smokers at the same age. Regular smoking by 13-year-old boys had shown a decline from 8 per cent in 1982 to 5 per cent in 1998, whilst amongst the female sample the percentage had increased from 6 per cent to 9 per cent during the same period (Goddard and Higgins, 1999).

The consumption of alcohol and the use of drugs by young people has also increased markedly in recent years. In the North-West study, most respondents had started to drink alcohol at the age of 10 or 11. Nearly a third (30 per cent) were drinking it weekly at the age of 14, over a half (57 per cent) by the age of 16, and over 80 per cent by the time they reached 18. In 1995, the Department of Health revised its guidance on *Sensible Drinking* – drinking which would not result in significant health risks. This replaced weekly limits by daily limits of 3 to 4 and 2 to 3 units for men and women, respectively. Research indicates that, by the age of 18 a third of the sample could be classified as heavy session drinkers, consuming 11 units or more the last time they drank (Parker *et al.*, 1998). Amongst 18-year-old male drinkers, more than half reported that they drank more than the previously advised 'sensible' weekly drinking limit of 28 units per week, with more than a third (36 per cent) of young women of that age exceeding their suggested limit of 21 units (Parker *et al.*, 1998).

The venues at which young people drink change according to age. When they are young, 14 and 15-year-olds drink mainly in their own, or friends' homes, although a considerable proportion (around two-thirds of drinkers) also report drinking outside on the streets, in parks or other public places. By the age of 16, the vast majority of young people were also drinking in licensed premises such as pubs (approaching 90 per cent of all drinkers). By the age of 17 or 18 this proportion declined as young people gained access to clubs and other leisure venues. By this age drinking outside on the streets covered less than 1 per cent of the age group.

Some studies that have examined the prevalence of illegal drug use amongst the young have made claims about the 'normalisation' of recreational use. 'Normalisation' refers to the contention that some involvement in using illicit drugs is now the experience of the majority of teenagers (Shiner and Newburn, 1997). Some regard talk of 'normalisation' as an exaggeration, as often 'headline figures' are based upon self reporting of 'ever having tried' an illegal drug rather than its regular use. The North-West study indicated that over a third of 14-year-olds will have tried at least one illicit drug, rising to nearly two-thirds (64 per cent) of 18 and 19-year-olds. However, the proportion of the age groups who report use within the past month is substantially smaller – one in five 14-year-olds and around one in three by the age of 18. At the age of 18, rates of drug use amongst young men are significantly higher than those for young women although, interestingly, there are no real differences between rates for young people from different class backgrounds. This is confirmed by the 1998 British Crime Survey which studied much wider age groups. This survey also points to a strong link between drug use and unemployment (Ramsey and Partridge, 1999). In the North-West study, rates of drug use by young people self-identifying as black are much higher than whites in all age groups, although Asian groups were much less likely to have tried drugs at all, or to have used them within the past month. The British Crime Survey indicates that the highest rates of drug use are amongst a relatively small group of rising urban professionals (Ramsay and Partridge, 1999).

Studies showing how many young people have ever tried an illegal drug have revealed some regional differences, with higher rates being reported in London, parts of Northern England and Scotland (Ramsay and Partridge, 1999). The Home Office study in the North-

East and West Yorkshire found that over half of 15 and 16-year-olds had tried at least one drug, with more than 60 per cent reporting use by the second year of the survey (Aldridge *et al.*, 1999). Young people in the North-East seemed to have first tried a drug at an earlier age than those living in West Yorkshire, although by their mid-teens differences between the two samples had largely disappeared. When the survey restricted the definition of 'drug users' to those who reported having used an illegal drug in the last year, this reduced the numbers involved by around two-thirds. Where 'drug users' was restricted to those who report use in the last month, this reduced the figures by a further third. Whilst the overall figures remain high, these reduced figures do not really support the 'normalisation' claim. Just under a third (30 per cent in Yorkshire and 35 per cent in Northumbria) report having used an illegal drug in the last month at the age of 16.

The use of school-based surveys has also helped to identify the early age at which young people are first exposed to illegal drugs. As part of the 'NE Choices' project (see below), a baseline survey was conducted with just under 2,000 pupils in year 9 (around 13-years-old) in ten schools in North-East England in Autumn 1996 (Stead *et al.*, 2000). Almost half (47 per cent) had been offered a drug by that age. This included a third who had been offered cannabis, a quarter solvents, around 15 per cent who had been offered magic mushrooms or LSD, and one in ten ecstasy. About a third had tried at least one drug by the age of 13 (mainly cannabis or solvents), although this was reduced to a quarter if the definition was restricted to those who had done so within the last six months. If taking drugs within the last three months was taken as an indicator of regular use, this accounted for around 15 per cent of 13-year-olds, with a third of these (5 per cent) reporting that they had taken drugs within the past week. Much drug taking amongst the young is experimental. Increasingly drug-awareness programmes have become attuned to the fact that they must target younger age groups and be aware of the distinctions between 'ever used' and 'regular users' and an appreciation of different 'career routes' into, and out of, drug use.

The North-West study sample of 18-year-olds provides the clearest large-scale analysis to date of 'drug careers'. This study splits the sample into four broad groups in their attitudes and behaviour on drug use. Just under a third (31 per cent) were current users; they had used illegal substances, intended to do so again and nominated themselves as 'taking drugs'. A further third (30 per cent) were abstainers; they did not take drugs, never had, and had no intentions of doing so in the future. A further 11 per cent had used drugs but had given up; they were former triers. The fourth group of 28 per cent are reported as in transition in that they had taken drugs in the past, did not currently identify as a 'drug user', but remained agnostic about whether they will become users in the future. The abstainer group reported on by Parker and colleagues was much smaller in size than that reported on by the British Crime Survey. The North-West study claimed less than a third were abstainers compared with the 50 per cent of 16 to 19-year-old abstainers claimed by the British Crime Survey (Ramsey and Spiller, 1997).

Most young people who use drugs do not regard this as problematic behaviour (Perri 6 *et al.*, 1997). Most surveys confirm that cannabis is overwhelmingly 'the drug of choice' for the majority of those using drugs, although many also mention LSD and amphetamines and ecstasy. Other studies report that ecstasy use is more common amongst young people in their late teens and is associated with clubs and dance music (Merchant and MacDonald, 1994). The use of cannabis, in particular, is regarded as bringing positive feelings of relaxation. Amphetamines are perceived as improving self confidence and making young people feel sexy, energetic and excited. LSD was reported by young people as the least predictable of the drugs commonly used, although negative experiences with any of the popularly used drugs were reported by less than one in ten users. Even amongst abstainers, cannabis was regarded as a safe drug and no more (and often less) dangerous than alcohol or tobacco. Indeed many young people report that, whilst alcohol sometimes makes them violent and aggressive, they find cannabis is calming and less likely to result in violent or anti-social behaviour (see also the cameo of the Freagarrach project in chapter seven). Parker reports that young people regard themselves as 'sophisticated about their drug of choice' whilst having negative images of 'drug abusers', regarding these as 'dangerous, diseased, dishevelled injecting "junkies" and "saddos" who commit vast amounts of crime to feed their habit . . . Taking hard drugs is an anathema; a Rubicon they will not cross.' (Parker *et al.*, 1998). In the late 1990s, however, there remained worries that more and more young people were using cheap, heroin based, drugs sold under different names and smoked rather than injected. The 1998 British Crime Survey reported significant increases in the use of cocaine based drugs (Ramsay and Partridge, 1999). One study in the North-East suggested that some estates had become flooded with cheap heroin and some young people did not regard smoking it as likely to lead to addiction (Johnston *et al.*, 2000). As we will see in the next chapter, the use of hard drugs is often linked to persistent offending. Yet what must also be recognised is that the production, distribution and consumption of drugs is a huge industry. Although the concentration in this chapter has been on drug use, the distribution and sale of drugs offers young people significant earning opportunities and represents a major route to developing alternative careers outside of the legitimate labour market (Johnston *et al.*, 2000). Too often the limited number of studies of 'drug careers' have concentrated only upon drug use in isolation from other aspects of young people's careers. Yet, often it is related to other behaviours, sometimes other risk behaviours, such as involvement in crime, but also to other more mundane activities. One small scale, ethnographic study in Scotland, for instance, showed that common events like splitting up with a girlfriend or dropping out of college can sometimes precipitate a change of friendship patterns and leisure activities. This can lead either to infrequent users becoming regular users or to young people changing their drug of choice (Bell *et al.*, 1999).

There are a number of known correlates of drug use. Current users are much more likely to have smoked tobacco in their early teens. Amongst abstainers, only a few had ever been regular smokers. Abstainers are just as likely to drink alcohol, although they were more likely to do so weekly and at a later age than others. In a large scale, longitudinal, survey of over a thousand young people in western Scotland (including Glasgow), smoking and drug taking were also found to be related to earlier sexual experiences (Sweeting and West, 1995). Young women who used drugs before the age of 15 were three times more likely to drink alcohol, smoke and have had sexual experiences. There were also connections between these four risk taking behaviours and family background. All four behaviours were more accepted as 'normal' by young people living in poverty or in poor neighbourhoods. Smoking and illicit drug use were also 15 times less likely to take place when young men lived in intact families. For young women smoking at the age of 15 was most likely where they lived in single parent households, including ones where a parent had died. Of those young people who had experienced the death of a parent, 27 per cent had had sexual experiences before the age of 16 and 40 per cent were pregnant before the age of 18. Of course, these are not suggested as directly causally connected. Rather this may be part of a set of factors related to living in poor neighbourhoods. Teenage pregnancy was also more common in those living in single parent families at the age of 15, and three to four times higher than in intact families.

Anti-drugs strategies

Government policy on drugs has had a chequered history with much public pontificating and moral condemnation but, until recently, little effective coordination of effort. Until the 1997 general election there was little attempt to coordinate policy between three competing government departments, the Department of Health, the Home Office and the Department for Education and Employment. There was some recognition of this in a report from the Department of Health in 1994 and the beginnings of a strategy was announced in *Tackling Drugs Together* in 1995. This was revised after the election as *Tackling Drugs to Build a Better Britain*. The latter also announced changes in the organisation of the Drugs Prevention Initiative which was replaced by a Drugs Prevention Advisory Service (DPAS) in April 1999. The former initiative saw 12 drugs prevention teams set up to coordinate community based prevention programmes. These were expanded in 1999 to cover all government regions. A budget of £2 million per annum was supplemented by a further large budget to carry out evaluations of the projects involved.

There is a now a widespread recognition that many of the old sources of information and guidance have been ineffective and regarded by many young people with contempt. Young people only listen to credible sources. Peer education programmes have been encouraged within the youth service and others engaged in outreach work. Within schools, policy now recognises the importance of early education (including primary schools) and that this is best integrated into wider programmes of personal, social and health education as well as at all stages of the National Curriculum (Blackman, 1996). There is also recognition that getting a message across requires dialogue and debate, rather than simply preaching to the converted, the agnostic and the disbelieving. Parents are known to be influential and need to be supported with confidential advice and support in terms of their own role. However, barriers to their involvement also need to be carefully thought through.

One interesting programme is described in the North-East Choices report. A summary is given below.

North-East Choices: The Intervention Programme

This is a multi-component drugs prevention programme for young people in the north-east of England developed by the Northumbia Drugs Prevention Team. It is being evaluated by a Home Office project that also incorporates a large-scale school-based survey on drug-related behaviour. This enables the evaluation to employ a quasi-experimental design, comparing the schools where the programme operates with schools where it does not. Young people in the 'control group' schools are exposed to only normal school-based drug awareness programmes. Those in the experimental schools are exposed to the full, multi-component, programme.

This has three main components:

- Interpersonal components: a three year programme of interactive drama workshops, classroom activities, sessions for parents, youth work projects and intensive work with high risk groups.
- Media-based information: including a magazine, a filofax-type reference file, a website and computer software, manuals for parents, teachers and school governors.
- Community awareness and support: work with community leaders, the drug awareness service and local community groups.

Overall the project aims to produce re-enforcing messages from different sources and is based upon a 'social influences' approach to drugs prevention. It tries to avoid an overt abstinence message. Rather it seeks to reduce exaggerated perceptions of peer use and illustrate how it is possible to step back from occasional experimental use. It also emphasises themes related to the consequences of different choices and provides opportunities to 'rehearse' social strategies and skills to deal with drug use. Other key components of the message it seeks to get across are strategies of 'harm reduction' and how to cope with an emergency situation.

The evaluation of NE Choices

The North-East Choices programme is tied to an evaluation using an 'integrated research design' which aims to examine its outcome and the impact of its components by continuous 'formative research' aiming to identify lessons for further refinement. This evaluation covers ten different schools, six of which will have received the intervention (three the full, year nine intervention programme and three a partial programme) and four further schools from neighbouring local authorities, matched to be as like the intervention schools as possible. Just under 2,000 pupils in year 9 filled in a 'baseline' questionnaire. This collects information about drug-related behaviours and is repeated annually. At the time of writing, the evaluation of the project has been confined to examining responses to the various elements of the process of intervention and the perceived impact it has had. Evaluations of the project also involve observation of the sessions, focus groups

with parents and with the drama team, interviews with teachers, PSE coordinators and year heads and a self completion questionnaire with pupils administered in schools two weeks after the interventions have taken place (Stead *et al.*, 2000). The evaluation reports very positive responses to the drama workshop and high levels of pupil participation. Half the respondents thought it would make people less likely to take drugs and more than 80 per cent thought it successfully emphasised the importance of considering choices and consequences carefully. One in ten, however, thought they would definitely continue to use drugs.
(Based on *Aldridge et al., 1999*)

Vulnerable groups are also targeted as these are more likely to experiment at an earlier age, and more likely to progress to hard drug use and addiction. Work with these groups requires earlier intervention and must be sustained over longer periods of time. Because vulnerable groups are the targets of so many intervention projects there is also a need for a coordinated response and effective multi-agency cooperation. Newburn and Elliot have reported on two innovative drug prevention projects based in youth justice teams in two areas in the Midlands. Overall, the projects worked with 113 known offenders, all of whom were under the age of 18. Self reported drug use amongst 30 interviewed was exceptionally high, with an average age of starting to use drugs as low as 10. The vast majority reported using cannabis, but half also reported heroin use and two-thirds the use of amphetamines or LSD. A third had been 'looked after' at some stage, although slightly over a half were still living with their parent(s).

The work of Youth Offending Teams will be described in more detail in the next chapter. Newburn and Elliot report that these offer significant opportunities to work on problematic drug use. Some major barriers to effective working, however, were also noted. Social workers who were part of the teams often failed to question offenders about their drug use and, even when this was brought to their attention, felt ill-equipped to address these needs themselves and reluctant to refer clients on to specialist drug workers. More positively, some workers, including drug workers, also found they were pulled into working more 'holistically', including working with other family members and parents. However, for drug workers, this created problems as it ran the risk of them becoming supervising officers, which was beyond their remit. Although the review of the youth justice system was intended to promote multi-agency working and a more holistic approach to need, some significant barriers to effective working still persisted. Even professional workers clearly need more training in identifying, and dealing with, the needs of problematic drug users. Drug testing of young people in young offenders institutions and prison is now routine. Indeed there are now real dangers that young people are being pushed from softer but easy to detect drug use (such as cannabis) to harder, more addictive drugs, such as heroin, which stay in the system for a shorter period of time (and thus are less easily detectable). Other areas being targeted include poor neighbourhoods and less obvious groups, such as those living in rural areas.

Young carers

The welfare of some young people can be as much affected by the ill health of other family members as by their own. Throughout the 1990s there has been considerable research and policy interest in young people who carry out significant caring tasks in and around the home for adults (usually their parent) or siblings. Surveys produce a range of wildly differing estimates of anywhere between 10,000 and 210,000 (Walker, 1996). Some of these discrepancies are due to differences in the way in which the term 'young carer' is defined. A survey carried out for the Department of Health claimed that the most appropriate definition should not include teenagers looking after their own children. Nor should it include those living with a sick or disabled adult where the young person only took on 'age appropriate' domestic tasks, and where others, including other adults or older siblings, did most of the caring, and where the young carer performed such tasks for less than ten hours a week. On the basis of this definition, an Omnibus Survey of households estimated that there were 32,000 young people aged 8 to 17-years-old who were young carers. Because this is only an estimate based upon a sample, however, this still means that the true figure could be anywhere between 19,000 and 50,000.

Other surveys have been based upon those contacted through young carers' projects and have produced data through which we can draw a profile of the characteristics of young carers – what they do, and what the implications of fulfilling this caring role are for their own welfare (Deardon and Becker, 1998). In all surveys it was found that young women are more likely to take on the young carer role than young men. They were also more likely to live in poor households and were twice as likely to live in lone parent families (Deardon and Becker, 1998). In their 1997 survey, mothers were the main recipient of care, accounting for three quarters of all carers living in lone parent families. However, of those living with two parents, a third of young carers were found to be looking after brothers or sisters. Many projects supporting young carers cater specifically for those from minority ethnic groups, although surveys suggest that young carers from minority ethnic groups are no more likely than their white peers to take on such a role (Shah and Hatton, 1999). The recipients of care were most likely to have a physical illness or disability (57 per cent), although mental illness and disability accounted for a quarter of all cases and learning disability a further one in ten (11 per cent). The type and severity of the illness and disability do, of course, influence the kinds of care that will be required.

In summarising the tasks young carers perform, Deardon and Becker use a five-fold typology: domestic tasks; general caring; intimate care; emotional care and child care. Domestic tasks include washing up, cooking meals and tidying up. General caring involves helping with medication, mobility about the house and getting dressed. Intimate care includes help with toileting and dealing with incontinence. Emotional care involves dealing with fluctuations of moods and depression. Child care means looking after the needs of younger children. The range of these tasks undertaken by young people is related to age and gender differences between young carers. The research indicates that the older the carer, the wider the duties they performed, with young women being more likely to take on a wider range of tasks as they got older. More than one in five young women carers were carrying out forms of intimate care, although this was almost exclusively for someone of the same sex (mainly mothers). Perhaps more disturbing was the finding that intimate care was being provided by at least one child under the age of 5 and in a further 79 cases (11 per cent of all young carers) by children and young people between the ages of 5 and 10. Other concerns were about young people being involved in lifting heavy adults without being properly trained on how to do so without sustaining injury. Some young carers also reported that their sleep was seriously interrupted by night-time duties.

Being a young carer can have an important impact on youth transitions. The vast majority of carers surveyed by Deardon and Becker in 1997 were of compulsory school age (86 per cent). Of these, a fifth were missing school, including a third (35 per cent) absent from secondary school (Deardon and Becker, 1998). Some of this absence was periodic rather than permanent, although the research did note that young carers were sometimes in trouble with school authorities due to persistent lateness or missing significant periods of schooling when problems at home were particularly acute. Such absence obviously affected their educational progress. Young carers were also severely restricted in the time they could spend with friends. Coping emotionally with the precarious health of a parent or sibling was also debilitating. These factors, together with the physical demands – such as lifting a parent – and working longer hours than their contemporaries, has an effect on their own health. The National Strategy on Carers also notes that their role can produce low self esteem and have an effect upon transitions to adulthood (Department of Health, 1999a). The Social Exclusion Unit also notes that 'some young carers often escape the attention of statutory services because by the nature of their responsibilities they spend much time at home, and they are not "creating problems"' (SEU, 1999b). Yet despite the huge difficulties they face, some young carers are successful with school qualifications and do go on to post–16 study and later to university.

Deardon and Becker have also completed an in–depth study of 60 young carers between the ages of 16 and 25 (Deardon and Becker, 2000). This confirmed some of their earlier findings about the circumstances in which they lived. Half were living in lone parent families and none of the parents who were ill or disabled were in work. The majority were living in rented accommodation. Two-thirds of those studied were caring for mothers and seven of the 60 were caring for more than one person. Most of those cared for had physical health problems or disabilities, but ten of the 60 carers were looking after someone with a mental health problem and five were caring for a parent with problems involving alcohol or drugs. Three of the sample had been 'looked after' at some stage. Two more had not been admitted to care but social services had made arrangements for them to be looked after by a neighbour. One had requested that she be taken into care but was refused. All these cases had a parent with mental health problems. Four other respondents had siblings who had been 'looked after', although because of their own behavioural difficulties rather than their parent's illness.

As was indicated by previous studies, the caring role had a considerable effect upon young people's schooling. A half of the sample had missed some school, often because of a fear of leaving a parent alone, and sometimes because a parent had previously experienced an accident or crisis when the young carer had been away at school. Sometimes absence from school was with the collusion of school staff and educational welfare officers. Despite significant educational disadvantage, some continued to study for their 16-plus examinations and three quarters of the sample got some qualifications, although a quarter had none. A remarkably high proportion continued with their education after minimum school leaving age. Twenty-three of the 36 studied in the 16 to 18-year-old age group were still in education, either in school or sixth form college (10), or in further education (13), either doing GCSE re-takes or vocational or academic courses. In the older 14 to 25-year-old sample, a quarter had gone on to university, one had obtained a first class honours degree, although two had dropped out because of problems with the parent at home. Of those who were not in education, a small number were either in, or about to start, a training programme. In the 19 to 25-year-old sample, a third were in full-time employment although four of the 24 were unemployed. In the younger age group five (14 per cent) were not in education, training or work, and some had dropped out of training or a college course because of their caring role. None of these were in receipt of benefit in their own right nor claiming Invalidity Care Allowance (ICA). Only in the older 19 to 25-year-old group were four young women claiming ICA, three of whom were full-time carers.

As outlined in chapter one, domestic and housing careers are also often considered key elements of the transition to adulthood. Of the sample of 60 young carers, seven had left home or were living independently. In five of these cases, leaving home had not been a positive or planned choice. One was married with a child and two were lone parents. These three with children were in secure rented accommodation. Many of the remainder were either in various forms of transitional housing (whilst at university, for instance), or remained in the parental home. Others, however, had left home because of not being any longer able to cope with their parent's illness. One was in a hostel for homeless women. Her mother had mental health problems and she herself had an eating disorder and was self harming. Another young woman who left home at 16 also had a mother with mental health problems and reported being on the edge of ending her own life. She had stayed with a teacher and other family members before getting a flat of her own.

In a variety of different ways, being a young carer required young people to take on domestic and other responsibilities at an earlier age than their peers. Some were running their household in their early to mid teens. Yet experiencing the suffering, and sometimes the death, of a parent was also a cause of considerable anxiety and stress. A number of the sample said they felt 'stressed out' and depressed. Five had been treated for depression by their GPs. Five more reported eating disorders, although only one had been treated for this. A number also recognised the restricted choice they had compared with their peers, especially in terms of going out with, and mixing with, other people in their own age group. Some of these 'social costs', when added to other forms of disadvantage, meant that the illness of others had a marked and long-lasting impact upon their lives.

Support for young carers

The Carers (Recognition and Services) Act of 1995 offers all carers, including young carers, the opportunity to have their needs assessed at the same time as those for whom they care. This was the first Act to include young carers and was accompanied by a Practice Guide. Prior to the 1995 Act they were only covered by clauses of the 1989 Children Act dealing with children in need. There are still complexities under Scottish law about carers under the age of 16. In England and Wales the Practice Guide stressed the need to consider:

- how to listen to children and young people, respect their views and give adequate time and privacy for them to express these;
- their needs which arise because of their caring role;
- the impact of this role on their educational progress;
- the impact of caring on emotional and social development; and
- the provision of a full range of support services including those of young carers groups.

Emphasis was also given to how a parent's strengths could be supported and not undermined, and the need to acknowledge that children and young people involved in caring might be an important means through which the family as a unit coped with illness or disability.

Despite the 1995 Act, a survey in 1997 suggested that little progress had been made, with only 11 per cent of young carers being assessed, and less than half of these assessed under the 1995 Act (Dearden and Becker, 1998). This report recommended further action on a number of fronts. Firstly, despite a considerable research effort in this area, there is still ignorance amongst professional workers about the needs of young carers. This leads to the lack of an informed response to the need to mobilise effective means of support. This is particularly the case for education-related professional workers including educational welfare officers and school nurses, as well as those involved in generic health services, including mainstream doctors and nurses. Despite their responsibilities under the 1989 and 1995 Acts, social service departments are still failing to provide proper assessments of the needs of young carers. Who gets assessed, where and when is still something of a lottery. Assessment and provision still need to be made more systematic and be carried out in a family-friendly and child-friendly manner. It is widely recognised that both health and social services are stretched in terms of the resources they feel they can allocate to this work, and their ability to provide appropriate packages of care and support. There are now more than a hundred different young carers' projects nationwide. The good news is that, where systems of support are in place, services for both the young carer and those being looked after mean a significant reduction in the need for young people to provide substantial care on a regular basis (Dearden and Becker, 1998). The bad news is that this is far from comprehensively and universally available and clearly more needs to be done.

Conclusions

This chapter has reviewed research, policy and intervention projects across four broad areas related to health. Hitherto, the impact of health-related issues has largely been omitted as a significant dimension of the youth transition model. Yet, as we have seen, the ill health of the young person themselves or that of a significant other in their lives, can be of fundamental importance. It can be life threatening, as in the case of accidents, chronic illness, or suicide and self harm. It can also be life shaping and can affect schooling and the qualifications attained. It can also be an important determinant in the course of youth transitions as in the case of young people who leave home prematurely to escape the stress and anxieties caused by caring for a parent with severe mental health problems or with problematic alcohol or drug use. The use of drugs by young people themselves can also be related to family tension and family conflict. This may also result in their leaving home early and/or becoming homeless. The use of hard drugs, especially, is linked to criminality that may result in custodial sentences which will considerably impact upon future life chances. This is discussed at more length in the next chapter. Ill health is not only an important causal factor in helping to determine youth transitions, it is also strongly related to other forms of disadvantage. As we have seen, many forms of ill health, accidents and childhood mortality are related to social class background, ethnicity, living in poor housing or deprived communities. Research on health inequalities suggests that, although the relationship between class and social background is complex, it is associated with a disproportionate amount of ill health amongst the poor (Achieson, 1999: Gordon *et al.*, 1999; West, 1999). Health may thus become an important mechanism through which patterns of disadvantage are passed on from one generation to the next.

One of the main reasons for including this chapter in the book is to increase the awareness of the impact of health issues on youth transitions amongst those who work with young people. Taking health issues seriously must be a key element in any holistic approach to meeting young people's needs. Until recently, there has been too little recognition that many problems associated with youth transitions are mediated through the ill health, risk behaviours and the caring responsibilities young people experience. The review of youth intervention projects in this chapter also points to major gaps in services for children and young people, particularly in the area of mental health. There are also significant training and re-training needs amongst professional workers. Some new opportunities are beginning to occur because of a government commitment to promoting more 'joined-up' and holistic approaches to meeting young people's needs. Many of these include the health-related issues covered in this chapter. Yet, if these opportunities are to be taken, much more is required of both health and other professional groups in seeking to understand the complexity of the needs of young people and in being prepared to work together to promote the welfare of young people.

Chapter seven

Youth crime and criminal justice

Tony Blair first came to prominent public attention as the shadow Home Secretary who promised to be 'tough on crime and tough on the causes of crime'. Many of the previous chapters of this book have covered issues known to be related to youth crime and so many of the policies and projects related, for instance, to educational disaffection, can be seen as addressing the causes of crime. This chapter focuses on research, policy and practice which is more directly related to young people's involvement in crime and the criminal justice system. Even before the election in 1996, the Audit Commission had published a hard hitting and influential report, *Misspent Youth* which reviewed what happened to young offenders. This report indicated that, of the seven million offences by young people each year, less than one in five were reported to the police and only one in twenty crimes were cleared up by them. Only 3 per cent of offences resulted in arrest and only 1.3 per cent resulted in a charge or summons. On the basis of this it might be concluded that whilst youth crime is widespread, it is only loosely articulated to the criminal justice system.

The Audit Commission also reported that the cost of youth crime to public services alone was around £1 billion and much of the processing of youth crime, although costly, was slow, inefficient and ineffective. In some areas it took 170 days between arrest and sentence with the average in England and Wales being 121 days (nearly four months). During this time an offender went on to commit many other offences (Audit Commission, 1996). Other estimates have suggested that, when such elements as private insurance and damage repair are taken into account, the total cost of youth crime is over £7 billion a year. The Prince's Trust have estimated that the cost in Scotland alone is £730 million (Prince's Trust, 1997). Clearly, vast amounts of money are being spent as a result of 'failed' youth policies in a number of areas. Being tough on crime and the causes of crime had, therefore, considerable potential to prevent wasteful public expenditure, through reducing the amount of youth crime and diverting those responsible for committing it from further offending.

Self-reported crime by young people and persistent offenders

Some Home Office tracking studies have found that criminal activity is alarmingly high, particularly amongst young men, with one in three of this group being convicted of an indictable offence before the age of 30 (Home Office, 1989). Much of what we claim to know about offending behaviour by young people is based, not upon an examination of the characteristics of convicted offenders, but on 'self report' studies of large samples of young people in the general population. The most quoted of these was carried out by Graham and Bowling in 1992 and published in 1995 (Graham and Bowling, 1995). This was based on a national random sample of 1,721 young people aged 14 to 25 and a booster sample of 808 young people from ethnic minorities. Respondents to the main survey were asked to admit whether they had committed one of a list of 23 different offences or whether they had used controlled drugs. A second stage involved in-depth interviews with a small sample of 'desisters' – young people who had offended in the past but claimed not to have done so within the past year.

The Home Office now conducts more regular surveys of young people. The Youth Lifestyles Survey covers a sample of nearly five thousand young people aged 12 to 30 with the most recent published in October 2000 (Campbell and Harrington, 2000). Key findings from this survey include:

- youth crime is widespread, with the majority of young men (57 per cent) and 37 per cent of young women admitting to committing at least one offence at some point in their lives;
- almost a fifth of those sampled admitted to one or more offence in the last 12 months. Men (26 per cent) were more likely to admit to offending than women (11 per cent). Those in the 14 to 21 age group were the most likely to be offenders;
- most youth crime does not result in young people being dealt with by the youth justice system. Only 4 per cent of young men and 1 per cent of young women reported that they had been cautioned or taken to court;
- the average age of offending was 13.5 for boys and 14 for girls;
- most admitted to only one offence in the last year, but 10 per cent of offenders were responsible for nearly half of all crime;
- offending amongst boys aged between 14 and 17 increased by 14 per cent between 1992–93 and 1998–99 but fell during the same period for 18 to 25-year-olds by 6 per cent;
- types of offending varied with age with fighting and criminal damage predominating amongst 12 and 13-year-olds but declining in later teenage years;
- amongst 12 to 17-year-old boys factors associated with persistent offending included drug taking, educational disaffection, and the influence of family and friends. Persistent offending was five times more common amongst this age group taking drugs than those who did not; and
- drug use amongst 18 to 30-year-old men was also the factor most predictive of persistent offending.

A similar study was carried out in Scotland between 1996–99 (Jamieson *et al.*, 1999). This employed both quantitative and qualitative methods, including in-depth interviews with three different age groups: 14 to 15-year-olds; 18 to 19-year-olds; and 22 to 25-year-olds. It involved a large questionnaire survey of 1,274 young people and was carried out in two areas. Respondents were asked about the same 23 named offences included in the Graham and Bowling study. An attempt was also made through in-depth interviews with a much smaller sample of 276 young people to explore three main groups within each age category: resisters – young people who had never offended; desisters – young people who had offended but claimed not to have done so within the past 12 months; and persisters – young people who had committed either one 'serious' or several less serious offences in the past 12 months.

In Scotland, most 14 and 15-year-olds reported that they had offended on at least one occasion but much of the self-reported offences were not serious. Amongst boys, only 6 per cent reported never offending, 3 per cent confessed only to minor offences and a further 10 per cent had not offended within the last year. Amongst girls, 18 per cent said they had committed no offence, 5 per cent only a minor offence and 11 per cent had not offended in the last year. Throughout Britain, therefore, youth crime and offending behaviour is very widespread.

For both boys and girls vandalism, fighting in the street and shoplifting were the three most common offences. Boys outnumbered girls in these and all other categories. Although these gender differences are statistically significant, a majority of girls still reported that they had committed the first of these offences (vandalism or property damage) and 49 per cent reported being involved in street fights. Nearly a half (47 per cent of boys and 41 per cent of girls) reported committing property damage or vandalism within the past year and 34 per cent of boys and 24 per cent of girls also reported shoplifting within the past year. Boys were also more likely to have committed more offences and to have been involved in violent offences. Nearly a half (47 per cent) reported beating someone up and 28 per cent hurting someone with a weapon, compared with 21 per cent and 11 per cent of girls admitting these offences, respectively. It remains an open question as to whether the connection between gender and crime suggests criminal behaviours are connected to aspects of masculinities although some authors have argued this strongly (Coote, 1994). The connection could be the result of other factors which are connected to both being male and criminality, such as patterns of truancy, parental supervision, gendered leisure or the influence of peers. The study in Scotland does not cover ethnic differences. In England and Wales, there are few notable differences in self-reported crime between white and African-Caribbean groups but less self-reported crime amongst Asian young people.

In Scotland, some of the offences (fighting and shoplifting) were more common amongst 15-year-olds than those aged 13 or 14. In England and Wales, the peak ages of offending are in the mid- to late-teens with different peak ages for different offences. Offending is most likely to start at age 15 for male and female (a year later than, for instance, running away, truancy and drinking alcohol). As we saw in chapter six, drug taking is more likely to start a year later. In England and Wales, most early offences are, what Graham and Bowling describe as, 'expressive property crime' (vandalism). Sixteen is the peak year for acts of violence (male and female). Involvement in property offences amongst young men is more likely in the late teens and early 20s. Young women's involvement in this is earlier (although much less). Offending amongst young women declines in their late teens. This is not the case for young men, where offending remains constant between the ages of 18 and 25, and, in the case of property crime, increases in the late teen years.

Whilst offending amongst young people may be widespread, there is also concern for the high number of crimes committed by a relatively few young people. Research by Hagell and Newburn has helped to identify some of the characteristics of persistent offenders aged between 10 and 16 (Hagell and Newburn, 1994). They report that most persistent offenders were male, although in their Midlands sample 16 per cent were female – twice as many as in their London sample. Amongst persistent offenders the most common offences were traffic offences, non-residential burglary and thefts from shops and cars. Self-report data from their sample of 74 convicted offenders suggested that there were high levels of unrecorded crime, especially disqualified driving, carrying offensive weapons and frequently buying drugs. Much of this is reported to have occurred in the month prior to the interviews. Many persistent offenders also reported that they often committed offences with others, mainly other persistent offenders, and sometimes whilst on bail. Amongst sample members, there was also a clear pattern of family disruption with half the sample known to social services. Initial contact with social workers had been concerned with the welfare of the young person rather than their offending behaviour. The majority had also left school and been 'status zer0' with nothing to do with their time (Hagell and Newburn, 1994).

In Scotland, Jamieson *et al.*, also have more recently examined factors associated with persistent offending. Some of the cases suggested that a number of 13 and 14-year-olds did try to avoid trouble by, for instance, trying to avoid situations in which they might get into fights. Others, however, reported that, if confronted, they would not back down from a fight, and others knew that the influence of alcohol meant they would soon get into trouble. By the time young people were in their late teens, involvement with drugs was a common reason for continuing with acquisitive crime – stealing to fuel a drug habit. In the older 22 to 25-year-old age group, drug use and addiction was also reported as the main reason for all the young women persisting in crime and for a majority of the young men.

Recorded crime

Another main source of evidence about crime is crime recorded by the police. In the 12 months up to June 1992 the police recorded a peak of 5.6 million incidents. On the same counting rules, recorded crime had declined to 4.5 million by 1998–99, but because of new counting rules the official figure stood at 5.1 million. New rules introduced since the 1997 General Election involved a principle of one crime per victim, so that if one person assaults two people in the same incident, this is now recorded as two crimes. However, not all crime is reported to the police and, for a variety of reasons, the police may not record an incident as a crime simply because it is reported. They may have reason to doubt the allegation.

Official crime figures in 2000 indicated that recorded crime had increased again to

5.3 million recorded offences, an increase of 3.8 per cent on the previous year. Under New Labour, some key crimes were targeted as areas where the police should make special efforts to reduce crime. Some of these, including domestic burglary and car-related crime showed some reduction, with a reduction of nearly 5 per cent in domestic burglary on the previous year. There was also a reduction of over 10 per cent in drug offences, although this might be as a result of some police forces effectively decriminalising possession of small amounts of cannabis for personal use. However, the most marked increases in official crime figures were for violent offences, with a more than 15 per cent increase in violence against the person, and a 26 per cent increase in robbery (Home Office website). The Home Secretary claimed that 80 per cent of violent crime was committed by offenders whilst under the influence of alcohol, including more than three-quarters of all assaults. Given that many areas around night clubs are now largely 'policed' by untrained 'bouncers', it is highly likely that violent offences around such venues are hugely under-recorded (Hobbes, 2000).

The victims of crime

Since 1982 the Home Office has also conducted large scale surveys (every two years) of potential victims of crime – random samples of the population aged 16 and over. The British Crime Survey allows us to examine the prevalence of particular types of different crimes across different groups. The crimes examined include burglary, car crime and violence. Respondents are asked to report on incidents they have experienced as victims in the previous 12 months. The 1998 survey estimated 16.5 million crimes against adults in households in 1997, a fall of 14 per cent from a peak of 19.1 million in 1995. The 2000 British Crime Survey reported a further 10 per cent reduction in crime, with significant reductions in burglary, vehicle-related theft and theft from the person. Crimes reported through these surveys are, however, much more widespread than crime recorded by the police. This is considerably greater than the number of crimes recorded by the police – four and a half times more, according to the 2000 survey. Some crimes reported by victims are, however, still increasing. Robbery increased by 14 per cent between 1997–1999, and whilst there was a reduction in being a victim of violence from someone known to the victim, violence from a stranger increased by 29 per cent. This might go some way to explaining why, despite reductions in crime in the late 1990s, the level of concern about crime has remained the same (Home Office, 2000).

The British Crime Surveys enable us to examine with a little more certainty who are the most likely victims of crime. In general terms the groups most like to experience violence are almost identical in characteristics to those committing offences. Men are more than twice as likely to be victims as women, young men more likely to be victims than those over 30, single men more than married men, and those living in inner-cities more than those living in other areas. Many of these factors are associated with 'exposure to risk'. Young men in inner cities and who are single are more likely to be in places where violence occurs and at times, and in circumstances, in which violence is most likely to occur. The only exceptions to these patterns concern women and members of ethnic minority communities. However, older women are just as likely to be 'mugged' (street robbery) as young women, and members of ethnic minority groups (especially Afro-Caribbean men), are more likely to be victims of violence than whites or those of Indian or Pakistani descent. Public places are where most violence occurs. Four-fifths of violence on the streets is against men. However, of the over 500,000 self-reported incidents of violence in the home, four-fifths are against women.

Young people as victims of crime

One major gap in our knowledge of who are the victims of crime arises because the British Crime Surveys do not cover young people under the age of 16. The only exception to this was an extension to the 1992 British Crime Survey. This covered a sub-sample of 1,051 12 to 15-year-olds with a booster sample of 299 drawn from minority ethnic groups (Maung, 1995). This sample was asked about six types of offences in the previous 6–8 months – since the beginning of the summer holiday prior to the survey. They were asked about six different ways in which they might have been a victim: theft from unattended property; theft and attempted theft from the person; assault; harassment from adults; harassment from other young people; and sexual harassment. The survey also covered a number of attitudinal and behavioural questions including attitudes to the police and offending behaviours.

Sixty per cent of the sample reported that they experienced at least one incident, with boys slightly more likely to report being a victim than girls. Assaults were the most commonly reported crimes (by 40 per cent of boys and 34 per cent of girls). These were generally school-related with seven out of ten taking place in, or around, the school. The victim was often with other friends, although in 20 per cent of cases the victim had been alone. Assaults against older boys aged 14 or 15, however, had a 'gang element' in 28 per cent of cases. Just under one in ten assaults were reported to come from strangers, with a much higher proportion of these away from school. Most assaults were written off as 'just something that happens' and only 12 per cent of those questioned regarding it as being a crime. The level of fear created by these assaults was highest amongst older girls at nearly a quarter (23 per cent), rather than younger pupils.

The 'harassment' reported included incidents which had frightened young people and included young people being threatened, shouted at, stared at, or followed. This was reported by around one in five of the sample and by slightly more girls (23 per cent) than boys. Half of this occurred around the school and patterns of harassment were largely the same as for assaults. Harassment from adults was mainly on the streets and where the victim and the perpetrator were alone. Perhaps understandably, this produced much higher levels of fear. Sexual harassment was covered by different questions and restricted to incidents involving the male perpetrator being over the age of 16. Incidents were more likely to be reported by girls (19 per cent) than boys (2 per cent). Six out of ten incidents of these involved men unknown to the victim and a third were perpetrated by a man acting alone, with the victim also alone. A third of the incidents involved men estimated to be over 30 years old. In a fifth of incidents, the victim was confronted by more than one man. Half of the incidents were thought of as crimes and the same proportion regarded by their victims as being very frightening.

The same survey reported that just under a quarter of young people experienced theft of personal property, mainly at school, with slightly more boys (28 per cent) reporting this than girls. This was often the theft of equipment (including sports equipment), clothing, books, food and drink, and it was the least likely offence to be regarded by young people as being a crime. Theft, and attempted theft, from the person was much more likely to take place away from school. It was reported by a much smaller proportion of the sample (6 per cent) and was much more likely to be from boys (8 per cent) than girls (3 per cent). In around two-fifths of cases this involved the theft of money, followed by bicycles (14 per cent), school equipment (8 per cent), and food and drink (8 per cent), these being the most common items under threat. Many young people did not know what was happening until after it had occurred and they had difficulty in identifying the perpetrator. However, force was involved in a third of incidents and, understandably, this left the young person very frightened indeed.

Multiple victimisation was also found to be common. The majority of victims of assault said that it had happened to them twice at least, with a fifth reporting it had happened 'too many times to say'. Nearly as high a proportion who reported that they had been the victim of harassment by adults (15 per cent) and sexual harassment (12 per cent) also reported that this was such a regular occurrence that they could not estimate the number of times they had been a victim. All this adds up to a significant section of young women under the age of 16 being terrified in the communities in which they live.

Young people from minority ethnic groups, especially those of African Caribbean heritage, are reported to experience most of the crime types more than their white peers, although, in general, not more than those living in the same areas or with the same lifestyles. This was true of all the six types except assault, where white young people reported more assaults (35 per cent) than either African Caribbean (24 per cent) or Asian (20 per cent) young people. White young people were also slightly more likely to suffer harassment from other young people. Yet this should be read in the light of other, more recent, studies of racial harassment in school, reported in chapter three (Ofsted, 1999).

Correlates and causes of youth crime

Being tough on crime and the causes of crime relies on having some certainty about who commits it and what the causes are. Some authors suggest that, based upon a number of longitudinal studies conducted in a number of different countries, we do know a considerable amount about the causes of youth crime (Boswell, 1995; Fergusson, 1993; Hagell and Newburn, 1994; McCord, 1979; Pulkkinen, 1988; Moffitt and Silva, 1988; Robins, 1979; Wilkstrom, 1987; Wadsworth, 1979). These are associated with a series of 'risk factors' clustered around issues to do with the family, education, the community and peers (Farrington, 1996; Utting, 1997). It should be emphasised, however, that some of the studies on which this analysis is based are quite dated, with one, much quoted, British source, being based on 411 boys born in south London in 1953 and studied between the ages of 8 and 32 (Farrington, 1995).

Family factors associated with young offending include having a teenage mother, experiencing harsh or erratic discipline or neglect, conflict between parents, separation from at least one biological parent, and having a parent whose own attitudes condoned lawbreaking. Condoning parents have also been reported as significant in a number of other studies. In the study of self-reported crime in Scotland, for instance, the vast majority of those who resisted offending (82 per cent) reported that, to their knowledge, no other family member had offended. This affected their own attitude towards offending. In the Graham and Bowling self-report study, those living with both biological parents were least likely to report being offenders (Graham and Bowling, 1995). However, more significant were family relationships, including parents getting on badly with their children, not knowing where they were, or who they were with when they were away from home. Fifteen and sixteen-year-olds who reported that they got on badly with either their mother or father were much more likely also to report that they offended. Where bad relationships with parents resulted in young people spending at least one night away from home, this was associated with respondents also reporting offending behaviour in the case of nearly half the young women and three quarters of the young men. The relationship between these factors is highly complex. For instance, on the one hand offending may lead to a worsening of family relationships to such an extent that the offender runs away from home. On the other hand, if a young person has run away from home, they may engage in offending as a means of quickly obtaining money or provisions to survive on.

Educational factors associated with offending suggest that children who perform poorly in primary school, those who indicate a lack of commitment to school (through, for instance, truancy), and those involved in persistent bullying were more likely to be offenders (Utting, 1997). Graham and Bowling also report an association between offending and school factors such as school work being below average, being involved in truancy or being excluded from school (Graham and Bowling, 1995). They reported that more than a third of males and a quarter of females skipped school for at least a day without permission. Amongst this group, offending was three times higher than amongst those who did not truant. Temporary exclusion was reported by just over one in ten young men, three-quarters of whom also reported offending. All of the males in the sample, and five out of eight of the young women, who had been permanently excluded also reported offending.

Utting reports on a number of community factors associated with offending, including living in a household with a poor income, or living in a poor neighbourhood with various forms of community disorganisation. This latter factor was indicated by a high turnover of residents and harassment of ethnic minorities (Utting, 1997). Jamieson *et al.*, in their study in Scotland, report that most of their sample thought that, overall, most of the adults in the communities in which they lived, disapproved of offending behaviour (Jamieson *et al.*,

1999). However, a significant minority reported that some adults who were also involved in offending, saw it as 'getting one over' on the police, and that some behaviour, particularly minor offending, was seen as acceptable, or at least, understandable.

The other major factor associated with offending, found in numerous studies, is being associated with a peer group who also offend. Graham and Bowling report that more than two-thirds of male offenders had friends who were also in trouble with the police and that a third of female offenders had friends who offended. Only a sixth of female offenders had no friends who were also in trouble with the police. However, although based on a small sample, Jamieson *et al.* report that many of those who persist in their offending were oblivious to the views of their friends and peers, especially when they were also involved in drug misuse. Friends were reported as hostile both to their drug habits and to their offending.

There are a number of protective factors which are thought to reduce the likelihood of young people becoming involved in crime or related to their dis-involvement. Utting, for instance, emphasises opportunities for involvement and feeling valued at home, in school and in the communities in which young people live. Connected to this is the importance of recognition and due praise being given for achievement at home and at school and the opportunities to develop social skills and thinking skills. It was through this more balanced appraisal of their behaviour that potential young offenders learned to recognise the widespread damage offending behaviour might cause.

Careers involving crime

A number of studies report on the staged sequences through which 'criminal careers' develop (Craine, 1997; Little, 1990; Hagell and Newman, 1994). Most early offending is reported as 'opportunistic', sometimes chaotic, silly and often involves little tangible reward (Little, 1990). Research also indicates that, as acquisitive criminal activity becomes prevalent, young people develop 'techniques of neutralisation' through which crime is not thought of as 'bad', or as 'seriously hurting' victims, who are regarded as either 'asking for it' (in the case of violence), or as not really suffering because they were insured against loss. As with taking drugs, where young people do not regard certain types of activity as being seriously wrong, illegality may not be a significant deterrent, especially when the chances of being caught are very low. If their crime can further be seen as 'victimless', or the victim as being not really seriously affected, this may allow offending behaviour to be redefined as justifiable.

The study of self-reported youth crime in Scotland asked young people to conduct an exercise on a lap-top computer in which they were asked whether they regarded a list of offences to be very serious, quite serious, or not serious. Within the youngest group, 13 to 15-year-olds, the majority saw most of the listed offences, as very serious offences. Yet, even within this group, 41 per cent saw stealing from school and 28 per cent stealing from a machine as not serious, with a further 24 per cent regarding a street fight, and 19 per cent beating someone up as not serious. There were also marked differences between resisters, desisters and persisters in how they regarded offences. Amongst persisters, some crimes were regarded as serious, such as hurting someone with a weapon, mugging, or snatching a bag. However, the following were only regarded as serious by a minority of persistent offenders: stealing from school (by only 10 per cent); or a machine (by only 12 per cent); shoplifting (by only 14 per cent); being involved in a street fight (by only 16 per cent); vandalism (by only 18 per cent); and beating someone up (by only 19 per cent). Even more startling, the majority of persistent offenders did not regard breaking into a property, setting fire to something, stealing from a car, picking someone's pocket, stealing a bicycle or stealing from work as serious offences.

These findings may appear to suggest a significant decline in moral standards amongst the young. Yet some groups of young people engage in highly principled behaviour. The findings do, however, suggest that different moral codes operate within groups of young people who offend. It is these that must be systematically targeted if young people are to desist from offending, rather than simply applying the rigours of the criminal justice system. As we will see when we examine the intervention projects, breaking down the neutralisation techniques associated with crime is often as effective as threatening young offenders with punishment. After all, most offending behaviour remains undetected, and those who are apprehended and punished often regard themselves as either victimised and picked on by police and magistrates, or simply unlucky to be caught.

Youth crime and the criminal justice system

The youth justice system was subjected to a fundamental review as a result of the 1996 Audit Commission report *Misspent Youth* and the 1998 Crime and Disorder Act. This section begins with a brief description of the system as it existed in England and Wales, prior to the 1998 Act, with comment made about differences between this and the system operating in Scotland. For instance, the age of criminal responsibility in England and Wales is 10 but in Scotland it is 8. Under that age a child may not be charged with a criminal offence. There is significant variation in the age of criminal responsibility throughout Europe. It is as low as 7 in Ireland, whereas in Spain and Belgium it is 16 and 18 respectively. It has also been subject to change over time. Until 1908, in England a child could be tried in an adult court for any offence and, if found guilty, hanged, deported or imprisoned in an adult prison. Since then a variety of different acts of parliament have introduced different regimes for children and young people, in recognition that their offending may be related to the social and familial conditions or a need for mental or emotional help. Because of this, much work with young offenders involves the intervention of social workers as well as the police. Under the 1933 Children and Young Persons Act, and the 1989 Children Act, social service departments are responsible for safeguarding and promoting the welfare of children in need, which includes most young people who offend. Yet there has been much variability in the degree to which SSDs in different parts of the country are involved in programmes of crime prevention, or diversion from the courts.

In England and Wales, when a young person, under the age of 17, is arrested, both a lawyer (under legal aid) and a 'responsible adult' (in the absence of a parent, often a social worker) are required to be in attendance before the police can legally conduct an interview. The custody officer normally asks the parent or 'appropriate adult' to be present. The 1996 Audit Commission review reported that in 30 per cent of cases, a social worker was asked to act in this role. Appropriate adults are drawn either from a panel of trained volunteers or social services or youth justice workers. Assuming that the young person is thought to be guilty of the offence, the police must then decide what action to take. In considering this, they take account of the gravity and circumstances of the offence. Marginal cases are sometimes referred to an inter-agency youth panel. In Scotland, evidence from the police and other relevant evidence from social services and education are considered by special 'Children's Panels'. Prior to the 1998 Crime and Disorder Act and 1999 Youth Justice and Criminal Evidence Act, the range of options that could be considered included:

- warnings;
- cautions;
- caution plus (attendance at centres or forms of community service);
- prosecution through a youth court; or
- prosecution through crown courts.

Young people were not normally tried in an adult court unless it was a very serious offence (for which an adult would be imprisoned for 14 years), or where the offence was committed with an adult over the age of 18.

Most offences are dealt with by warnings or cautions. The 1996 Audit Commission report found that three out of five offenders who were apprehended were cautioned (although the proportion varied significantly across the country). Cautioning seemed to work well on first or second offences. Seven out of ten young people cautioned were not known to offend again. Yet after the second caution, prosecutions and cautions had an equal effect and after the third caution, cautions were more likely to result in later offences than prosecutions. Prosecutions are expensive, however, costing around £2,500 per case in 1996.

The Audit Commission report concluded that prosecution procedures were not only very expensive, but too long drawn out and, as a consequence, ineffective. The research it conducted calculated that, on average, a single prosecution involved 40 different forms being filled out, various reports on the educational and social welfare of the young person, and around four different appearances in court (Audit Commission, 1996). In England and Wales, decisions to prosecute are eventually taken by the Crown Prosecution Service, and not the police. The independent Procurator Fiscal plays this role in Scotland. The Audit Commission reported that, prior to 1996 in England and Wales, of cases in which a prosecution was being prepared, a quarter were either dropped or dismissed at an early stage. Most of these cases resulted in at least one appearance in court, and if proceeded with, a further three appearances were necessary, all adding to the delay and the expense. There was also an unclear division of responsibilities between the probation service and the social service 'youth justice' teams. Prior to 1998, patterns of responsibility were negotiated locally.

In practice youth justice services mainly dealt with 10 to 15-year-olds and those aged over 16 already known to them, whilst probation dealt with other 16-year-olds and most 17-year-olds.

Youth Courts replaced Juvenile Courts in October 1992. They are intended to be less severe, less formal, and to have more control over the publication of proceedings. Youth Courts have three magistrates, a clerk, a crown prosecutor, a defence lawyer (mainly from legal aid), an usher, representations from the youth justice service and/or probation and parents. Between hearings, young people are often put on remand in either local authority accommodation, secure accommodation, or in adult prisons (see below). Many are released on bail, although around one-third of these re-offend whilst on bail. Most young people plead guilty, though the proportion declined in the 1990s from 65 per cent in 1989 to 55 per cent by 1994. In some cases the pleas change at the last moment (often when they find that witnesses have turned up). Because of this, courts (like airlines) systematically overbook. The Audit Commission report that many cases collapse or are postponed because of absences or delays and that this is one reason for the huge cost of bringing young offenders to trial (Audit Commission, 1996).

In the mid 1990s and before the 1998 Crime and Disorder Act, outcomes of youth courts included:

- absolute or conditional discharge (28 per cent);
- supervision orders (12 per cent) (equivalent to probation for young offenders);
- fines (10 per cent) Fines had a maximum of £250 under the age of 14 and £1,000 for 14 to 17-year-olds;
- attendance centre order (9 per cent). These were available for sentences which would be imprisonment for adults. Attendance Centres must be within reasonable access to offenders. Attendance involves a maximum of 12 hours for under 14s, 24 hours for 14 to 16-year-olds and 36 hours for 16 to 17-year-olds;
- custody (6 per cent) For 15 to 21-year-olds this should be in a Young Offenders Institution (YOI) rather than an adult prison. Under the Criminal Justice and Public Order Act of 1994, since early 1995 young people may be given a Secure Training Order (for between six months to two years). Young 10 to 14-year-olds convicted of very serious crimes such that it would be inappropriate that they be sent to Young Offenders Institutions, may be sent to Secure Accommodation (usually in a local authority residential home);
- community service order (4 per cent);
- probation order (3 per cent); and
- other (2 per cent).

(Source of statistical breakdown: Crown Prosecution Service 1996 *Criminal Statistics 1994*)
(Quoted by the Audit Commission 1996)

The 1991 Criminal Justice Act also gave courts the permissive powers to fine parents or to bind them over for up to £1,000 for the future behaviour of their son or daughter. Such measures have consistently been opposed by pressure groups on the grounds that they punish parents, many of whom are unable, rather than unwilling, to do anything about the behaviour of their child. They also potentially undermine, rather than support, the parent-child relationship and may lead to even more family breakdown. In practice few parents have been penalised in this way. Indeed fines of young offenders themselves declined in the 1990s, with less than one in three ordered to pay any form of compensation.

The reform of juvenile justice from 1997 under New Labour

Before the 1997 election, New Labour set up a task force drawn from a variety of different agencies and different sectors which spent time devising an alternative strategy. This was outlined in the (relatively short) White Paper *No More Excuses: a new approach to tackling youth crime in England and Wales.* The main proposals were incorporated into two wide-ranging Acts, the 1998 Crime and Disorder Act and the 1999 Youth Justice and Criminal Evidence Act. Many of the provisions of the Acts came into force in April 2000.

The Bills and Acts are hugely complicated and far-reaching. The main strands, however, are:

- Tackling delays in processing young offenders. (The Home Office has produced a new target of reducing the time from arrest to sentence by a half and this is monitored by the Audit Commission and the Home Office). It has also introduced the 'fast tracking' of persistent offenders (those who have committed three or more offences in three years).
- Addressing offending behaviour more effectively. This includes a number of initiatives, including reparation orders and schemes, described below.
- Developing multi-agency working. This is to be achieved by a number of means, including making it the duty of local authorities to develop multi-agency anti-crime strategies, and addressing young offending through Youth Offending Panels and Youth Offending Teams (see below).

The 1998 and 1999 Acts created new institutions and orders and extended the responsibilities of the Youth Court. The new institutions include the following:

- The Youth Justice Board (YJB). This is a national agency for the supervision and funding of youth justice, including Youth Courts, Youth Offending Teams (YOTs) and Panels (see below) and Young Offenders Institutions (YOIs).
- Youth Offender Panels. These were set up by the 1999 Act. They deal with referrals from Youth Courts of young (first time) offenders (10 to 17) who are (or plead) guilty and include a member of the local YOT. They consider inquiries and propose a contract with a young person and their family, to address offending behaviour. This may include making an apology and/or reparation (see below), family counselling or drug rehabilitation.
- Youth Offending Teams. The Crime and Disorder Act made it a duty of local

authorities (including education and social services) to enter into a partnership with the police, probation officers and health workers. YOTs include representation from social services, probation, the police, from the health service and education. They work to an annual local youth justice plan agreed with national YJB.

Examples of new orders include:

- A new Final Warning Scheme. This includes police reprimands and warnings for 10 to 17-year-olds. This is dependent upon the evidence available, admission of guilt and the seriousness of the offence. The Final Warning is followed by immediate referral to a YOI and a rehabilitation programme.
- A Detention and Training Order. This is a single new order for 10 to 17-year-olds. It involves a period of detention in a YOI including education and/or training, followed by a period of community service (with further education and training). The intention is also to produce continuity of planning and supervision between YOIs and YOTs. A supervising officer (SW, PO or YOT) is appointed at the start of the order and expected to follow this through to the completion of the order.
- Parenting Orders. These are for parents of those convicted or subject to a child safety or anti-social behaviour order. They involve counselling or guidance, and a requirement to exercise control. The Youth Justice Board report that the pilots of parenting orders have been very successful with parents requesting more help.
- Permissive powers for LAs to issue Child Curfew Orders between 9pm and 6am for 90 days). Much to the disappointment of the Home Secretary, there has been only a low take-up of these powers.

The overall aim of these reforms was to try to ensure that the criminal justice system for young people was more integrated and more effective in making them confront their offending behaviour. The 1997 White Paper also proposed reforms to the Youth Courts so that they too were more active in engaging with young offenders rather than simply adjudicating guilt or innocence and dispensing punishment. It proposed that magistrates involved in Youth Courts should be trained about the importance of talking directly to young offenders, even when young people had legal representation. It also proposed changing the Magistrate Court rules to permit this and so allow magistrates to explore with the young person the reasons for their behaviour before reaching final decisions about a sentence. Changes in court lay-out were suggested with this aim in view.

Even tougher on crime? The impact of locking up children

Much of the policy agenda reviewed so far has been concerned with diverting young people from offending where the nature of the offence does not result in them receiving a custodial sentence. Yet, as we have seen, some serious offences, including violent offences, are becoming more prevalent, and Government has also begun to get tough on young people who are persistent offenders, with harsher sentences promised for them. Increasingly, Government has been encouraging sentencing along the lines promoted in the US of 'three strikes and you're out'; prison or custodial sentences for persistent offending. At the end of 1999, over ten thousand young people between the ages of 15 and 21 were in custody, with over two thousand aged between 15 and 17. There are nearly five hundred young women in custody including 83 under the age of 18 (Lyon *et al.*, 2000). There are no Young Offenders Institutions for young women, so, as NACRO has reported, young women under the age of 18 are incarcerated in adult women's prisons in contravention of the UN Convention on the Rights of the Child (NACRO, 1998).

The 1997 White Paper made it clear that the Government regarded custodial arrangements for young people to be unsatisfactory. Four main types exist:

- Secure Units.
- Secure Training Centres.
- Young Offenders Institutions (YOIs).
- Youth Treatment Centres (run by the Department of Health).

Secure Units were introduced in 1998 for 12 to 16-year-olds awaiting trial where courts regarded it as necessary for the protection of the public for them to be kept under lock and key. Prior to this, they would be received into the care of the local authority but whether this was in secure accommodation varied. A review in 1998 suggested that some children under the age of 16 were, at that time, being kept in YOIs including Feltham (Pitt, 1999). Secure Training Centres were introduced in 1997 and were designed for 12 to 14-year-olds who were persistent offenders. The vast majority of young people who are in custody are, however, in Young Offenders Institutions. Yet in 1998, the Youth Justice Task Force reported that many of these were too large, that bullying and abuse was widespread, and that the level of education and training given was often poor. A report on one of these indicated that over-crowding was such that 192 children were confined to 96 cells, each initially designed for a single adult (Pitts, 1999). Feltham YOI fell under the spotlight, yet again in October 2000, following the conviction of one inmate, described as 'an openly racist psychopath' for the murder of his Asian cellmate. Apart from accusations of widespread racism which followed this incident, attention was again drawn to endemic violence (5,000 prisoner on prison assaults), seven suicides within the past ten years. Reminders were also given of the findings of the Chief Inspector of Prisons in 1998, ('conditions and treatments . . . completely unacceptable') and complaints from psychologists working there of the 'basic brutality of banging up 15-year-olds' (including some described as 'acutely psychotic') for twenty three and a half hours a day (Kelso, 2000).

Youth Treatment Centres were designed to offer long term care for difficult and disturbed children who have been charged under section 53 of the 1933 Children and Young Persons Act of an offence of such gravity that it would incur a life-sentence for an adult. These Centres were extremely expensive and although some research suggests that positive outcomes were achieved for even the most disturbed young people (Bullock *et al.*, 1994), the last one finally closed in 2000.

Research on young men and women in custody has recently been conducted through a number of focus groups with young people serving custodial sentences (Lyon *et al.*, 2000). These examined young people's accounts of their lives before, and leading up to, custody; their experiences whilst inside; and their hopes, fears and plans for their future. Most blamed themselves as being responsible for their plight and believed their parents, especially their mothers, had tried their best to intervene to prevent their offending. This is particularly important given the introduction of parenting orders that appear to blame and penalise parents for the offences committed by their son or daughter. Despite accepting self-determination, however, it is also clear that young offenders in custody do come predominantly from difficult and deprived backgrounds, live in 'rough and nasty' areas where violence, crime and drug use is rife, and where unemployment and poverty are the norm. As we saw in chapter five, care leavers, especially children who had not had continuity of care, are highly over-represented in the prison population. Many young people in custody either couldn't or wouldn't go to school, with many of them reporting repeated exclusions from school. The research reports that only a small minority had remained in school up to minimum school leaving age and even fewer had gained any qualifications. A high proportion of those in custody were also involved in taking drugs prior to custody and many from an early age. They considered soft drug use as normal and part of a lifestyle witnessed amongst older groups – a lifestyle to which they aspired. Older friends within the communities in which they lived were also reported as influential in moving a substantial number of young people on to hard drug use; they witnessed older friends getting a bigger high and wanted to experience it for themselves. Hard drug use was also sometimes used to explain offending behaviour; they had to steal and rob in order to fund their habit.

The young people were, perhaps inevitably, critical of their experience of the criminal justice system, although some of their comments are revealing. Most perceived the police negatively, some accused them of violence and many thought them immune to any effective means of complaint. Others complained of racial abuse from them. The courts were seen as unprofessional and inconsistent, with magistrates, especially, regarded as not understanding their circumstances and often ignoring reports about them. One young man commented 'They're just normal people off the streets; you know what I mean . . . 18 months in prison from shopkeepers.' They were equally dismissive about probation officers and community service orders. All this suggests a fundamental alienation from a criminal justice system trying to influence their behaviour.

They were also critical of the custody regimes. They complained of bullying and racism, the humiliation of induction, and being given little constructive to do with their time. They asked that they should be treated with respect and given education and preparation for work when they leave. They called for prison rules and procedures to be clear and fair with efforts made to ensure that these are understood. They wanted the illegal use of drugs within prison to be tackled more effectively and called for improvements in health care and emotional support. They also thought more could be done to prepare them for release, and for better contacts with families and carers on the outside whilst they are in custody. Interestingly, many of their comments are also reported to be in line with the new Prison Service Order for dealing with under-18-year-olds and with many of the reforms being introduced in April 2000 (Lyon *et al.*, 2000).

The track record of youth custody in terms of preventing future offending is not good. Of young male offenders released from custody in 1995, 16 per cent were reconvicted within three months and 77 per cent were reconvicted within two years (NSO, 2000). Despite repeated calls for a much safer environment for vulnerable young people there were 15 suicides of young people in custody in 1998, five of these in YOIs (NACRO, 1999).

The known causes of crime and youth intervention projects

In discussing the causes of crime two main factors have been outlined: social background factors associated with the family, education, the community and peer groups, and cultural factors associated with the ways in which young people distance themselves from the harm their activity caused. Previous chapters of the book have described a number of initiatives that attempted to deal with educational disadvantage and disaffection. Utting has provided a useful review of intervention programmes that try to reduce youth crime, covering interventions in the family, in schools, in the community and through sport or leisure, often targeting very specific age groups (Utting, 1996). This will be further explored in the next chapter. Many of the more successful attempts to address youth crime do so in 'holistic' ways by combining support within school, with support for the family and in the community (Vulliamy and Webb, 2000); many involve multi-agency working. Because this has been a general theme in intervention projects across a number of different areas reviewed in this book, issues concerning multi-agency working will also be reviewed in the last two chapters.

There are thousands of youth projects nationwide which claim to be addressing youth crime. Many projects run by the youth service and voluntary sector organisations, including play and recreation projects during school holidays, are regarded as important 'displacement' activities. Housing managers are all too aware that, if no provision is made for young people, especially during holiday times, then they will bare the brunt of the consequence in terms of vandalism and complaints from residents (Coles *et al.*, 1998). A policy action team set up as part of the Social Exclusion Unit inquiry into poor neighbourhoods also emphasised the need for appropriate leisure facilities for young people (PAT 12, 2000). This, and the work of the Youth Service, will also be covered in the next chapter. Here we concentrate on intervention projects which are specifically directed at confronting offending behaviour. The first of these works exclusively with young people referred to it by other agencies because they are known to be at risk of offending. This is largely youth work based, although it differs from other youth work projects in specifically focusing on young offenders, or those at risk of offending.

SPACE: Positive alternatives to crime in Leeds

Space was a project run by Leeds City Council Department of Community Benefits and Rights and was based in East Leeds Family Learning Centre. It started in 1992 under the Home Office Urban Crime Fund but much of the funding of the project now comes from a Single Regeneration Budget (round 1) grant for seven years starting in 1995. It started with one manager and administrative support but has since expanded. When visited, there were 11 part-time and three full-time workers mainly working in area teams. Some had a more specialised function in working with particular groups or in particular settings. Most had a youth work background and many have formal youth work qualifications although some have been seconded from the Training Department. One of the part-time workers worked with Asian young people and another was concerned with progression and occupational and training guidance.

Mostly the project worked with naturally occurring groups within neighbourhoods which meant that different age groupings within a single neighbourhood could be involved. Referral was mainly from different agencies such as the police, social services, education or educational welfare, which referred particular individuals. There was a referral form to ensure that agencies only referred young people who were appropriate to the project's aims. These young people were allocated to groups according to age, gender, culture, neighbourhood or type of offending behaviour. There were some girl-only and gender-mixed groups although boys did predominate. All referrals must be through an agency and neither young people nor their parents could directly refer. Although involvement did depend upon parental consent no direct work was done with families. There was an emphasis on the project working with young people within their own neighbourhood in recognition of the importance of territoriality to young people.

The general aim of the project was to divert young people aged 10 to 18 involved in, or at risk of, offending. It did this by: creating an environment in which young people examined their attitudes and behaviour with regard to offending; providing alternative activities and encouraging participation in educational, social and leisure activities and employment. Those involved in the project were engaged in a number of 'purposeful activities' which could vary from time to time according to the interests of the group. However, despite some of this being consumer-led, all activity groups were expected to be 'challenging, confronting and educative'. 'Taking on' attitudes and behaviour with regards to offending was always on the agenda. Although some of the activities were intrinsically interesting or exciting (grass track car racing, for instance) they did also allow issues to do with vehicle-related offences, such as illegal driving, to be discussed. Some of the skills they gained in working with cars also became the means through which they could gain accredited training qualifications. The emphasis (about 70 per cent) was upon challenging criminal and related behaviour rather than activity based youth work.

The project did recognise a range of risk factors related to the likelihood of young people offending, such as truancy, school exclusion, family conflict and poor supervision. It also liased with other agencies dealing with these issues more directly, such as educational welfare, pupil referral services and social services working with families. The main work of the project, however, was on individual and peer group attitudes and behaviour. There was a concern with 'progression' and involvement in post-16 education and training and there was a guidance worker within the project to promote these links.

Multi-agency working was mainly carried out through networking with individual front-line workers. The project did report, quarterly, to a Steering Group dealing with Youth Crime and Community Safety through a Community Safety Partnership that included the directors of the main LA departments. There were also monthly meetings of workers within groups of LA divisions to which SPACE reports.

The project did collect information through an exit questionnaire and claimed that young people self-reported an improved attitude to offending and offending related behaviours and a reduction in their convictions and cautions. It also claimed to have helped young people maintain attendance at school, interest in sports, leisure and other youth work activities. The project was evaluated in 1995 by Leeds Metropolitan University Policy Research Unit.

The second project works with young people already known to the authorities as persistent offenders. As with SPACE, the aim is to confront the offending behaviour and divert young people from offending in the future. But this project targets more 'hard core' and persistent offending. It is more 'contractual', more wide-ranging in the interventions it makes, and exploratory of the social and familial background problems related to offending.

Barnardo's: Freagarrach Project

This project started in March 1995 and came about because of a concern of the Chief Constable of Central Scotland Police Force for the rise in juvenile crime. He got together with chief officers in education and social work and the Reporter's Administration for Children's Panel* in 1993 to develop a more strategic approach to try to tackle juvenile crime. Initially this was based on a hunch about the connection between crime and truancy from school. An initial pilot and research in the town of Denny in Falkirk suggested school exclusions was a more important factor but it also drew attention to persistent offenders and showed that 1.6 per cent of offenders were responsible for 20 per cent of juvenile offences. It was accepted that there was a need for agencies to work together and the chief officers formed a Young Offenders Strategy Group which still exists. They developed a proposal for a community based project to work with persistent young offenders which was approved by the Scottish Office. Barnardo's won the subsequent tender and the project started in March 1995 with five years funding.

It was thought that the project benefits from being in the voluntary sector because it is not associated with a fear of 'social workers'. Social workers were often thought of as a profession that take children away from inadequate families whereas Barnardo's workers were regarded by many parents as 'on their side'. The staff on the project had a mixed professional background, some social work trained and others trained in youth and community work. From the beginning it had been well funded, employing nine full-time workers who work with around twenty 12 to 16-year-olds at any one time. Over time, the group with whom the project works had increasingly been with young people in their mid-teens (15 and 16-year-olds) who were better able to respond to attempts made to make young people think and self-reflect upon their offending behaviour. The ethos of the project was to treat the client group with respect, and in a non-judgmental way. Its five main aims which determined the areas in which the project works were to:

- challenge offending behaviour;
- raise awareness of the impact of crime and offer opportunities for reparation;
- support educational involvement so as to maximise potential through education, training and employment;
- encourage and help parents and carers to provide appropriate levels of care and control; and
- encourage young people to make a constructive use of leisure pursuits.

The minimum length of time on the project was six months although the average was around ten months. Referral to the project was through social workers. Referral included the consent of the young person and family members who were also expected to cooperate and sign a contract to attend. The contract covered all five main areas of work, although assessment was an important first stage of work. The police gave the project a weekly update on all offences committed by juveniles in central Scotland. To meet the referral criteria young people needed to meet the definition of a persistent offender – having been charged with five separate incidents of offending within a 12 month period and as having committed an offence within two months of referral. The average number of offences of those involved had declined over the duration of the project but in 1999 the average was still 27. The predominant age group was 15 to 16-year-olds. Most offenders were young men, with the main crimes involved being property crime. Violent offenders have, however, also been referred. Many of the young people had had connections to the care system. A significant connection was also reported between offending and young people suffering loss and rejection, including the death of a parent or someone close to them. Often, what proved to be highly significant events in young people's lives were either not in official reports, or had been not investigated thoroughly. Sometimes this had involved allegations of child abuse. There was also often various degrees of violence in the backgrounds of those referred.

Much of the work done was based upon being positive about the strengths of both young people and their carers. Sometimes this involved young people's abilities in a leisure activity where achievements in school were not obvious. Each young person was attached to a key worker and usually stayed with that worker for their duration at the project. During the assessment period, the young person and a key worker tried to identify what problems needed to be addressed in the five main areas covered by the project. Reparation was often done through community work rather than with the victim, although the project did work with Victim Support. Some of the work done with them was through 'role-play' based around real cases. This helped emphasise that crime was rarely victimless and often involved severe trauma to victims. It was sometimes accepted that all offending may not cease, but involvement in crime, and the seriousness of the offences might be reduced.

The project involved a mixture of individual work (one young person and a key worker) and group work programmes. The latter were developed by staff to meet the perceived needs of a group of young people who were currently part of the project. In 1998–99 group work included work on drug and alcohol awareness, masculinity, as well as victim awareness and attitudes towards the police. Some of this involved the imaginative use of role-play (including court-based drama) and videos in which the tape was stopped so that discussion could take place about what was likely to happen next. They also ran a programme which involved a visit to a Young Offenders Institution (Glenochil). The programme was intended to de-glamorise crime and imprisonment so that young people could be made aware of the conditions, the loss of privacy and dignity as well as freedom. After the visit, young people also discussed what further offending might mean in terms of their future and the likely restriction of opportunities. A group of no more than four at a time, took part in the programme. It also involved group discussion with inmates who had been sent to a YOI for similar sorts of crimes.

Initially, work with families was part of a holistic approach to issues. Often families simply did not know what to do with a boy in his mid-teenage years who was too big to be physically chastised or stopped from going out and who may orchestrate family rows to precipitate leaving. The project offered help to parents on anger management and self-awareness so they could defuse conflict situations before they occurred. Examples included offering positive encouragement and support to young people who, so often, only experienced adults as agents of constraint and control. Parents were also encouraged to develop diversionary activity. They might politely ask for help, or show affection through a hug, a hand on a shoulder, or words of affection. Such positive action was rarely heard by young people. Parents were given role-play exercises so they could try out different types of response. Continuous work with parents was more pronounced when the project worked with a young age group. In 1999, when the average age was very close to 16, no Parents Support Group was operating, for the first time in the history of the project. Instances were also reported of parents simply leaving the parental home and leaving the young person to manage the tenancy. In Scotland, parents are not legally bound to maintain parental responsibility for children on reaching the age of 16 years as they are deemed adults by law. Those who had been 'accommodated' were similarly detached from all systems of support

Many of the young people taking part in the project had experienced difficulties with their education since primary school with many problems starting on the transition to high school. The majority of young people on the project were not in mainstream, full-time education with some of those getting only a few hours education per week. There was an education unit for those excluded from school in the same building as the project and this had places reserved for those placed with Freagarrach. Others were involved in Skill Seekers – post-16 training for which they received £50 per week. There was also an Apex scheme specifically offering pre-vocational and basic skills training for ex-offenders. Both these schemes were the only real way in which young people could legitimately obtain money. Many of the young people were described as bright and well able to work out the financial implications of post-16 choices. For a variety of reasons re-integration into mainstream education was not a viable option for those on the project. So education, though part of the problem, was not always able to play a significant part in any solution. Young people on the project largely had modest ambitions to work, have a house, a partner and a family. Yet there were few legitimate means through which they could finance such ambitions. A number of them were parents either at the time of being on the project or during their stay, and sex and relationships education was part of the work they did on the project. This was likely to increase in future years.

Encouraging the constructive use of leisure began with assessment, with some recreational activities (such as a pool table) located in the project building. The young people on the project were predominantly not involved in other, mainstream youth work activities. Many felt they would not be welcome amongst their non-offending peers. Key workers would often encourage the development of leisure activities. Community facilities are also hired for football. One group had formed a band that had performed in Stirling, the proceeds of which were donated to Victim Support. Some residential work was also arranged through Venture Scotland which often took place late in their involvement with the project.

The project was responsible to both Barnardo's and the Young Offenders Strategy Group to which it reported. The strategy group involved representation across three local authorities from the police, social work, education, Apex, Children's reporters and Barnardo's and met four times a year. SACRO also got the minutes of meetings. Community Education (youth work) was not involved.

The project also reported to the Scottish Executive which, together with the local authorities and Barnardo's, was the major funder of the project. The project was being independently evaluated for the Scottish Office by Professor David Smith. This is examining its long-term effect up to four years after taking part in the project. The project's own indicators of success involve outcomes such as attendance and re-offending as well as the number of referrals, assessments and completions. As well as these statistics the project also produces cameos of 'success stories' and the project leader emphasised the qualitative changes in young people's lives as a result of their involvement. Young people started the project unable to look staff in the eye, self-reflect or hold conversations. They also had low self esteem. The project helps their social skills and self confidence and trust of adults. But this is not measured, formally.

The core funding from the Scottish Office was secure only until March 2000 although it was expected that the three local authorities were committed to ensuring that it continues. A similar project working with 8 to 12-year-olds was being discussed. Total income for 1998–99 was over £335,000 and the project worked with 91 young people (including nine girls). In March 1999 Baroness Linkater contrasted the average cost of £330 per week of a young person being involved with Freagarrach which had a re-offending rate of less than 40 per cent with the average cost of Medway Secure Training Centre of £2,400 where re-conviction rates were 100 per cent.

New developments in 1999–2000 included an extension of the service to work with 16 to 18-year-olds and female offenders. The latter visit Cornton Vale Prison.

•Children's Panels in Scotland review evidence from the police concerning young offenders together with other relevant evidence from social services and schools. It also reviews evidence concerning children in need or at risk.

A number of projects visited whilst researching this book were already putting into practice a number of the guiding principles which lay behind the Crime and Disorder Act. One of these involved the use of reparation, requiring offenders to apologise and, if appropriate, try to make amends for their offence.

Thames Valley Police: Restorative Justice
The project started from discussions in the mid-1990s about the failure of the criminal justice system to really fundamentally impact upon re-offending or indeed anything for the victims of crime. A Criminal Justice Audit in Milton Keynes in 1994, undertaken by Sheffield University showed that of the annual cost of juvenile criminal justice (£16 million) only 1 per cent was spent on actually working with offenders and less than 1 per cent spent on work with victims. This was consistent with national findings published in 1996 by the Audit Commission. This coincided with the police wanting to conduct a radical review

of its approach to problem solving rather than continuing with past practices. There were also links to New South Wales police in Australia who were invited to discuss the work they were doing. As a result a pilot scheme was set up in Aylesbury in 1995.

The initial pilot was small scale but showed very significant decreases in re-offending. NSWP came back to the force in 1996 to give some training to those involved and TVP had developed its own training programme. The project started in earnest in 1997 under the quasi-independent Restorative Justice Consultancy. Of critical importance to the success of the project was the training of the facilitator and the preparation of all parties for the process. Amongst the defining principles of the Thames Valley Police Restorative Justice project were that it should:

- involve victims, their family, the community, offenders and their family;
- empower victims as active participants, giving them real choices;
- achieve mutual agreement through dialogue;
- work in partnership with other agencies;
- seek to reintegrate rather than stigmatise;
- require professionals to facilitate rather than prescribe solutions; and
- safeguard all involved in the process.

All young offenders taking part in the scheme had a choice as to whether the victim was present and where they were this was called the restorative conference. Where victims were not present this was called a restorative caution. All offenders were initially subject to an inquiry by a multi-agency panel supervised by the area liaison officer. Multi-agency panels operated in all police areas and were the pre-cursors of Youth Justice Panels in 2000. Those involved included representatives from education (mainly from educational welfare), youth justice, social services, the police and also included victim liaison officers in three of the police areas. These considered all the things that had happening in young offenders' lives, including background factors. The panel examined what the victim wanted to happen, the type of offence and, on the basis of this review, a decision was reached about whether they should go to court, or have a restorative conference or restorative caution. The whole process was overseen by the Consultancy, which was responsible for quality assurance and answerable to an Assistant Chief Constable.

To be eligible, young offenders must also have admitted the offence and be regarded as suitable for the cautionary process rather than other dispositions. This meant that offences did not include the more serious offences but were more likely to cover crimes such as theft, burglary, criminal damage and minor assaults. Male offenders outnumbered females by around three to one with the over-whelming majority of offenders being white with Pakistani young men (the largest non-white group) accounting for just over 3 per cent of all male offenders.

During 1998–99, there were 2,762 restorative cautions and 650 restorative conferences. Conferences required the consent of both the victim and the perpetrator. It was thought that the vast majority of victims welcomed the opportunity to take part.

The two main aims of the project were to reduce re-offending by getting young people to take responsibility for what they have done and give something back to the victim to repair the harm done by the offence. Proper preparation and research into the background to the offence was regarded as essential before the caution or conference takes place. For the most part, the schemes had been working with offences where a primary victim can be identified even where, in the case of shoplifting from a major firm, that victim may be someone responsible for the security of property rather than the direct owner of it. The preparation for the caution or conference was also important in identifying a range of significant adults to take part in the process.

The actual caution or conference was described as a highly structured process with the facilitator mainly ensuring that the structure is followed. At conferences, young offenders spoke first, giving them the opportunity to admit what they had done and to accept it as wrong. The victim then gave their response followed by the others also taking part. The offender was then afforded the opportunity to respond to this by suggesting how they might put things right. Other participants were then asked what they thought should happen. Conferences and cautions were not regarded as a 'soft' or 'easy' option to other forms of disposition. The young person often suggested reparation which was far in excess of what the victim wanted. The latter often merely wanted to hear a confession of guilt, to hear remorse 'from the heart' and to feel that the crime would not happen again. More than a thousand victims had received a written or verbal apology since the project began.

The process had been described as 're-integrative shaming' in that it showed disapproval of offending whilst avoiding stigmatisation and maintained a relationship of respect. The presence of parents was often thought to be very important in that admitting guilt was being done in front of someone who is highly significant to them. Sometimes other adults who were significant in the young person's life were also involved.

Evaluation

One of the key indicators of the success of projects such as this is re-offending rates. Both the police and the Oxford Centre for Criminological Research are monitoring this. Whilst it is still early in the life of the project to provide a definitive verdict, early results are promising with overall reported reductions in re-offending of a third or better in a 12 month period, and much higher reductions in some areas. These are long-term measures, however, and subject to fluctuation over time. Victims too reported that they gain from the experience in terms of reducing their continued fear of crime and feeling that the conference or caution finally brings an end to a traumatic experience. The independent evaluation also reports on how far participants feel satisfied with the process, whether they thought they had not been treated fairly and whether they had been properly prepared for the conferences. Around a half of these studied reported that they thought they had not been given a choice in the process and less than a fifth had asked for legal advice prior to taking part. However, nearly all those taking part did feel safe doing so, and many thought it helped to break down stereotypes.

The involvement of police officers in the project was also thought to have helped in the cultural change being required of the police service in the light of the 1998 Crime and Disorder Act. The project is now working in all TVP areas with first and second time offenders. However, it has now widened its scope beyond working with offenders and victims to work with other professional groups, with schools and in prisons and YOIs dealing with offenders prior to their release. TVP also runs a Crime Intervention Service which runs other intervention programmes. Taking part in restorative conferences and cautions can therefore link to other programmes and following reparation, the young person may be asked to take part in other crime prevention programmes. By no means all young offenders are good communicators and the process does sometimes identify communication skills which require further work after the conference or caution.

The project now has a strategic partnership with Nottinghamshire and Surrey police forces which are following the Thames Valley model in their forces.

Other projects were trying to keep young people out of custody by supporting offenders within the community before they came before the courts for sentencing.

Barnardo's, Nuneaton Albion Court Project

In many ways this project was two projects in one with both sharing the same management and support structures. One was called BRICS (Bail and Remand Intensive Care and Support) and the second was 'Key Moves' which was a leaving care scheme. Only the former will be described here. BRICS was developed in response to an initiative of government to develop provision for young offenders to develop alternatives to secure accommodation in 1994. The application from Warwickshire Social Services Department for government funding was not successful, but the proposal, developed in partnership with Barnardo's, was thought important enough by the SSD to continue with internal funding. This was not sufficient to justify a project in its own right, so the leaving care project was added to make it viable. (Barnardo's has criteria that distinguishes between 'projects' and 'schemes' with projects requiring at least four workers and a project leader).

Because of the dangers of 'stigma by association', the two projects have been kept separate. Over both strands of work, the project had four project workers, a project administrator and a project leader but also employed a number of sessional workers. Two project workers were involved in BRICs, one male and one female and both social work trained. Within BRICs, two forms of support were offered: a remand foster care with families; and a bail support scheme where extra support for young people was necessary if bail was to be given.

Remand foster care offered through BRICs was intended as an alternative to custody. Under the scheme, young people were placed with families rather than sent to a YOI or secure accommodation. Each placement cost around £500 per week compared with up to £3,000 per week for secure accommodation. The project had five families, mainly in the north of the county. The families were not 'employed' but they did receive payment of around £300 a week whether they had a young person placed with them or not. When they have a placement they received around an additional £20 per day. They also received four weeks holiday pay per year. The families must have one adult carer available 24 hours per day, although sessional respite relief was available for up to 20 hours per week to take the young person off their hands. All families were paid the same regardless of how difficult their placement proved to be. In the three years of its existence, it had had no trouble recruiting the families, had never had to advertise for them, and none had dropped out. There was a carers day once a month for training and support.

The bail support scheme operated for those on bail but lower down the tariff scale than offenders on the remand foster care scheme. These offenders still lived with their own families whilst on bail, but one of the conditions was that they must have extra support. This was given by 11 sessional workers employed by the project. These support workers were paid just over £8 per hour and some were on part-time contracts. They were not regarded as 'mentors' but people trained to work with young people on the project. Their remit was to work with the young offender although some also work with families. Often, as in the Freagarrach project, the 'real problem' was found to be something other than the 'presenting problem' – the young person's offence. The majority of those dealt with were either non-attenders at, or had been excluded from, school. The project had also recently linked into the county psychiatric services with someone coming into the project once every six weeks to give support on mental health problems. It also had connections with 'Double Take' described in chapter three.

Under the bail support scheme, 'creditable provision' was offered to around another six or seven young people at a time although the project had worked with around 40 young people in 1999, five of whom were girls and four from 'mixed heritage' families. The dominant age group had been 14 to 16-year-olds. Sessional workers tried to explore how young people see their own problems, their problematic behaviour, whether this involves crime or not. Attempts were also made to develop their skills, and good relationships had been developed with the education service to address issues concerning the re-integration of young people into some form of education. This had been aided by new patterns of working through the multi-agency Youth Offender Teams.

Being part of the voluntary sector was also seen as important in ensuring that urgent matters were dealt with promptly by statutory services. Often the extra time available to voluntary sector workers meant that suspicious events could be properly investigated and dealt with. Magistrates had initially been suspicious of some aspects of the scheme following the failure of a similar project run by another voluntary organisation. Initially the conditions of bail were proposed by managers who set unrealistic conditions for carers and young people. Barnardo's had resisted some of these (for instance about the time a young person had to return to their carer's home) and the reputation of the project was thought to have been enhanced as a result.

The project reported that 85 per cent had not re-offended whilst the young person had been on the project. However, once young people left the scheme, re-offending rates had been significantly higher. At the time of the visit the project had just begun to try and address this. It was also negotiating with the Youth Justice Board to explore the possibility of introducing reparation schemes working with young people after sentencing.

The final project was trying to work with young people who had already received a custodial sentence. The main concern of this project was to encourage young offenders to take a positive and serious attitude to potential routes back into mainstream careers involving training and work. The strategy adopted was to offer positive role models. These were used to try to encourage more positive thinking, action planning and training whilst the young person was in custody, and support following their release. The project involved the use of a form of 'mentoring' which, as we have seen, is also a method employed in working with other groups of disaffected young people.

Feltham: Trailblazers

This project started in September 1998. It was based on a recognition that careers guidance for young offenders was extremely limited but that having a positive employment goal may well be of importance in diverting offenders from an extended career in crime. The aim was to give offenders serving their sentence in Feltham Young Offenders Institution a 'mentor' in an occupational area in which the offender may be interested in working when released. The mentor was also a source of information, guidance and practical help with training whilst in Feltham and support on release. The project started in September 1998 with a budget of just over £100,000 for two years to cover the cost of project managers and the day-to-day running costs. It worked with young offenders age 16 to 21 who volunteered to take part in the programme. Although it was working with only 27 young men at the time of my visit in May 1999, it aimed to cover around 120 young offenders.

The 'mentors' were all adult volunteers who had had significant employment experience and were relatively experienced and established in their field. At the time of writing there were about 50 or so on the books. They attended a short training course at Feltham YOI and were given a comprehensive briefing pack as well as having continuing support from the project managers. Advice was received early in the development of the project from other mentoring projects working with 'young people at risk'. Mentors were expected to be in regular written correspondence with offenders, although early experience suggests that they also liked to meet the mentees in order to put a face to a name. All correspondence was scrutinised by the project managers whilst the offender was in custody, although the mentor was also expected to keep in contact for about a year after release. Matching was done according to occupational area and compatible personality. An attempt was being made to extend the range of occupational ambitions (often thought to be highly restricted for young offenders) and to engage them in 'action planning' and working towards the achievement of occupational goals.

The mentoring relationship and intervention was intended to be 'holistic' covering all aspects of the young person's life. It was also intended to be both confidential and non-judgmental. The prison's security imposed strict rules about what could and couldn't be sent to the offender whilst in custody and all mentors were 'police checked'.

As well as mentoring, which was central to the project, one-to-one work between the project managers and offenders was also seen as integral to developing positive and realistic thinking and planning. This one-to-one course lasted for ten to twelve hours over three or four weeks and covered a variety of topics. Examples included: planning, consequences; communication skills; career guidance; interview technique; budgeting; and information about alcohol, drugs, healthy eating and exercise.

The project was working with a group of young people where recidivism (being re-convicted within two years) could be expected by around three-quarters of offenders once they had been released. Not all young offenders could be expected to go straight into employment and training courses and work experience was also actively explored. It should be recognised that this project had much less intensive forms of support than was offered by others such as Youth at Risk and the Dalston Youth Project. However, these latter projects worked with young people on a face-to-face basis in the community where more issues would need to be addressed.

Trailblazers had to work within the prison regime with most of the mentoring done through the medium of letter writing. At the time of writing it is estimated that the eventual unit cost would be around £1,000 per offender and was, therefore, an extremely low cost intervention, relying as it does on free time and effort of volunteers. An external evaluation of the project was taking place late in 1999

> with the recidivism and employment or other constructive activity being the key indicators of success to be examined. The project was also thought to have had a positive impact on the 'culture' within Feltham.

Several things should be noted about the five projects outlined. Firstly, there was a huge difference in the costs involved, even though not all projects were willing to openly discuss the financing of the project. Secondly, and very much related to costs, there were also major differences in the degree to which projects relied on trained and qualified staff. There were also differences in the type of professional training given to those involved. The two Barnardo's projects relied upon professionally qualified social workers who also had other experience working with vulnerable groups. The combination of youth work experience and social work was regarded as one of the reasons for the success of the Freagarrach project. The Trailblazers mentoring project, however, relied mainly upon volunteers who received little, or no, training. This contrasts markedly with the mentoring of career leavers discussed in chapter five and serves to emphasise how the single concept 'mentoring', means very different things to different projects. Thirdly, the importance of being in the voluntary sector seemed of considerable importance in all the Barnardo's projects. This also enabled some distancing from other interventions identified with 'social work' – something that was seen by many vulnerable families as threatening. Being part of the voluntary sector also enabled staff to take a firm stand with statutory services in making demands for changing practices. Finally, it should be noted that the projects differed significantly in the type of young people they tried to engage. At one extreme, were young people recruited to SPACE who were only 'at risk' of offending. At the other, Trailblazers was working with those serving a custodial sentence. BRICs and Freagarrach were also working with either persistent or serious offenders, but making a concerted attempt to prevent them being consigned to custody.

Conclusions

This chapter has reviewed research and policy about young people involved in crime and criminal justice. As we have seen, not only are a significant proportion of young people involved in committing crime but the majority are also likely to be the victims of crime. Indeed those living in some communities are subjected to persistent assault and harassment which is likely to seriously impact upon other aspects of their lives. Too often young people are only regarded as the perpetrators of crime, with too little attention given to the impact crime has on young people as victims. When young people live in communities with high levels of crime and where they are constantly subjected to violent behaviour, bullying and harassment, they too can be seriously harmed and disadvantaged by such experiences.

In examining young offenders and the known causes of crime, the chapter has examined a number of risk factors including educational disaffection and under-achievement, family factors, and involvement with a peer group also involved in crime. We also pointed to a range of cultural factors through which young people distanced themselves from the seriousness of their offending and the damage it might cause to victims. In reviewing policy since the 1997 General Election attention has been given to more integrated local planning of crime reduction strategies. This now involves a number of different service providers through Youth Offending Panels and a number of different professions being brought together within Youth Offending Teams. The new orders brought in under the 1998 Crime and Disorder Act and the reform of the Youth Court are also clearly trying to remedy under-achievement in education and training. A more systematic attempt is also being made to make offenders confront their offending behaviour and the damage and distress this causes to victims and the communities in which they live. The chapter has also reviewed a number of intervention projects, some of which anticipated the new reforms instituted in 2000. Some of these claim to have an impressive track record in diverting people from further offending. Reparation and diversionary projects certainly seem to be more effective than custody in preventing further offending, especially when these take place early in a young person's criminal career. Those in custody, however, were more likely to be persistent or serious offenders. Whether the new Detention and Training orders will be any more successful in redirecting this group to more legitimate employment careers is too early to say.

Young people's involvement in crime has also been closely linked to other forms of disadvantage and disaffection. In areas associated with youth crime and criminal justice the Home Office has been taking the lead. However, in many other associated areas, the Social Exclusion Unit has been instrumental in trying to promote more joined up government and a more 'holistic approach' to youth policy generally. One of its reports, to be reviewed in chapter nine, also promises that this will now be fostered within local, as well as central, government. When joining-up government and promoting multi-agency work is being promoted by different parts of government, there is clearly a danger that policy yet again pulls in contradictory directions. For instance, it is possible to construe many of the policy developments promoted by the SEU to be part of the efforts of government to be tough on the causes of crime. Yet the Home Secretary and the Prime Minister still wish to bang the drum about being tough on crime itself and are increasingly tempted by rhetoric from the US along the lines of 'three strikes and you are out' – with incarceration and new Detention and Training Orders. Despite the failure of custody to divert young people from further offending we continue to build more institutions for locking up children and young people. And the one thing we should have learned is that, when custodial places are available, magistrates will fill them.

Chapter eight

Holism and joining up youth policies and practice at a local level

This book has been concerned to examine not only the youth policy agenda at a national level but youth intervention projects delivered locally. The next chapter will examine how national youth policy is attempting to be more 'joined up' and holistic. As we have seen in previous chapters, many local projects also claim to have a holistic perspective. Chapter one outlined ten key principles of a holistic approach. In this chapter these will be used as a template for an evaluation of the degree to which these are being realised through the projects covered in the chapters of the book. Additional projects will also be described.

The theory and practice of holistic approaches

Chapter one offered a critique of the youth transition model and outlined ten main principles for the development of a more holistic approach. These are repeated below.

Principles of a Holistic Perspective

1. Including childhood experiences.
2. Including the experiences of the 'young adult'.
   Taken together, these two principles emphasise the importance of integrating the youth transition model into a more developed 'life course perspective'.
3. Avoiding linear assumptions.
4. Avoiding normative assumptions.
5. Focusing on both sides of the careers equation – young people, and the opportunity structures afforded to them.
6. Examining both sides of the careers equation holistically.
7. Including young people as full participants in the process.
8. Realism – extending the three main transition strands to include the full range of factors impacting upon transitions.
9. Understanding patterns of difference.
10. Being inclusive of all groups, not merely focusing on those defined as vulnerable or at risk.

There are a number of ways in which the value of following these principles have been illustrated in the main policy areas covered in the chapters of this book. Its main focus has been on patterns of disadvantage which is why it is worth emphasising the importance of the tenth and final principle if we are to begin to chart an agenda for a more holistic approach to future research, policy and practice. Chapter two reviewed research, policy and practice on youth unemployment. This demonstrated that disadvantage and dis-involvement in the labour market are closely linked to earlier, and similar, patterns throughout childhood. Unless disadvantage and disaffection are adequately addressed within schools and, some would argue, prior to children reaching school age, then this becomes further compounded throughout the life-course. This illustrates the importance of early intervention. Sociologists have repeatedly emphasised the importance of social background, regarding youth transitions as a 'trajectory' in which the successes and failures are highly determined by class, gender, ethnicity and locality (Banks *et al.*, 1992; Roberts, 1993). The importance of these factors is recognised within the ninth principle of holism outlined above. However, there are dangers in this being overstated. Whilst not wanting to deny the influence of these factors, there are dangers in turning strong influences into inevitabilities. Many of the projects described in this book bear testimony to the fact that much can be done to militate against patterns of disadvantage and 'risk' factors associated with social and cultural background. Some young people living in deprived circumstances survive and thrive despite the odds. For instance, as discussed in chapter six, some young carers go on to have successful careers in higher education despite predominantly coming from poor, lone parent families and coping with the adversity of playing significant caring roles within the family. Some continue with their education after the age of 16 to try and make up the ground they had lost because of their caring role.

The discussion of young carers in chapter six also illustrates the powerful way in which health issues impact on youth transitions. As was pointed out in that chapter, ill-health, whether this is experienced by young people themselves or by other family members, can be crucially important. Yet health-related behaviours are rarely considered as key strands influencing transitions through education, training and employment, household formation or transitions to independent living. Whilst for decades academics have drawn attention to the social inequalities of health, comparatively little attention has been given to the way in which health is a factor mediating inequalities of opportunity in education, employment and patterns of leaving home. Mental health problems are also known to be widespread amongst the young. These are often related to family and social background, and are important factors producing forms of social exclusion, through educational under-achievement, family conflict and breakdown, running away from home and becoming homeless. Chapter six also pointed to the importance of drugs in a large minority of young people's lives. This, together with the link between some drug use and involvement in crime (discussed in chapter seven), emphasises the importance of the eighth principle in order to round out and develop the old youth transition model beyond the three main strands.

Chapter two documented the fact that a significant minority of young people complete the years of compulsory education without formal qualifications and become unemployed. It also reviewed the policy agenda for trying to re-integrate this minority into the world of work through, for instance, New Deal for the Young Unemployed (NDYP). Two features of the New Deal system are of significance here. Firstly, the Gateway stage of NDYP involves a holistic assessment of need over a period of up to four months. This involves the exploration, with a personal adviser, of the barriers to employment that lie beyond skill and training needs. NDYP recognised that the young unemployed, with their advisers, may have to address drug or alcohol dependency, debt problems, homelessness and housing issues, or other aspects of their lifestyle that make them not yet 'job-ready'. The Gateway system thus offers one practical example of a holistic approach being put into practice. When it is working at its best, young people are engaged as partners, assessing needs and seeking means through which these can be addressed. Sometimes this involves other agencies in trying to help them do so – principles four to seven. When NDYP was designed, the maximum period of time on Gateway was four months. In practice, this has been found to be too short for some young people and some have stayed on for longer in order for realistic stepping stones to be found for them (principle eight). By no means all starts on New Deal lead eventually to a 'successful outcome' if this is defined as securing a sustainable job in the open labour market. Some 'new dealers' drop out. Others become unemployed again at the end. Some do get work, only to become unemployed again within a few weeks of starting their job. Three related points are important here. First, we should question the evaluation of initiatives such as New Deal against single 'hard outcomes' measures such as sustainable employment. Perhaps given the explicit targets for New Deal of reducing unemployment this is sometimes understandable. But there are surely other 'welfare' outcomes for young people of their participation in NDYP, such as its impact upon their health, self-confidence and self-esteem, for instance. Secondly, if NDYP does have a wider 'welfare' impact, then it seems perverse to return young people to a further period of debilitating unemployment (as punishment?) before they qualify for another period on Gateway. Thirdly, as we have noted in several chapters of this book, the careers of vulnerable groups often involve long, complex and non-linear pathways – as summarised in principles two, three, four and eight. Accordingly, there is a need to take a longer term, as well as a holistic, perspective. Especially for some groups, and in some labour markets, sustainable open employment in the short-term may be an unrealistic target. Furthermore, an over-reliance on a single strand, 'hard outcome' assessment of 'success' runs the risk of only addressing problems associated with labour supply, when the underlying cause of unemployment may be labour demand – a failure to recognise the importance of principles five and six.

Similar points could also be made with regard to young people's domestic and housing careers outlined in chapters one and four. Particularly important for these transitions are that, for the majority of young people, these are often long and non-linear. A large minority of young people are dependent upon their parent(s) and continue to live at home well into their mid-20s. Domestic and housing transitions especially serve to emphasise the importance of principle two – seeing youth transitions within a longer life-course perspective. Much government policy, however, assumes family dependency, despite the fact that young people have no legal right to live at home after the age of 18 in England and Wales, and after the age of 16 in Scotland (Jones and Bell, 2000). Chapter four concentrated on the minority of young people who become a parent and/or leave home in their teenage years. Teenage pregnancy was shown to be correlated with many forms of disadvantage including performing badly, or being disaffected, at school, being in trouble with the police, and family related issues such as living in a poor neighbourhood and having a mother who had a child in her teens. Care leavers are also hugely over-represented amongst teenage parents. The policy agenda designed to reduce teenage pregnancy includes both preventative measures, including better sex and parenting education, and education, training and other supports for those who do become parents. This is to be welcomed and suggests that, in principle, a more holistic perspective is being adopted. It also takes a longer term view of the need to support young parents, rather than simply seeing early motherhood as effectively ending education, training and employment aspirations. Whether this policy perspective turns into actual and effective support is too early to tell. It should also be remembered that much of the support offered by the voluntary sector is dependent upon short-term, and often precarious, funding.

For those who leave home in their teenage years, unless this is to pursue courses of education and training which also offer intermediate housing support, appropriate housing provision is in short supply. Chapter four demonstrated that housing policy, together with the changing shape of the housing market, has exacerbated the problem of young people gaining access to appropriate accommodation. Homelessness was one of the first moral panic issues that gave recognition to the 'joined-up' nature of vulnerability. Foyers have made some attempt to try to address the 'no-home-and-no-job' syndrome. But, as discussed in chapter four, many of these are not really catering for the needs of homeless 16 and 17-year-olds. There remains a lack of provision for this age group and, in most parts of the country, suitable 'move-on' accommodation for those in hostels is also a problem. The young homeless may be provided with a bed but, outside of the voluntary sector, little is done to make any holistic assessment of their needs or to effect long-term planning for their housing needs. The breakdown of family support, often resulting in homelessness, remains a major cause of social exclusion amongst young people. Yet adequate, long-term housing provision does not yet seem to be part of the solution.

Those 'looked after' in public care, discussed in chapter five, figure prominently in all vulnerable groups discussed within this book. Most of the public scandals surrounding young people in care have been around issues concerning the abuse, including sexual abuse, of children and young people whilst they are in care. But what has been the real national scandal in the past is that those children and young people for whom the state stands *in loci parentis*, should be so readily abandoned at the age of 16. We have long known the consequences of the inadequate system of public care. It is associated with a shameful checklist of 'negative outcomes', such as the lack of qualifications, unemployment, teenage pregnancy, homelessness and imprisonment. To be sure, children and young people who do become 'looked after' have already suffered ('joined-up') constellations of disadvantage. But the very few studies which have compared the fortunes of those 'looked after' with other groups living in similar, deprived, circumstances seem to demonstrate that being brought up in care further exacerbates disadvantage, rather than compensates for it (Baldwin, 1998). One of the (albeit strangely muted) triumphs of youth policy since 1997 has been the willingness of the Government to confront the failure of the care system and, more especially, radically amend policy and provision for young people leaving care. Many of the proposals contained in the Care Leavers Bill are to be welcomed and are broadly in line with the principles involved in a more holistic approach. Especially important is the amendment to the Bill that will make it a duty of local authorities to assess and meet the needs of young people 'looked after' up to the age of 21 or until they complete their education, whichever is the longer. So too are the proposals for pathway plans and systems of continuous support through personal advisers.

The reforms surrounding youth crime and the youth system were outlined in chapter seven. These too indicate a broad commitment to developing a more holistic approach through better partnerships between the police and local authorities and through the work of Youth Offending Panels and Teams (YOPs and YOTs). Many of these now involve specialist workers dealing with drug-related issues. Young people's use of illegal drugs was examined in chapter six as part of a review of risk-taking behaviour. So called 'recreational drugs', especially cannabis, are widely used, and seen by many young people to be largely harmless and less likely to result in violent or anti-social behaviour than the use of legal drugs such as alcohol. As reported in chapter six, most young people have their own mental maps of what is harmful, and the use of heroin and other hard drugs is seen as an anathema. Drugs are part and parcel of a significant minority of young people's lives. Two other aspects of drug-related behaviours also need to be addressed if we are to understand routes into, and out of, serious offending. Firstly, the sale and distribution of drugs is a large industry and one in which GCSE results do not figure prominently as passports to lucrative careers. For some young people, dealing may be the best job they will ever get, and not one from which they will be enticed away and into the legitimate labour market by the offer of a National Traineeship or a place on New Deal. Secondly, the supply side of the drugs industry is increasingly enticing marginal young people into the use of hard drugs, less detectable by routine screening, and used in a way which is regarded by young people as unlikely to lead to addiction. Being involved in the drugs industry and sliding towards problematic hard drug use is also related to persistent offending and needs to be addressed by multi-disciplinary teams working with vulnerable groups. Yet, as was noted in chapter six, there remains some doubt about whether professional training and patterns of working are sufficiently well developed to adequately do this. This suggests that, whilst some of the youth policy development is informed by a holistic perspective, questions remain about whether the structures and the skills are in place to deliver this in an effective manner.

The final chapter will review the potential of some of the national initiatives being introduced by the New Labour Government to coordinate better youth policy and practice at a national level. This will include a discussion of the potential and problems that lie ahead for the Connexions Service. What the development of the service means for the future of the Youth Service in England, however, remains unclear. At the time of writing, it seems that Wales and Scotland will not follow England as seeing a brand new Connexions Service as the main instrument through which to deliver enhanced patterns of support for young people. Both countries will do something, but in Wales the mantra seems to be about 'extending entitlements' rather than inventing a new army of advisers. There also seems to be greater belief in the value of building on already established patterns of working within single-tier local authorities. There is more than semantics to the distinction between 'entitlement' and 'advice'. The former suggests a young people's rights agenda. The latter seems more connected to meeting needs – defined, identified and met by professionally qualified 'experts'. The two do not necessarily have to be dichotomous. But extending entitlements does suggest that young people will be active partners in choosing to access services rather than have their needs identified and remedied by professionals intervening in their lives. The implicit theme of 'voluntarism' within the emphasis on young people's rights and entitlements also sits more comfortably with the youth work agenda. Up and down the country youth workers have been instrumental in delivering a variety of different services and patterns of support for young people in ways which many would claim to have been holistic.

W(h)ither the Youth Service?

It may seem strange to have delayed any review of the Youth Service until the last but one chapter of this book. In September 1996, the United Kingdom Youthwork Alliance published *Agenda for a Generation* which proclaimed three major imperatives:

- building the capacity of young people through promoting their skills, self worth, creativity and enterprise;
- promoting social inclusion through supporting more disadvantaged young people, re-engaging them in learning and thereby enhancing their employability; and
- encouraging active citizenship and developing in young people an awareness of their rights and responsibilities to the wider community.

These are, of course, central to many of the themes addressed in the book. Youth work has, however, had a chequered history, has suffered from having only a flimsy statutory base, and has constantly been starved of stable and secure funding. (For an excellent and comprehensive history of the service see Bernard Davies' two volumes published in 1999). As Davies makes clear, one of the defining features of youth work has been its voluntary nature; young people must opt into it. Whilst many do, most do not. When the statutory Youth Service was last audited in England at the end of 1997, it was estimated that it weekly reached around 600,000 11 to 25-year-olds, 400,000 of whom were between 13 and 19-years-old, no more than 10 per cent of the age group. Davies concedes that, at best, all youth work reaches only around 30 per cent of the age groups and that this declined in the 1990s. Moreover, it has been less successful in reaching young women and members of minority ethnic groups.

Yet, as some of the examples given below demonstrate, the Youth Service has been impressively flexible in the way it delivers services, both in the statutory and voluntary sectors. It has been particularly imaginative in patterns of provision in rural areas (through the use of 'mobiles', for instance) (Fabes, 1999). Sometimes, from the outside, youth work might appear like low-cost leisure provision in an era when young people really crave the more glamorous venues and more exciting activities provided by the private sector. As we saw in chapter seven, persistent young offenders are either excluded or self-exclude from most Youth Service provision. Yet, as we also saw in the cameo of SPACE in that chapter, some youth work-based projects have specifically targeted young offenders. Youth work has been persistently misunderstood. Davies provides an excellent review of many of its dilemmas. The ministerial conferences held on its future and purpose in the late 1980s and early 1990s only served to confuse things further. For instance, how could a service reaching so few hope effectively to 'redress all forms of inequality'?

Yet the Youth Service has many workers with the skills and capacities that it is hugely important to harness if the new youth policy agenda is to be adequately addressed. Below we provide three, very contrasting, cameos of youth work activity.

Youth Café: Fort William

This youth café was one of the first established in the highlands of Scotland and has been in existence for five years. It was set up largely with funding provided by the Rank Foundation. It also had support and encouragement from the local Community Council. The café is in the main street of the town and has two floors; a cellar disco and ground floor café. It also provides a social centre and informal drop-in centre for 12 to 25-year-olds in the area. The café has three games machines, a juke box and pool table. It is open five evenings a week (everyday except Mondays and Wednesdays) and is normally open until 10.30 at night, and later at weekends if there is an event, such as a disco. There are also some local youth clubs supported by Community Education, although these largely cater for the younger age group.

The café does have a code of conduct attempting to ensure that it is an environment free of alcohol, drugs and violent or threatening behaviour. Users violating this can be suspended or banned. The café has a management committee made up of local residents, three young people and a non-voting representative from Community Education. There is also a members' committee made up of eight members. It is staffed by one full-time project manager, a second full-time 'volunteer' worker (funded by Rank's GAP programme) and other part-time sessional workers or volunteers who help out at busy times. On busy nights around 80 members may be present and even during the week a regular handful of eight to ten can be expected to use the premises.

It is not intended to be a one-stop shop offering information and advice. It does offer a summer programme of activities for young people and has a mini-bus to facilitate visits and activities out of Fort William. Its staff also gain valuable

---

experience in running the café and training in supporting them to do so. But the café is essentially a social centre for young people to meet.

The youth café idea is now being promoted by The Prince's Trust which aims to help promote similar ventures in other areas of the Highlands and Islands, – safe, secure, alcohol free environments' for young people to meet. The Prince's Trust intends to provide: training and support to management committees; volunteers and staff; an exchange of good practice and networking; financial 'seed corn' funding for new projects; and to involve young people in developing the projects. There is still, however some tension in the funding of such projects between initial capital and continuous revenue funding. Rank's five year support for the Fort William Youth Café is coming to an end and it must now seek alternative core funding support.

The café does have links to other local groups including Lochaber Crime Prevention Panel, Drug and Alcohol Forum, Citizens' Advice, Sports Council and Action on Disability. The disco is accessible through a chair lift.

Perhaps the youth café cameo might reinforce the image of youth work as leisure provision. Yet, the next two projects help to correct this. The first is well established and one of the success stories in supporting young people in a deprived area of Glasgow. The complexity of the second project was just beginning to emerge when visited in 1999. But it did involve a joining up of services for young people within local government through a partnership with the voluntary sector.

Castlemilk (Glasgow)

Castlemilk Detached Youth Work Project has been in existence since 1989. The bulk of its initial funding was through the Urban Programme, although at the time of the visit much of its funding was through Glasgow City Council. One full-time worker was funded by the Tudor Trust. This was a voluntary sector project and had charitable status. Its voluntary sector status meant that it had seven years of funding, whereas local authorities' funding for such work is less likely to be secured over such a long time. It had always had a relatively large staff – five full-time, and one part-time worker. It also had a number of sessional workers working between 12 and 15 hours per week.

Like many other detached youth work projects, it aimed to 'build trusting relationships with young people . . . on their territory . . . on the streets, up closes, in the bookies, at the shops, wherever they are'. Castlemilk, like many other areas of social housing, is situated on the edge of the city and has experienced widespread problems of educational disadvantage and disaffection, very high levels of unemployment (double the Glasgow average), and high concentrations of lone parent families. Until recently, it had very poor locally based provision in terms of shops, banks, or community centres. There was little space where people could congregate, meet, or receive information, help, advice and support. Since October

1994 the major exception to this has been the Castlemilk Youth Complex, an impressive facility built at the cost of £1.3m with funds from the Scottish Office and the former Strathclyde Regional Council.

The estate has changed considerably during the existence of both the detached youth project and the new Youth Complex, with many millions of pounds spent on its physical regeneration. However, several tower blocks still dominate the skyline. As elsewhere, these have proved to be associated with many of the intractable problems of the estate.

The Youth Complex was said to have grown out of the work of the detached youth work team on the estate. The detached project at the beginning was called the Youth Forum Project, one of a series of youth development teams within Glasgow. There was general recognition at the time that there were a number of acute problems on the estate concerning drug misuse, crime, unemployment and homelessness, gang rivalries and violence. It was also thought that young people were not accessing mainstream services. Young people's experience of adults was often very negative. Detached youth work was one means through which the disadvantaged, disaffected and disinvolved could be re-engaged. Detached youth work also acted as a conduit between the disengaged and the council and helped to identify need.

One of the projects undertaken as part of the old Youth Forum was to conduct questionnaire surveys of young people asking them to identify their own needs and gaps in services meeting need. One of the perennial problems of this 'expressed wants' approach to identifying need is that young people will demand the unobtainable – an international swimming pool; a purpose-built youth centre with recording facilities for bands; a theatre; a suite of computers; regular cheap discos; a bar with free booze; drugs and ice cream!? Castlemilk is the strange case of where, aided and abetted by detached youth workers, young people not only researched and drew up a wish-list of 'the unobtainable', but they eventually got what they asked for – except for the bar, free booze, drugs and ice cream. Following the survey work, DYWs organised conferences which attracted 150 people, to try to help articulate their demands. The eventual result was the successful application for Urban Programme money, albeit with a budget trimmed from £4.5 million to £1.5 million.

A second area in which this project can claim success is in helping young people confront issues involved in the running of supported accommodation in 'scatter-flats'. This was 'independent' accommodation for young people in a number of single bedroomed flats. Tenants also had housing support workers. Young people had their own keys (young people can legally be tenants in their own right at the age of 16 in Scotland). Support workers also had keys. Young people complained to DYWs that support workers frequently let themselves into their flats without their permission and whilst they were not there, often leaving behind notes and instructions about being tidier. The DYW team was able to assist tenants in ensuring that support workers respected a young person's right to privacy.

The detached youth work on Castlemilk was organised in five teams. Four were based in different areas within Castlemilk. The fifth was dedicated to work with young women. Each of the full-time team members operated with part-time and sessional workers. They met with young people three evenings per week. At the time of the visit, they were about to experiment with weekend shifts. Much of the current work had focused on a 'Fair Play' football league between the areas. Some of this was based on football competitions – all young people in Castlemilk were described as obsessed with football. Many identified with the Celtic-Rangers rivalry that also mapped on to 'territories' within Castlemilk. The football competitions were supplemented by others with a more 'developmental youth work' agenda. These took the form of education and quizzes in areas such as health education, young people's rights, territoriality, violence and drugs. Scores on questionnaire quizzes counted as 'goals for' in the Fair Play league. The women, described as just as football-obsessed as the young men, were involved in the quizzes and also supported the football teams. They also said they wanted to play football themselves, and this was something the project said it would address.

Sometimes, even the most well-organised and imaginative of youth work projects can either fail or go wrong – sometimes in spectacular fashion. Castlemilk DYWP was no exception. Two weeks before the visit, a friendly Fair Play football competition with over 200 spectators had erupted into violence. Amongst the spectators was a small group of older young people who were highly competitive, territorial, loyal – and fighting-drunk. In the heat of the conflict, banter, support and name calling erupted into serious and dangerous violent behaviour. One supporter drew a long knife from his tracksuit and was intent upon using it on the opposition. At times like these, a sympathetic and supportive partnership with the police can prove very useful, and in this case a tragic resolution to the competition was avoided. Following the incident consideration was given to changing the names of its teams to ones that provoke less obvious territorial loyalties.

Existing as it has for more than ten years, the project had been involved in several inter-agency partnerships. This took the form of The Youth Services Group. It involved representation from the Detached Project, the Youth Complex, Community Education, and the Castlemilk Economic Development Agency (CEDA). This latter organisation had been targeting 16 to 18-year-olds who were unemployed, with some success. The partnership had been developing a coordinated youth strategy which was focusing on issues of youth housing, young people's health (including mental health) and youth (un)employment. Noticeably absent from the partnership was representation from the city housing department, social services, local secondary schools and education. However, some housing issues were being addressed through work with Scottish Homes and the housing associations present on the estate. There was also a separate Children's Services Planning Group with social services and education as the main partners. This too was set to address issues round young people's health.

Detached youth work was also important in helping to identify issues and problems in a more informed way than front-line intervention services. Drug (mis)use was one such area. In Glasgow, as elsewhere, the received wisdom used to be that there was a wide, bipolar spectrum of drug use, from widespread use of marihuana at one end, to a small hard core of heroin users at the other. At the time of the visit, detached workers were signaling that this spectrum was narrowing and that these boundaries were being blurred, especially by poly-drug users. For instance, young people using ecstasy and speed for raves and clubbing, had also become associated with the smoking of heroin to 'come down'. This was not perceived by them as dabbling dangerously with addictive drugs, but youth workers were very concerned.

The project is also part of Young People's Voice, at which representatives of local young people meet to identify, discuss and promote young people's interests.

The detached project produces an annual report and monthly reports to Glasgow City Council through the management group. Workers collect and provide both qualitative and quantitative information on the numbers of young people with whom they are working and the sorts of issues which form the basis of their work. These are, however, largely 'through-put' rather than 'outcomes' measures. However, indirectly there are 'more objective' signs of success. Youth unemployment in Castlemilk is now more in line with the average across all Glasgow.

In Scotland as a whole, there is a National Development Project, funded by the Scottish Office and evaluated by Cartmel et al. in phase one, and the YMCA in phase two (Cartmel et al., 1997). Because young people on estates such as Castlemilk tend to stay in the same area throughout their life course, a long-term evaluation, using a life-course perspective, would be quite feasible.

The Castlemilk project may be thought to be highly unusual. But throughout Britain, there are similar sorts of projects. For instance, The Guardian newspaper and the think tank, Institute for Public Policy Research (IPPR) held a Public Involvement Award in 2000. The winners, Cambridge Youth Participation Scheme, employed similar techniques to those used in Castlemilk to identity young people's needs (Dean, 2000). Initially, using surveys and seminars they identified concern about drugs, alcohol and crime as the major worry, together with the lack of things for young people to do in Cambridge. Together with local councillors and managers from leisure services they then identified 32 proposals for change. Many of these were concerned with enhanced leisure provision for young people, a cyber-café and a free summer party. But, as happened on Castlemilk, often such provision can be extended to meeting the needs of the most disadvantaged and excluded.

The third youth work project was suggested by the Wales Youth Agency as an example of a well-run youth information service. As it turned out, it was much more than that.

Wrexham Youth Information Shop

This service was offered in a newly renovated building in the centre of the town by the Youth Service. The base was open from 1–4.30 pm four days a week. At the time of the visit, it was staffed by only two paid workers and some volunteers. Its main focus was in giving information and advice but there was also a limited amount of counselling on an appointment basis. The centre gave access to a wide range of leaflets, many of which were produced by the Wales Youth Agency. There was also access to some community databases – again supported by the Wales Youth Agency. Four main things were thought to make information shops work. The first of these is having an easily accessible location. The second is the quality of service provided which then becomes known to young people by word of mouth. The third is having a good network to other agencies through which they can refer young people and know both the quality and the limits of what is being offered. The fourth element concerns marketing and in this project this was admitted to be still in its early stages. Its target was to deal with four and a half thousand enquiries a year and with full-time opening it would expect around six thousand enquiries.

At the time of the visit, enquiries fell into a number of broad categories including housing, family relationships, benefits and education and training. The most significant amount of time was being spent on housing issues – between 25 and 35 per cent of enquiries. These also turned into case work which accounted for around three-quarters of the workers' time. Housing was often a 'presenting problem' and young people were encouraged to 'bump into' other important aspects of information and advice on, for instance, support for teenage parents, ante-natal care and nutrition and benefits. This service was intended to be 'young-people-friendly' and seen as a generic service that could support young people and provide an indirect means of accessing statutory services. In this sense, what was offered was not just information, but support, counselling, 'advice' and advocacy. The age range mainly covered young people in their late teens, although it was open to all young people over the age of 13.

The shop was increasingly becoming a gateway to other services located in the same building. A Youth Access Initiative (YAI) also operated from the centre. This was the equivalent to what in England is called New Start which was reviewed in chapter three. Part of this was funded by the Welsh Office and catered for around 30 disaffected young people between the ages of 14 and 17 who were likely to leave school with no, or few, qualifications. Significant groups within this were young traveller children. Through the Youth Service, YAI offered a mentoring scheme from trained mentors over a 12 month period. It also offered support for 18 young people going through a Pupil Referral Unit, offering them alternative

---

curricula activities and programmes leading to Youth Achievement Awards.

The base also offered a lunch-time 'drop-in' support service for around a dozen young drug users between 1–2.30pm, often dealing with people referred from a detached youth work project also being run by the Youth Service. The Youth Service called it the 'Day Services Project' although young people refer to it as 'The Power Project'. There was a café at the back of the building which operated at lunch-time and offered basic food. Young people could also get a shower in the building – particularly important to young people who were sleeping rough. Washing machines were also due to be provided when the project was visited. Membership of the group was largely 'self-defining' and increasingly it catered for young people either injecting heroin or on methadone. They were largely trying to manage their own 'detox'. The main age group was 18 to 23-year-olds. Workshops were offered in the afternoon, including a popular acupuncture clinic for young drug users. Some young people were reported to be reluctant to access college-based student support services as they thought that divulging information might impact upon their academic careers within the college.

There were reported to be close links between the shop and other services, including Careers Plus, the local TEC, probation services, the police and the Health Authority and Trust, all of which had different boundaries. There were plans to increase services in the mental health field that would provide access to the community psychiatric team and a health visitor offering sexual health advice from the centre. Problems did exist with unfilled posts, particularly in the community psychiatric team. There was also a new, purpose-built Foyer in Wrexham run by a housing association and part of the Foyer Federation. Some information services were also offered through the Foyer. There were also contacts with voluntary sector projects, such as Shelter, and an active Children's Rights organisation. Together with Children's Rights, the Youth Service also was coordinating consultations with young people and it had a joint responsibility for developing a Youth Forum.

The local council has a Strategic Planning Group for Young People. One of the issues it tried to address was the mismatch between the number of street homeless young people and the number of council owned properties that were boarded up. One of the ideas considered was some form of supported tenancies for young people. There was also no emergency accommodation for young women apart from a women's refuge and no local accommodation for teenage mothers. Drug users and young mothers were being referred to other areas, often isolating them from systems of support and leading to delays in their benefits. The planning group identified a need to offer better housing support for young people as a priority.

> **Barnardo's**
> **Compass Project**
> The project was further developed in 1999–2000 during which Barnardo's took over the management. The Information Shop continues to offer generic information and advice services and the Power Project continues to offer services for young people involved in drug and substance abuse. The main elements that have been added are a range of services for meeting young people's housing needs and a leaving care service. Under Barnardo's, the project manager (with a background in youth work) is supported by an administrator. The Supported Accommodation Service has a staff of five, including a half time volunteer coordinator to support a 'Night Stop' scheme similar to that described in chapter four. This will provide emergency accommodation in the home of a volunteer for up to four nights, during which time the housing and social services department will be expected to arrange more permanent accommodation. A housing advice worker also runs a Bond Guarantee Scheme and offers some debt counselling. The project also plans to have a half-time 'street worker' working with young women at risk of being drawn into prostitution and sexual exploitation, and social services plans to second a member of staff who is a trained psychiatric nurse as well as a trained social worker.
>
> Out of a Youth Service initiative, therefore, a multi-disciplinary team was being assembled to cover a very wide range of issues.
>
> The building, which was leased from the Temperance Society, was also used for other purposes. A Welsh language playgroup used it in the mornings, there was a Sure Start project, a youth club operated in the evening and several voluntary sector organisations used it for meetings.

The Wrexham and Castlemilk projects serve to remind us of the ways in which youth work can be strategically important in identifying wants, needs and rights and in helping secure the entitlements of young people to have their basic needs and rights met.

The role of the voluntary sector in joining up youth policy and practice

In the course of researching this book a number of other projects were examined which claimed to be implementing a 'holistic' approach. Some of these have been covered in previous chapters. The NCH project in Kings Lynn (described in chapter five), for instance, grew from being a support scheme for care leavers into a project offering a whole range of services for young people from a single base. This and the projects described below offer different examples of the part played by the voluntary sector in helping to join up services for young people at a local level. However, there are major differences between projects in the ways in which needs are identified and met.

Barnardo's

The Base, Whitley Bay

The Base is a centre for young people between the ages of 15 and 25. Initially set up in 1987 by Barnardo's and supported by funding from the EEC anti-poverty programme, its activities and services have continued to be focused on issues related to poverty, unemployment, homelessness and social exclusion. Since 1987 it has received further funding from, amongst others, North Tyneside Health Care Trust, the Mental Health Foundation and North Tyneside Council. Overall its annual budget is over £200,000.

From its inception, the objectives of the project were to develop services in a holistic way based upon a voluntary relationship and in a welcoming environment. The services it has developed were regarded as appropriate to the needs of unemployed young people and in accordance with an agenda developed with young people. In developing a profile of services and activities it had responded to both young people's expressions of need and to national and local funding opportunities. The success of The Base was due, in part, to the range of activities and services offered in a 'one-stop-shop', its 'word-of-mouth' reputation in the region and perhaps its location away from, but adjacent to, inner city Newcastle and its tough peripheral estates. The project also valued its voluntary sector status as this had enabled it to maintain its commitment to a holistic approach and not be simply driven by short-term specific funding initiatives. Its current activities included:

- a café where young people can get a cheap meal from 9–5 Mondays to Fridays;
- cheap laundry facilities;
- help and advice on homelessness, housing, benefits and employment;
- advice, counselling and support on personal problems including health, sexual health and substance misuse;
- a support group for young people with mental health problems – the 'Reach Out' group;
- support for young people who have been 'looked after' in liaison with other agencies;
- help with young offenders;
- support for young parents using a High/Scope approach and including a creche;
- support in child protection work;
- a range of activity sessions covering creative arts, photography and computers and an outdoor activity programme; and
- promoting participation and citizenship;

The Base had four full-time project workers as well as a cook, secretary and domestic and sessional workers. It also worked in partnership with other projects and agencies. Annually it dealt with over 400 young people and tried to keep in contact with them. It collected some data on young people who used the centre, their background, and how they learnt about it. It was less equipped to evaluate the outcome of the contacts except through vignettes and case studies. It also did not seem to reach members of the (albeit relatively small) minority ethnic communities.

The Base and other projects described in this book are often instrumental in encouraging local authorities to review their own structures and practices. Utting reports that some local authorities have used the opportunities provided by becoming a single-tier authority to rationalise services (Utting, 1998a). He reports that Milton Keynes, for instance, combined education, social services for children, leisure and community services, museums and libraries under a single Learning and Development Directorate. Poole also gave directors of services mixed portfolios and moved them around every two years to try and encourage better knowledge and communication between departments. Another way in which integration is being encouraged within local authorities is through the Communities that Care (CtC) programme.

Communities that Care (UK) is an intervention programme which was devised and developed in the United States, initially as a drugs prevention programme. In the US, it was piloted in the states of Washington and Oregon and is now running in over 300 locations. Although CtC (UK) is now a company with charitable status, it has received core funding and support from the Joseph Rowntree Foundation which has invested more than a £1 million in its development in the UK. Its claim is that it 'produces a comprehensive package of training, technical assistance and practical support'. Initially it set up three 'demonstration projects' although, at the time of writing, several more projects are being developed, with more than 20 likely to be established nationwide by the time it becomes self-funding in June 2001. Projects seek to work with communities of around the size of three local authority wards. Although working to an organisational and methodological template designed by CtC, each project is developed and implemented through local partnerships involving local authorities, organisations and agencies. The aims of CtC are slightly wider than 'youth' policy and interventions *per se*. It aims to provide 'a long-term programme for building safer neighbourhoods where children and young people are valued, respected and encouraged to achieve their potential' (CtC, 1997).

CtC seeks to build from research about the nature of the problems it is seeking to address, promoting intervention projects which have a 'proven' ability to be effective. It claims this involves a 'holistic' approach to adolescent problem behaviours and accepts that multiple problems require multiple solutions. There are four broad phases to the development of the CtC projects: community involvement; a risk and resources audit; action planning and implementation; and evaluation (Utting, 1998b). Community involvement requires the development of a partnership involving local authority and community leaders, other agencies such as the police, schools, the Youth Service and residents. Without a commitment from all these groups, key policy-makers and stakeholders, it is recognised that the investment would not be worthwhile and the project would not be supported. Key partners are arranged in the form of a three tier management structure involving a Key Leader Group concerned with strategy, a Community Management Board, and Area Coordination Teams concerned with implementation. Each project is also expected to appoint a coordinator responsible for day-to-day administration and implementation.

The methodological template for the project is based upon an understanding of 17 'known' 'problem behaviours' and 'risk factors' associated with school failure, youth crime, drug abuse and teenage pregnancy. These cluster around four institutional zones: the family; the school; the community; and individual peer networks. The 17 risk factors identified by CtC are listed in the box below.

Communities that Care (UK)
Adolescent problem behaviours and associated risks

a) Family
1. Poor parental supervision and discipline
2. Family conflict
3. Family history of problem behaviour
4. Parental involvement/attitudes condoning problem behaviour
5. Low income and poor housing

a) School
1. Low achievement beginning in primary school
2. Aggressive behaviour, including bullying
3. Lack of commitment, including truancy
4. School disorganisation

a) Community
1. Disadvantaged neighbourhoods
2. Community disorganisation and neglect
3. Availability of drugs
4. High turnover and lack of neighbourhood attachment

a) Individuals, friends and peers
1. Alienation and lack of social commitment
2. Attitudes that condone problem behaviour
3. Early involvement in problem behaviour
4. Friends involved in problem behaviour

At first sight, this list might seem unsurprising. It might also be thought to be highly prescriptive (and possibly restrictive). Where, for instance, are special needs issues, emotional and behaviour problems, or dyslexia also known to relate to problem behaviour at school, and involvement in crime? The claim of CtC is that the 17 risk factors it identifies are based upon a systematic review of 30 years of research in the UK, US and other Western countries (Farrington, 1996; Utting *et al.*, 1993). Much of the quoted evidence, whilst powerful, is, however, largely quantitative. Many of the authoritative studies were also carried out under conditions and at a time, fundamentally different to those existing now. Given the widespread use of recreational drugs, questions must also be asked about what level of use is significant in relation to 'problem behaviours'. Is having friends who smoke cannabis of the same order of magnitude as having parents who are addicted to heroin? The initial impression is that CtC employs a remarkably 'deductive', 'positivistic' and 'normative' approach to problem identification and problem solving. It suggests that social science is supremely confident that it knows the causes of problem behaviours and poor outcomes during youth transitions. This might be a very questionable assumption. A second major worry about the model is that it seems to identify young people's problems as mainly located at only one side of the 'careers equation'. In other words the problems, and therefore the solutions, are clustered around young people, their family, friends and communities, rather than the opportunity structures available or inadequacies in service delivery.

The apparent 'top-down' appearance of the methodology is misleading however. The second stage of the CtC programme involves a systematic needs and resources 'audit' through which risks are identified and prioritised through community surveys. This stage is anticipated to take at least six months, although, in practice, some of the pilot projects have had difficulties with the data and analysis and have taken much longer. Many have identified issues to do with the early years of education, broadly in line with the first principle of holistic approaches to youth identified in this book.

The third phase of CtC involves identifying from a menu of 'promising approaches' those that seem best suited to tackling the priority problems identified in the risk audit. The projects are intended to enhance 'protective factors' which might act as a buffer against risk for those living in adverse circumstances. Two things about the list are worth noting. Firstly, many of the programmes listed are thought to be influential across more than one of the main institutional zones. (For convenience of presentation in the box below, the projects have not been sub-divided according to the 17 problem areas.) Secondly, the CtC manual divides the projects between three different grades of confidence and quality assurance. First are projects for which guidance and exemplars are available and, according to CtC, there is some confidence in their effectiveness as they have been piloted extensively and are subject to evaluation within the UK. The second ranked projects are ones for which there is guidance and a network of support, but where the evaluation of effectiveness has not been carried out within the UK in a way which CtC regards as conclusive. The third rank of projects are those, which may be extensively used and for which networks and exemplars exist, but for which CtC regards there to be no conclusive evaluation of their effectiveness.

Communities that Care (UK) Promising Approaches:
A menu of intervention programmes

a) Family

Prenatal services
Family support using home visitors
Parenting information and support
Family literacy
Pre-school education
After-school clubs*
Housing management initiatives**

b) School

Pre-school education
Family literacy
Reading schemes
Reasoning and social skills education
Organisational changes within school
After-school clubs*
Mentoring*
Preventing truancy and exclusion**
Youth employment with education*
Further education for disaffected youth**
Youth work**

c) Community

Organisational change within schools
After-school clubs*
Community mobilisation*
Community policing*
Youth employment with education**
Housing management initiatives**
Youth work**
Peer-led community programmes**

d) Individuals, friends, peers

Parenting information and support
Reasoning and social skills education
Organisational change within schools
After-school clubs*
Mentoring*
Preventing truancy and school exclusion**

Further education for disaffected youth**
Youth employment with education**
Youth work**
Peer-led community programmes**

* indicates evaluation has taken place but not within the UK
** indicates practice guidance only – no real evaluation.

In the light of the projects outlined in this book, the listing and ranking of projects may also be thought to be controversial. Mentoring gets one star, because it is deemed to have been positively evaluated elsewhere. Youth work gets two stars; any evaluation of its impact is not deemed to stand up to CtC standards. This certainly raises questions about what the criteria are for success and the nature of 'evidence' used to evaluate interventions. The Connexions Service, the SEU and the DfEE and the adjudicators of Comprehensive Spending Review may all be a little concerned to note that Personal Advisers are not even on the radar screen.

Participation and young people's rights

In trying to develop a perspective on youth and social policy some five years ago, one central theme this author promoted was the notion of 'citizenship' and a distinctive set of young people's rights (Coles, 1995). An appendix to that book outlined a catalogue of rights based partly upon the UN Convention of the Rights of the Child, and partly on the Regulations and Guidance issued following the 1989 Children Act. These rights were grouped around four main headings: entitlements – the right to know or have something; protection rights – the right to be protected from exploitation and abuse; representational rights – the right to be involved in decision making; and enabling rights – the rights to adequate resources through which all rights can be translated into real opportunities. Without wishing to return to all of these here, one issue which is of considerable importance is the way in which young people can be consulted and involved in the design, management and evaluation of youth welfare systems. For there is little doubt that the involvement of young people is part of a holistic identification of problems and that full-hearted involvement is also more likely to make interventions succeed. The main questions concern who should be involved, how are they to be best chosen or selected, through what forums (or mechanisms of representation) are they most likely to be listened to, and how can we ensure that young people's voices are heard, understood and accorded proper respect. The active involvement of young people is central to ensuring that all other young people's rights can be ensured. Even protective rights become merely paper charters full of empty promises unless young people believe that their complaints will be listened to, believed, investigated and remedied.

Forms of 'participation' are sometimes conceptualised as a ladder; from the manipulation of young people's opinion (the bottom) through to involving them in initiating and setting the agenda and in all stages of decision-making (at the top) (Landsdown, 1995). Various forms of 'participation' have been described in the pages of this book, from the involvement of young people in ministerial task groups reforming the care system, through to choosing the name of a project being run in school or in the community. Some structures of participation are known to be more effective than others. Adult-dominated formal meetings, in, for instance, estate and community regeneration, are known not to work (Hastings and Fitzpatrick, 1998). Yet children and young people form a large minority of residents and deserve to have their views heard and respected. Other alternative means, involving listening through intermediaries such as detached youth workers and by consultation through surveys, and seminars (as described earlier in this chapter) are sometimes more effective (Coles *et al.*, 1998). Other means involve the development of youth forums and youth parliaments. The Carnegie Young People Initiative has commissioned research to map the various means through which young people are involved in decision making throughout the UK. One of the major worries that remains is that formal democratic means of involving young people is often restricted to the voices of young people who are privileged and articulate, and excludes the voices of the most vulnerable and disadvantaged.

We are repeatedly told that most young people have low levels of interest in politics, find the subject boring and are cynical about politicians (NCSR, 2000). Yet when given the opportunity to do so, many make an intelligent and constructive contribution in shaping services with their own, and other young people's, welfare in mind. This book is about politics and the ways in which a new agenda for change is being developed for young people. Many, but by no means all, the intervention projects that have been described have developed means of listening to what young people want and determining what they need. Being listened to and heard is as much a right and entitlement for young people as being properly looked after. The final chapter examines how the New Labour Government has set about this task and some of the possibilities and problems which lie ahead for youth policy and practice for the future.

Chapter nine

Holism and joining up youth policies in national government: Prospects and problems for the new agenda

Within much youth research literature, accepting the wisdom of adopting a 'holistic perspective' is commonplace. This final chapter examines how holistic approaches to youth policy have been developed in national government. First, it examines the influence of the Social Exclusion Unit in developing youth policy. Secondly, it describes and evaluates proposals for embedding within government better and more coordinated means of addressing youth issues in the future. Thirdly, it returns to a discussion about the potential of the Connexions Service and a national network of Personal Advisers. Finally, it reviews some of the problems to be faced by these new structures and services and what these mean for the new agenda for youth policy in the future.

National youth policy and the work of the Social Exclusion Unit

The Social Exclusion Unit was set up shortly after the 1997 General Election and, at the time of writing, has produced five reports. The detail of these has been reviewed in previous chapters. Three of the five SEU reports are exclusively about young people and youth policy. Of the other two, significant attention was given to young people. In this sense it is tempting to argue that the Social Exclusion Unit has been the Ministry for Youth some of us have long advocated (Coleman and Warren-Adamson, 1992; Coles, 1995). Despite welcoming the work of the SEU in developing and coordinating youth policy, it is also important to evaluate its distinctive style of working and ask questions about what might take over this role when, inevitably, its gaze and focus move elsewhere. It should be recognised that the SEU has a remit for England only and many of its recommendations are being followed through only in England.

In undertaking this review it is perhaps important at the outset to recognise something about its remit, size, resources and responsibilities, before turning to an analysis of its style of working. The SEU addresses topics chosen by the Prime Minister. It has only a small staff and it has neither a large budget nor executive powers or responsibilities. But it does, however, have power and influence and a mission to transform the business of government. It has done this in two main ways: through providing summaries of what research can tell us about problem areas that span across government departments; and by developing new ways in which these problems can be addressed in the future. As far as youth policy is concerned, however, it has also produced an important and more long lasting legacy – by proposing new structures within central government through which youth policies can be produced and coordinated in the future. Because it has been so influential in producing this, it is worth reviewing its key characteristics in using research and developing policy.

The first characteristic of the work of the SEU is in fulfilling the drive within government to base policy upon a systematic review of social science evidence. On a more negative note, however, as was illustrated in chapter two, some forms of 'evidence' seem to be preferred to others and 'hard' statistical evidence is clearly preferred to qualitative studies. This may be all well and good where the quality of evidence is widely accepted as reliable. But on topic areas that are new, or poorly researched, the SEU clearly has had problems and has been less than open and frank in admitting this. Chapter two illustrated that, in trying to identify the size and characteristics of that group of young people who were not in education, employment or training between the ages of 16 and 18, over-reliance on Youth Cohort Survey data made that picture very distorted and unreliable. It may have been the best evidence available, but it was deeply flawed. Despite this, rather than admit that we still have only a partial understanding of the characteristics of the group, the SEU report proceeded to present an apparently authoritative analysis of the issues and a radical policy agenda for change.

Secondly, the SEU has the topics it investigates chosen by the Prime Minister. Government departments are expected to respond immediately to its demands for evidence, no matter what their own internal priorities. Because it has a direct line of command from the Prime Minister it has been able to make demands of other departments and produce reports and policy recommendations in double-quick time. So far, the SEU has worked with a very tight timetable – reviewing and summarising evidence and producing a policy agenda for change in the space of six to nine months. Yet, there is little scope within such a timetable for new research to be commissioned and carried out, even though, on occasions, this might have seemed vitally important. Collecting new evidence is often a long and expensive business, especially where this involves using large-scale surveys and studying young people over time. At least three government departments sponsor such surveys and a new longitudinal study of young people has been under active consideration within DfEE. Yet it seems little attention is being given to how better and more collaborative research might be undertaken jointly by government departments, or to how this might be better used to address policy initiatives which are intended to be 'joined-up'. Departmentalism in commissioning research continues to be the order of the day.

A third characteristic of the work of the SEU has been its concentration on highlighting the 'joined-up' nature of social problems. What was striking in the biographical material included in the *Bridging the Gap* report, for instance, was that it did provide powerful illustrations through individual case studies of the complex dynamics through which social exclusion occurs. It might be hoped that this may be instrumental in convincing government that crucial evidence does not always have to take the form of statistics, tables based on large data sets or nationally representative samples. Yet the qualitative study quoted in *Bridging the Gap* was based upon only 25 in-depth interviews conducted by a market research firm (DfEE, 2000). Despite the SEU, government sponsored research that explores the 'joined-up-ness' of youth problems is still very rare.

Promoting 'joined-up' solutions is a fourth defining feature of the work of the SEU. The *Bridging the Gap* report even included its first 'joke' – a map of institutional funding and responsibilities for young people – a truly laughably complex web of muddle and confusion. In reviewing the aims of the SEU when it was initially set up, Polly Toynbee described it as a unit for banging departmental heads together and, with reservations, that is what it has tried to do (Toynbee, 1997). The Policy Action Teams (PATs) set up following the SEU report on poor neighbourhoods and overseen by the SEU itself, are certainly a concerted attempt to promote better coordination of policy development across government departments where responsibilities are shared (SEU, 1998c). Other 'action plans' following SEU reports have, similarly, required the coordination of policy across departments and a closer integration of national and local initiatives. Wedded as it is to 'third way' politics, the SEU has also promoted the involvement of the private and voluntary sectors in policy development and delivery. Indeed, as we saw in the last chapter especially, the voluntary sector is often instrumental in forcing more 'joined-up' thinking within local authorities. 'Third way' solutions also sometimes mean setting templates for the principles through which initiatives should be developed, whilst allowing variation in the ways in which this takes place according to particular local strengths or conditions (Benington and Donnison, 1999). The two SEU reports published in 1999 promote this by suggesting local initiatives in their appendices. These are intended to be examples of 'promising approaches', 'best practice' and 'what works', many of which are voluntary sector led projects. Yet, the viability of these projects needs to be treated with caution in that many are subject to short-term funding, discontinuities of staffing, and little genuinely independent evaluation.

A fifth characteristic of the work of the SEU has been the increasing use of geographical mapping techniques to identify spatial concentrations of the problems it identifies. In the report on teenage pregnancy, for instance, it examined the relationship of spatial concentrations of under-18 conceptions to indices of local deprivation as well as examining links within national data sets between pregnancy rates and a range of risk factors. This focus on local clusters of disadvantage clearly also has congruence with the development of 'action zones' and 'pilots' through which scarce funding is targeted at those areas thought to be in most need and policy initiatives tested before they are rolled out nationally. But again such an approach needs to be treated with caution. Local authorities have been quite adept at what the Americans call 'boon-doggle funding' – re-packaging and re-labelling the things which they do already (or are about to do even without extra funding) within the language and criteria demanded by the funders (Websters, 2000). Many 'action zones' may be zones in which little new is being done, other than producing funding applications with multiple signatures.

Sixth, the SEU has been instrumental in setting bold targets: reducing truancy and school exclusion rates by a third by 2002; reducing rough sleeping by two-thirds by 2002; halving the rates of conceptions among under-18s by 2010. In striving to achieve these, the SEU has also confronted some long standing and intractable institutional issues in youth policy, including the ineffectiveness of some of the statutory services in targeting vulnerable young people. Targets can, however, become hostages to fortune without clear mechanisms through which they can be achieved. Many organisations and institutions are well known for being able to massage the figures, in, for instance, simply not recording crime, or in encouraging 'voluntary' school exclusion.

Its seventh characteristic is being prepared to slay a few limping and ineffective sacred cows. For instance, as we saw in chapter two, educational disaffection and disadvantage increased in the 1990s, despite educational welfare, the Careers Service and the Youth Service. The SEU's response has been to propose/support the development of the new Youth Support Service (Connexions) to be discussed later in the chapter. It has proposed the development of better systems of coordination and planning in post-16 provision. It has long been known that there are different funding regimes and use of outcome targets for providers of education and training for 16 to 18-year-olds (Pierce and Hillman, 1998). The DfEE (with a little cajoling from the SEU?) decided to confront this, making schools, colleges and training providers more accountable to the communities they serve, and more cooperative in area planning through Learning and Skills Councils (LSCs). TECs and the FEFC are to be abolished, although whether many of the same staff will be recruited into the new structures is still unknown. As we saw in chapter two, the SEU has also been instrumental in trying to address the financial problems young people from poor backgrounds face. Higher rates of participation in education and training are being promoted through Education Maintenance Allowances and the 'Youth Card'. Yet notably, the SEU did not recommend the re-instatement of benefit entitlements for 16 and 17-year-olds, long campaigned for by many pressure groups, although it did call for an examination of a discretionary 'youth allowance' (COYPSS, 1999).

The SEU's eighth defining feature has been the use of its authority at the heart of government to jostle and police departments into deadlines and targets they might otherwise have been reluctant to accept. Here, one must raise questions about whether its main 'hits' are based upon a prime ministerial perception of departmental intransigence. More than one department has a track record of dragging its feet. Why, one might ask, are many of its initiatives 'joining-up' only the DfEE and the DETR to other departments? Why have other, equally obvious, departments, such as the Department of Health and the Home Office been given more of a free rein in sorting out their own patch? The track record of the Department of Health in its responsibility for those 'looked after' or the Home Office in presiding over the inefficiencies in youth justice could equally have led to investigations by the SEU. The Home Office and the new Drugs Prevention Advisory Service (DPAS) have been producing their own radical agenda on youth crime and drug misuse. As we saw in chapter seven, the known correlates of youth crime and drug use are far-reaching and often critical elements involved in other 'joined-up' problems. Yet policy on crime and drugs has been developed outside of the scrutiny of the SEU. Promoting and coordinating policy on youth crime and criminal justice has been made the responsibility of the Youth Justice Board. But this runs the risk of providing 'joined-up solutions' at odds with those developed under the watchful eyes of the SEU.

One of the main criticisms of the work of the SEU is, therefore, not to what it has attempted to do, but to what it has not done. For, whilst it has been promoting 'joined-up' government, other parts of government have been attempting to do the same, sometimes strangely out of tune with the proposals emanating from the SEU. As discussed in chapter two, some of the reforms for those 'looked after' in residential and foster care are strangely at odds with those devised for the young homeless and those not in the care system but living in similarly disadvantaged circumstances. Whereas the voluntary sector has been busy combining services for care leavers with other groups who share the same sort of needs, the DfEE and the DOH (presumably with the collusion of the SEU?) have been designing different systems of support with different entitlements. Some of this suggests that the SEU 'could have done better' as a surrogate Ministry of Youth, although it would be churlish not to welcome many of its achievements in developing youth policy. But the SEU's remit is much broader than the development youth policy and we must now look to other structures within government to take on the role it has so far played.

The Ministry for Youth argument

Chapter one pointed out that the UK was alone in Europe in having no minister or Ministry for Youth, no parliamentary committee and no body responsible for cross-governmental policy on young people. When first writing a draft of this chapter, the outcome of the deliberations of one crucial Policy Action Team (PAT) was unknown. PAT 12 was set up following the third SEU inquiry into poor neighbourhoods and was specifically asked to address policy for young people. In writing a first draft of this chapter, and before the publication of this report, four main options for the better coordination of youth policy within government were considered. These are reviewed in order to examine whether the proposals contained within the PAT 12 report, and due to be implemented towards the end of 2000, will overcome the problems inherent in the four options discussed below. The four options were:

- Giving someone within the Cabinet Office responsibility for promoting youth policy and coordinating the efforts of departments in research, policy development and implementation – The *Minister* for Youth option.
- Creating a *Ministry* of Youth – this would involve a whole new department, rather than merely adding to the responsibilities of one cabinet minister.
- Creating a cross-ministerial 'working group' on young people.
- Appointing an Ombudsman for Children and Young People.

The reasons for considering someone within the Cabinet taking responsibility for youth issues was to try to build on the power and influence the SEU has had on separate government departments and to seek to develop better coordination between them. However, there are doubts about whether merely being a member of the Cabinet will carry such authority. Were the Minister outside of the Cabinet this risk would be even greater. The appointment of a Minister for Women, for instance, is not regarded by many to have been a huge success.

The second option of claiming a whole new ministry runs the risk of other competing client groups making similar claims. Why should there not also be a ministry for children, for older people, for minority ethnic groups, or for the family, for instance? Furthermore, the arguments for a separate ministry have sometimes been unclear about precisely what functions it should have. Should it have executive authority and a budget? What power would it have in making competitive bids for money from the Treasury compared with some of the other large departments? Or might it merely take on an advisory role? Much of the argument for a Ministry has centred upon the need for a 'coordination' role – co-ordinating research, policy development and being responsible for producing a 'youth audit' to monitor the effect on young people of the policies of government departments on such matters as education, crime, social security and health, etc. The experience of the impact of the SEU does illustrate that, with appropriate authority and gravitas at the centre of government, a Ministry or Unit can be hugely influential without having either executive power or a large budget.

The third option was to try to obtain many of these same outcomes through a cross-ministerial team of ministers, all of whom would be given a specific youth policy brief. The danger of this option was that cross-ministerial groups may founder under the pressures of in-fighting for departmental responsibility and the defence of perceived departmental territory and budgets.

The fourth alternative was to create something autonomous or independent of government, perhaps in the form of a Children's and Young People's Ombudsman, with a watchdog role. But this option runs the risk of it being required to act in only a responsive and auditing role rather than proactively developing policies (perhaps in partnership with other departments) – the sort of role developed so successfully by the SEU. It is interesting to note that in the government-commissioned review of the work of the SEU, the suggestion is that, to maximise its effectiveness, the Unit needs more power and resources rather than less (Cabinet Office, 1999). This would allow it to follow through its recommendations and ensure that these were delivered by relevant government departments. Failure to chase and harry departments into the full implementation of its recommendations has potentially restricted the role of the SEU to one of being a mere 'think-tank' (Cabinet Office, 1999). There are clearly dangers that the new structures could be reduced to this role.

PAT 12 and beyond

PAT 12 was set up to review policy for young people and has now reported. It made 24 separate recommendations. Many make reference to the need to establish youth policy priorities within the Comprehensive Spending Reviews by the summer of 2000 and this does appear to have taken place. Many of the proposals are about ways through which new Youth Inclusion Objectives can be established, reviewed and progressed but they also include strategies to coordinate better government youth policy both within national and local government. The report provides six youth inclusion objectives, although it is stressed that these are illustrative only, in that Ministers will need to meet and agree them. These include putting young people at the centre of policies that affect them, and organising services around their needs (and rights?), including the consultation with, and the involvement of, young people in policy development. This is in line with the seventh principle of holism described in chapters one and eight. This is a strong theme throughout the recommendations, suggesting that young people's rights are not completely off the agenda. Also prominent is a commitment to ending child poverty, supporting vulnerable young people, especially at vulnerable times in their lives, and supporting those who face discrimination because of ethnic origin, disability or gender.

The proposals of PAT 12, accepted by government, include the creation of the following:

- A Cross-departmental Committee on Children and Young People.
- A designated Champion Minister for Youth.
- A new Unit on Children and Young People.
- A 'Children's Fund' to help resource programmes that will help to meet the social inclusion objectives.

The Chancellor, Gordon Brown, has agreed to chair the Cross-departmental Committee with David Blunkett (Secretary of State for Education and Employment) as vice chair. This should ensure sufficient weight and gravitas is given to this committee and, hopefully, ensure that its policies are properly resourced. Having a Cross-departmental Committee also potentially means several ministers becoming ministers with a 'youth policy' brief. Paul Boateng, who is a minister at the Home Office, is designated as the new Minister for Youth, although, at the time of writing the remit and responsibilities of this role are unknown. The new Cross-departmental Committee is also to be supported by a new Children and Youth Unit. This is intended to be a common resource for departments, bringing together staff from other departments and from outside Whitehall. This Unit will have the task of assembling knowledge on: young people; policies and services for them; good practice; risk and prevention; the implications of gender, ethnic origin and disability; and likely future trends. In addition, it will be responsible for producing an annual report on the Government's strategy for youth inclusion which is also to be debated in parliament. The Unit may also be given a role in promoting better coordination at a local level and good practice in the identification of need, especially in the case of vulnerable and special needs groups. This Unit will, however, be located within the DfEE.

Several anxieties remain about how these new structures will work out in practice. The first of these relates to the joint responsibility of the Committee and Unit for young people and children. On the one hand, this does recognise what this book has argued for in terms of a holistic approach to youth – encompassing a wider age group than merely the years covered by youth transitions. It therefore meets the first principle of 'holistic' thinking certainly. On the other hand, there are doubts about whether it will encompass principle two, a concern with young adults. At the time of writing there is uncertainty about whether the responsibilities of the Unit and Committee will extend beyond the age of 19, the upper age for the responsibilities of the Connexions Service. If this is to be the case this would severely limit the ability to address the full range of youth issues.

There are also dangers that the interests of children will overshadow youth issues so that the 'and young people' responsibilities of the Committee and Unit may, in time, become marginalised. This anxiety is compounded by the location of the Unit within the DfEE. This raises questions about whether the Unit will be able to sustain its independence and a holistic vision, rather than have its agenda and paramount concerns driven by the department in which it is located. A similar worry remains about how the new Children's Fund is to be administered and what issues will be prioritised. Ominous is the exclusion of 'young people' from the title. Certainly the press releases surrounding the Comprehensive Spending Review seemed to link the fund with an expansion of Sure Start, even though its brief suggests a much broader social exclusion agenda. The Connexions Strategy is also expected to attract significantly more funds than that previously allocated to the Careers Service. Yet the worry remains that issues surrounding children, education and disadvantage will dominate government thinking and spending rather than more holistically conceived youth matters. The appointment of a Home Office Minister as Minister for Youth might be thought to answer some of the worries that the DfEE, as hosts, will unduly influence the Unit. But, as we have already commented, issues concerning youth crime and criminal justice have, in effect, been delegated to the Youth Justice Board. Elsewhere within government DPAS has its own agenda for delivering a more coherent drugs strategy, the Department of Health redesigning support for young people leaving care and the Pregnancy Unit coordinating policy on teenage pregnancy.

In reviewing the work and influence of the SEU, whilst broadly welcoming its attempt to join up youth policy across government departments, it was pointed out that there were grave dangers of a lack of coordination of SEU led initiatives with others. Other departments and units were also attempting to join up policy and practice. It might be argued that, in evaluating the role of the SEU in developing more coherent and holistic youth policy, I did so unfairly, by ascribing it a role it was never really given. Yet surely that was the role taken on by PAT 12 in which the SEU took the lead. Its recommendations were explicitly designed to:

- provide 'new objectives and structures, to improve the way government develops and implements policy for young people;
- shift the balance of effort and resources over time into preventing young people

from encountering the worst problems rather than fire-fighting when they are already in deep trouble;
- improve individual services for young people; and
- design policies around the needs and priorities of young people – not least through involving them in thinking about policies and services and their delivery.'
(PAT 12, 2000)

It is far too early to see whether its proposals for new structures within central government will achieve such bold ambitions. In doing so, the stern tests to be faced, include curbing departmentalism with government, overcoming professional intransigence amongst those expected to deliver the new initiatives, and developing new attitudes towards, and ways of working with, young people as partners in their own futures.

One of the perennial problems faced by national policy-makers is how to link the ambitions of central government with what is delivered at a local level. There are hints that the new Children and Young People's Unit will be expected to use its influence to encourage more joined-up thinking within local government. How it will do so remains unclear. Surely if national government needed first a Social Exclusion Unit and then new structures to ensure youth policy coordination, local authorities need something similar. Many local authorities are often as fiercely departmentally-driven as central government. In the late 1990s, a number of policy initiatives were developed to address this problem, and to do so in ways that embraced a holistic perspective. These initiatives changed the lexicon of public policy. First central government sought greater control over patterns of service delivery by local authorities by requiring a plethora of plans for everything – hence Children's Service Plans, Early Years Development Plans, Education Development Plans, Behaviour Support Plans, Crime and Disorder Plans and Youth Justice Plans (Utting, 1999). Simultaneous with this, we added to the responsibilities of professional workers by adding 'plus' to everything – hence housing-plus, schools-plus, mentoring-plus (Ball, 1998; PAT 11, 2000). Action zones too fell thick and fast, although often not quite in the same place through a peculiar mismatch in the administrative areas they covered (PAT, 12). At the beginning of a new century, it is the turn of young people's 'advisers'. The various chapters of this book have detailed any number of different advisers either already in place, or being planned, to help better manage youth transitions. NDYP Gateway offers Personal Advisers to help the young unemployed prepare themselves for New Deal Options. Care leavers will now be offered named Personal Advisers to develop 'Pathway Plans'. The new 'big idea' for the delivery of youth policy on the ground, it seems, is through an army of personal advisers.

Making Connexions work

The proposals of PAT 12 made clear that the Connexions Service of Personal Advisers will lie at the heart of policy delivery in England. Connexions will not, however, be the only service for young people and PAT 12 also makes clear that much more could, and should, be done to develop awareness of issues faced by young people across a range of other professional groups. So, for instance, the DfEE, DOH and HO are asked to publish proposals on initial and in-service training of social workers, teachers, youth workers, the police, probation and health professionals. The DSS and DfEE are also asked to review the information to be made available to young people and the role and training of personal advisers on benefits and allowances and the administration and staff training. They are also asked to commission research on how the JSA Severe Hardships Payment is administered. Here too, there are considerable training needs if a more holistic approach to youth policy is to be effectively delivered at a local level.

From 2001, under the Connexions strategy, all young people in England between the ages of 13 and 19 will be offered Personal Advisers. The main structures and targets for the new service were outlined in chapter two. This indicated that the service would operate through a variety of different agencies as well as schools and colleges; through YOTs (with offenders) and social services (with care leavers) and through community and voluntary groups. But who are these advisers? What are the key skills they will need? What training (and re-training) will they receive to prepare them for such a critically important role?

Although Connexions is to be a new service, it is clearly going to have to build upon already existing professional workers, and those within the Careers Services especially. The 1990s were a time of considerable change for Careers Services, including being privatised and having to respond to more direction from government and new targets to meet. Although many still try to provide, through partnership with schools and colleges, a comprehensive service to all young people, much 'refocusing' has been required in order to reach out to, and try to meet, the special needs of disengaged groups. At the time of writing, the soon-to-be-disbanded Careers Services are expected, through contracts with the DfEE, to use a significant proportion of their resources (often as much as 50 per cent) on meeting the needs of such groups. It is expected that Connexions will at least match this. Yet there is deep anxiety amongst both careers officers and careers teachers, that the needs of all young people facing a plethora of new qualifications and routes through post-compulsory education will not receive the attention they deserve (Wilce, 2000). What is fundamentally different about the new Connexions Service from the responsibilities of the old Careers Services is that it is expected to give continuous support between the ages of 13 and 19; *and* to be able to keep in touch with, and offer a service to, *all* young people; *and* be a key service provider in preventing disengagement by a minority. For those experiencing serious problems, Connexions will also be expected to act as advocate and broker in relationship to other services. There is clearly some tension here between designing a service for all young people and tailoring specific variants of it to meet the needs of specific groups. Whether all this can be accomplished remains to be seen, but at least four crucial issues need to be successfully addressed.

Firstly, the new service must be based upon a new range of skills. The new profession requires a major cultural and technical transformation of the services currently operating within the Careers Service. Making contact with disengaged young people, and tracking all young people between the ages of 13 and 19 presents both technical and human relationship challenges. At present children and young people not in school or who disengage post-16 can, and do, simply disappear from official records. There is some discussion about all children being given a unique identification number and using a variety of different data sources to track their whereabouts. But to do this smacks of electronic surveillance, involves overcoming data protection issues and presents a professional challenge to those who will be expected to make contact with and work with the disengaged. Professional workers who have worked with vulnerable groups, whatever their institutional base or training, know that one key element which is the basis of effective work, especially in a tough environment and with difficult groups, is the development of trust and respect. This often takes a lot of time and effort and requires continuity of staffing if it is to be maintained over time (Coles *et al.*, 1998). To be successful therefore, Connexions will need to do much more than re-brand the Careers Service, or require a forced and unhappy marriage between careers officers, educational welfare officers and workers from the Youth Service. The new service will need strong and radical leadership with strong guidelines on effective ways of working. But professional groups often suffer from 'change fatigue' and something will need to be done to avoid professional complacency if real cultural change is to be achieved.

Thus, the second factor important to the success of the new service is the (re)-education and training of those who are being asked to carry out these difficult tasks. The Connexions Strategy document does recognise the need for cultural change within and between current services. It suggests a recruitment drive to widen the pool from which Personal Advisers will be drawn, and new forms of education and training through which new, enhanced and different skills can be fostered and developed. The suggestion is that this should be done on three fronts. First, it is proposed that there be a 'foundation qualification' to enable those already in youth work of some kind to gain accredited training in the range of skills the new service will require. This may also provide those already working within the communities with appropriate skills and aptitudes to gain accreditation. Secondly, there is a need for a programme through which already qualified professional groups can be given additional training to extend their core skills so that they can fulfil the full range of duties and responsibilities required of Personal Advisers. Thirdly, there should be a management programme, at post-qualifying level, for already existing managers (and those wishing to become managers) to prepare for the new demands that will be made of them. All this will require careful consideration of national accreditation and standards.

The third major factor that is critical to the success of Connexions is whether new funding will be provided and whether this will be adequate for the huge task of creating the new profession. Some extra money was announced in the Comprehensive Spending Review in July 2000. Indeed it seems as if the Connexions budget may be double that allocated to the old Careers Services. But whilst this might seem generous, it should be recognised that Connexions seeks to maintain a service for a much wider age range and through a range of different institutional settings. It is expected that Connexions will have an army of 20,000 Personal Advisers, but this might leave each with a case load of 20 or so 'challenging' young people and hundreds more who, despite not being troublesome, will still expect an enhanced service and continuity of support. Whether either the budget or the planned size of the personnel will be adequate to the tasks remains to be seen. Building a new structure, developing new tracking technologies, delivering new commitments, managing change under new leadership, and basing this on new personnel requiring accredited training or re-training does not come cheaply – or quickly.

The fourth important consideration is highlighted by the fact that, as was outlined in the last chapter, Scotland and Wales have not embraced the Connexions panacea. Wales seems more inclined to build on already existing partnerships developed within single tier local authorities. 'Third Way' policies seem to embrace and encourage local diversity within the overall objectives of a national plan. Within England there is also a diversity of provision and, as we saw in chapter two, some careers companies have already blurred the edges between careers advice and detached youth work. Whether Connexions can embrace local diversity whilst still delivering a cultural shift in working with young people is another of its many challenges.

Beyond Connexions: The mentoring solution

As well as the new model army of Personal Advisers, battalions of mentors have also been created in recent years. Only a few mentoring schemes have been reviewed in this book, ones for care leavers (in chapter five) and ones for young people involved in crime (in chapter seven). It was also noted that there were major differences in the training, supervision and support offered by different schemes. Strict boundaries are often set as to what issues can be discussed and supported within a mentoring relationship. In this sense it is more restricted in its ability to be holistic compared with the more open-ended agendas being addressed by Personal Advisers. Compared with Personal Advisers, however, mentoring is often a cheap solution; for the most part mentoring relies on volunteers rather than professional workers. A Research, Policy and Practice Forum on Young People held in 1999 illustrated the widespread use of mentoring in a variety of settings and a variety of different groups (National Youth Agency, 1999). It also illustrated a stark polarisation of strongly held 'opinion' as to whether it has been proved to be effective. There were disagreements about whether mentoring has been adequately evaluated. The last chapter indicated that, according to Communities that Care, mentoring still has to prove its worth and effectiveness in Britain. What is also unclear is how the various very different mentoring schemes will relate to the Connexions Service.

A new agenda for change? Some of the main problems that lie ahead

The subtitle of this book suggests that youth research, policy and practice has a new agenda for change. But has it? What is it? And what challenges does it face?

This book has outlined the ways in which, since 1997, youth policy in the UK has been taken seriously by government, and developed holistically, probably for the first time. What is perhaps strange is that this has not been the subject of public pronouncement and has hardly been recognised within the media. It is unlikely that producing more coherent youth policy will be one of the claims made by New Labour in the next general election. To be sure some youth issues continue to catch public attention. But these are largely the continuing moral panics about 'troublesome groups': young offenders; under-achievers at school; those 'looked after' (and abused) within the public care system; teenage parents; the young homeless; and the young unemployed. The work of the Social Exclusion Unit and other government bodies has attempted to address these 'problem' groups and to do so in new ways. This has involved adopting a holistic perspective and developing more joined up solutions. This book has reviewed these and broadly welcomed this more coordinated approach. This chapter has reviewed the proposals to embed such an approach within the structures of government decision making and has been positive about this new approach. But huge problems lie ahead and it is important to recognise them if they are to be overcome.

Throughout this book attention has been drawn to the fact that, whilst the SEU has been the major lead player in joining up youth policy, other arms of government have been attempting to do so too. Where there is delegated responsibility for developing joined-up solutions, as is the case for the Youth Justice Board, the Teenage Prenancy Unit, the Drugs Prevention and Advisory Service, and the Connexions Service, there are dangers that each of these separate initiatives may begin to develop their own agendas for change and begin to pull in contradictory directions. The Cross Ministerial Committee and the Children and Young People's Unit have a major and difficult job in ensuring that this does not happen. Ensuring youth policy coordination across government is the first problem that still requires careful monitoring.

Secondly, as illustrated throughout the book, the SEU has played a leading role in trying to ensure that policy is developed on the basis of the best available evidence. Yet, as has been illustrated, this is not always easy when the evidence either does not exist, or where it is flimsy or flawed. There remains a need for better, more reliable, and more holistic data about young people if policy-making is to be more securely evidence based. The bulk of information about young people's lives is still collected by the separate government departments, such as the DfEE, Home Office, Department of Health etc., aided and abetted by academia and the private sector. There is an urgent need for ways of producing more coherent and holistic sources of research data and data which is not simply driven by departmentally specific demands. Government still needs more joined up research. The proposed new longitudinal study of young people being discussed within the DfEE is one opportunity. The mapping and tracking systems proposed within the Connexions strategy represent another.

Thirdly, there is a continuing tension between the drive to have more and better information systems about young people and whether this new form of surveillance and intrusion will impede the work of professional workers trying to gain the trust of, and work with, young people. If, as the principles of holism suggest, young people are to be partners in the shaping of services and in developing policy, relationships of trust must be established and maintained. This might be threatened by the instruments of surveillance implicit in mapping and tracking technologies, including the use of the youth card. This too needs to be carefully monitored as these systems are developed. Government would do well to remember that some of the more powerful messages from research on vulnerable groups have come not from large scale quantitative surveys but from small scale, intensive, ethnographic studies. For instance, clear messages for the challenges facing the Connexions strategy, are to be found in a study of a hundred young people on a difficult estate in Teesside rather than the secondary analysis of the Youth Cohort Surveys (Johnston *et al.*, 2000).

Fourthly, an uneasy and unresolved tension still exists between the development of universal services for young people based upon rights and entitlements, and the targeting of services on vulnerable and 'at risk' groups defined on the basis of needs. Much of the drive towards more coordinated youth policy has been based upon an assumption that it is better to intervene early to prevent young people sliding into social exclusion, than to pay the cost of this later when things have spiralled out of control. There is a temptation to act to 'rescue' and 'remedy' young people's lives to prevent long-term harm and in their interests. Yet such a 'tough love' approach runs the risk of being based on stereotyping communities and groups. If we spend all our time, attention and resources on fire-fighting with vulnerable groups, the fire may well break out elsewhere. The Connexions Service must be a universal service for all young people facing difficult decisions. We ignore the needs of ordinary kids with mild ambitions at our peril. Extraordinary kids with huge ambitions also have needs and have a right to support.

Fifthly, this chapter has drawn attention to the problems inherent in trying to join up national policy to how that is delivered on the ground. Many tiers and structures of decision making lie in between. Mention has been made earlier in this chapter of what appear to be the Government's preferred strategies for tying policy at the centre to implementation at the periphery: demands made of local authorities for 'plans' for everything; targets they must try to meet; systems of blame and shame when they don't; and extra resources through action zones if they promise to do 'the right thing'. This, of course, produces huge amounts of paperwork and encourages institutions from local authorities to schools to fiddle the books. We may be able to reduce school exclusion rates by encouraging troublesome children to disappear from the register, but that is hardly a positive outcome for the social exclusion agenda. Third way approaches to welfare have been claimed to encourage diversity at a local level. Yet such an approach relies heavily upon a culture of trust between the centre and the periphery which is at odds with systems of surveillance based on plans and targets. Even if 'joined-up' works in Whitehall, there remain problems of whether such joined-up policies are implemented in Whitechapel, White City, Whitehaven or Winchester.

The problem of joining-up youth policy at a local level remains and many areas of the country have to address this. Some progress has been made but it is still too early to evaluate the success of initiatives such as Youth Offending Teams and Panels or multi-agency work in local authorities or on particular estates. What we do know is that often different professional groups have their own agendas, working practices and protocols and priorities for action.

Few, if any, local authorities have anything akin to the Social Exclusion Unit working at a local level, and it is too early to say whether any will follow the lead of central government in developing a Cross-departmental Committee serviced by a Children and Young People's Unit. Progress towards joining up youth policy within local authorities is a sixth area in which vigilance is required.

Many of the youth projects described in this book have been led and (at least part) funded by the voluntary sector. Several have experimented with holistic approaches to meet the needs of young people. Sometimes this involved combining services for different groups of young people, or extending periods of support beyond that which would be available in the statutory sector, or being more holistic in the assessment of need. Sometimes it has involved trying to develop generic services for young people, as illustrated by the projects discussed in the previous chapter. Many voluntary sector projects have been developed in partnership with local authorities and sometimes those involved had been instrumental in insisting that things should, and must, be done differently by statutory services. The changes in youth policy described in this book suggest that the whole landscape of support for young people is being transformed. This will require a review of what the voluntary sector can, and should, do in providing services for young people and in using its influence to shape what others do. One of the strengths of the voluntary sector is that, because many of its projects work closely with young people, it is adept at recognising gaps in services, and failures to meet need. Given such a widespread and rapid re-configuration of services, this monitoring role must be carried out even more vigilantly. As we have seen, part of the new agenda involves relying upon multi-agency partnerships and ensuring that partners work together rather than against each other. There is a wealth of experience within the voluntary sector in doing such work and avoiding disciplinary or professional blinkers, and bickering. The voluntary sector is in a strong position to take the lead on this as well as to monitor the problems that lie ahead.

Conclusions

This book has reviewed a wide range of youth research, policy and practice and at a time when all three have been subject to far-reaching and radical change. This review cannot, of course, claim to be comprehensive. It has largely concentrated on research, policy and practice focusing on disadvantaged young people, whilst insisting (within the tenth principle of holism) that due care and attention should be given to all young people. It has argued that, whilst in recent years public policy has focused, perhaps understandably, on those deemed to be vulnerable or at risk of social exclusion, there are dangers that the legitimate needs and interests of the majority might be overlooked. Much of the focus has been on patterns of disadvantage and disaffection. Within this, it has attempted to cover a wide range of youth issues rarely brought together in a single volume and, all too often, compartmentalised by researchers, policy-makers and practitioners alike. When the book was first planned it was hoped that it might be influential in breaking down some of the barriers